CAMBRIDGE SURVEYS OF ECONOMIC LITERATURE

RESOURCE AND
ENVIRONMENTAL ECONOMICS

# CAMBRIDGE SURVEYS OF ECONOMIC LITERATURE

*Editors:*
Miss Phyllis Deane, University of Cambridge, and
Professor Mark Perlman, University of Pittsburgh

*Editorial Advisory Board:*
Professor A. B. Atkinson, London School of Economics
  and Political Sciences
Professor M. Bronfenbrenner, Duke University
Professor K. D. George, University College, Cardiff
Professor C. P. Kindleberger, Massachusetts Institute of Technology
Professor T. Mayer, University of California, Davis
Professor A. R. Prest, London School of Economics
  and Political Science

The literature of economics is expanding rapidly, and many subjects have
changed out of recognition within the space of a few years. Perceiving the
state of knowledge in fast-developing subjects is difficult for students and
time-consuming for professional economists. This series of books is intended
to help with this problem. Each book will be quite brief, giving a clear
structure to and balanced overview of the topic, written at a level
intelligible to the senior undergraduate. They will therefore be useful for
teaching, but will also provide a mature yet compact presentation of the
subject for economists wishing to update their knowledge outside their own
specialism.

*First books in the series*
*E. Roy Weintraub:* Microfoundations: The compatibility of
microeconomics and macroeconomics
*Dennis C. Mueller:* Public choice
*Robert Clark and Joseph Spengler:* The economics of
individual and population aging
*Edwin Burmeister:* Capital theory and dynamics
*Mark Blaug:* The methodology of economics or how
economists explain
*Robert Ferber and Werner Z. Hirsch:* Social experimentation
and economic policy

# Resource and environmental economics

ANTHONY C. FISHER

*Energy and Resources Group*
*University of California, Berkeley*

CAMBRIDGE UNIVERSITY PRESS

CAMBRIDGE

LONDON   NEW YORK   NEW ROCHELLE

MELBOURNE   SYDNEY

Published by the Press Syndicate of the University of Cambridge
The Pitt Building, Trumpington Street, Cambridge CB2 1RP
32 East 57th Street, New York, NY 10022, USA
296 Beaconsfield Parade, Middle Park, Melbourne 3206, Australia

First published 1981

Printed in the United States of America

*Library of Congress Cataloging in Publication Data*
Fisher, Anthony C.
Resource and environmental economics.
(Cambridge surveys of economic literature)
Bibliography: p.
Includes index.
1. Natural resources.  2. Environmental
policy.  3. Pollution – Economic aspects.
I. Title.  II. Series.
HC59.F558   333.7                    81–9951
ISBN 0 521 24306 8 hard covers   AACR2
ISBN 0 521 28594 1 paperback

# CONTENTS

*List of tables and figures*                    *page* vii
*Preface*                                               x

1  **Introduction**                                      1
   1.1  Scope of the study                               1
   1.2  Plan of the study                                5
   1.3  A word about organization                        8
2  **Exhaustible resources: the theory of
   optimal depletion**                                  10
   2.1  Introduction                                    10
   2.2  Plan of the chapter                              11
   2.3  Key results in the theory of
        optimal depletion: an informal
        introduction                                    12
   2.4  A model of optimal depletion                    23
   2.5  Monopoly in resource markets                    37
   2.6  Uncertainty and depletion                       44
   2.7  Exploration                                      55
   2.8  Equity and exhaustible resources:
        the intergenerational problem                   67
   2.9  Concluding remarks                               74
3  **Renewable resources: the theory of
   optimal use**                                        75
   3.1  Introduction                                    75

3.2 A model of optimal use 79
3.3 The common-property problem 86
3.4 Concluding remarks 89
4 **Resource scarcity: are resources limits to growth?** 90
4.1 Introduction 90
4.2 Physical measures of scarcity 92
4.3 Economic measures of scarcity 100
4.4 Demand and supply: empirical results 113
4.5 Concluding remarks 125
5 **Natural resources and natural environments** 127
5.1 Introduction: the transition from extractive to in situ resources 127
5.2 Irreversibility in economics and in environmental processes 129
5.3 Evaluating irreversible investments 133
5.4 An empirical application 139
5.5 Concluding remarks 162
6 **Environmental pollution** 164
6.1 Introduction 164
6.2 Pollution externalities and economic efficiency 166
6.3 Pollution-control policies: a comparative analysis 179
6.4 Pollution damages and control costs 203
6.5 Concluding remarks 231
7 **Some concluding thoughts: the role of economics in the study of resource and environmental problems** 233

*References* 241
*Author index* 277
*Subject index* 283

# TABLES AND FIGURES

**Tables**

2.1 A comparison of optimal-depletion
and optimal control conditions *page* 34
2.2 Optimal OPEC price path 41
2.3 Effects on depletion of different
kinds of uncertainty 48
4.1 World oil reserves 93
4.2 Physical measures of availability of
selected minerals 98
4.3 Unit costs of extractive output,
United States 100
4.4 Relationships between prices of
important minerals and costs of labor 104
4.5 Real prices of selected important
nonfuel minerals, 1969–79 106
4.6 Average real exploration costs for
U.S. oil and gas, 1946–71 109
4.7 U.S. crude oil price per barrel 110
4.8 Marginal exploration costs for oil
and gas in Alberta, 1972–8 111
4.9 Estimates of industrial energy-
demand elasticities 117
4.10 Estimates of residential energy-
demand elasticities 118

4.11    Estimates of factor-substitution
        elasticities                                 120
4.12    California residential-sector retrofit       122
5.1     Costs and benefits, Hell's Canyon
        hydroelectic projects                        148
5.2     Recreation activity, Hell's Canyon           150
5.3     Initial year's preservation benefit
        needed to equal present value of
        project                                      152
5.4     Bituminous coal, average value
        per ton                                      156
6.1     Estimates of the value of saving a
        statistical life and averting associated
        illness and disability                       212
6.2     Selected estimates of U.S. air- and
        water-pollution damages                      216
6.3     Costs of water-pollution abatement
        under taxes and direct controls,
        Delaware estuary                             230

**Figures**

2.1     Relationship between marginal cost
        and price for an exhaustible resource         13
2.2     Time path of price and its relationship
        to resource and backstop costs                18
2.3     Time path of output                           20
2.4     Time path of price with unanticipated
        discoveries                                   56
2.5     Influence of discovery and technical
        change on price                               61
2.6     Time path of crude oil output in the
        United States                                 63
3.1     Biological growth law                         80
3.2     Stock size as a function of time              81
3.3     Derivation of catch locus                     83
3.4     Equilibrium stocks and yields                 84

4.1 Mineral and coal resource and reserve categories 94

4.2 Tonnage-grade distribution for a mineral 95

4.3 Availability diagram for uranium 96

4.4 Trends in unit prices of extractive products relative to nonextractive products in the United States, 1870–1957 103

4.5 Behavior of price-trend coefficients over time 105

5.1 Production possibilities and preferences for produced goods and environmental amenities 134

5.2 Energy use versus purchase price for a number of existing and proposed refrigerators 160

6.1 Externality, nonconvexity, and multiple equilibria 177

6.2 Coase theorem 181

6.3 Minimum-cost tax 190

6.4 Tax and standard compared 200

6.5 Steps in going from activity to costs 204

6.6 Compensating-variation measure of the value of an environmental improvement 220

6.7 Hedonic price-function equilibrium 222

6.8 Marginal costs of BOD discharge reductions in petroleum refining 229

# PREFACE

This book is intended as a response to the recent explosion of interest, both popular and scientific, in resource (especially energy) and environmental issues. I sought to deal with some of these issues in two recent survey articles, one in the *Journal of Economic Literature* ("The Environment in Economics") and one in the *Economic Journal* ("The Exploitation of Extractive Resources"). This book was originally conceived as an extension, but I soon came to realize that the survey format would not be adequate for the needs of students and others wishing to examine the detailed empirical findings and learn something of the structures and solutions of economic models used to address the issues. The book in its present form seeks to provide a self-contained development of selected portions of this material. However, the purpose originally conceived for the book has not been totally sacrificed. Footnotes and an extensive list of references at the end of the book serve as guides to the literature for those interested in further study of the questions treated here, as well as related questions not considered here. For the most part, references are cited in the text only when they are relevant to discussion of various positions on a controversial issue.

Why this particular book? Other books dealing with resources and the environment have appeared in recent years, but I believe this one offers some distinctive, even unique, features. First, it is almost evenly divided between the topics of resources and the environment. Thus it should appeal to those seeking a concise and balanced treatment, whether for a quick personal review of the field or for use in a one-semester course.

Second, the book is fairly evenly divided between theory and empirical materials. The concerns that motivate economic investigations in this field are essentially empirical: Are we running out of key extractive resources? What are the benefits of the various environmental programs proposed? To address these concerns in a useful way, a fairly heavy dose of theory is needed, and I have not shrunk from providing this. But substantial attention is also given to empirical methods and findings. Chapter 4, for example, concerns measures of resource scarcity, how they have behaved in the past and what they portend for the future. Chapter 6 includes a lengthy discussion of methods for estimating the benefits of environmental programs, with a sample of the findings in some key studies.

Third, this volume presents a careful heuristic development of the major mathematical results in the new and often forbiddingly technical theory of optimal resource depletion. The first substantive chapter (Chapter 2) begins with a simple example of exhaustible-resource depletion: oil. Given a structure of demand for the resource and the costs of extracting it, I show how a fixed stock should be allocated over two periods to maximize the net social benefit from its use. A numerical solution is obtained using only elementary calculus. Results are progressively extended until we arrive at a general statement of the conditions of optimal depletion. A very little further manipulation shows these conditions to be a special case of the conditions of optimal control, the rather advanced mathematical method used in the modern treatment of both exhaustible- and renewable-resource allocations over time, as well as in treatment of some environmental problems. Yet only elementary calculus is used throughout. This gives readers, and especially students, the best of all worlds. The exposition is pushed to the point where formal dynamic conditions of optimal resource use are presented; one must be familiar with these conditions in order to understand much of the literature. However, these conditions are carefully derived, step by step, in the context of a depletion problem, and so they do indeed become understandable, and even usable.

Still another distinctive feature is that I stress the economic logic, and sometimes the policy implications, of results. Although informal mathematical methods are used and results obtained, this is never sufficient. What I consider most important is the economic common sense of the results, and accordingly I have tried to bring this out, to make the results accessible to those who, like me, are not primarily theorists and are not comfortable with a primarily theoretical exposition.

Chapter 1, the Introduction, explains the scope and plan in some detail. Chapter 2 concerns optimal depletion of exhaustible resources. Following the development of the basic theory, Chapter 2 provides discussions of the behavior of resource cartels (like OPEC), the effects of different kinds of uncertainty on patterns of depletion, and the intergenerational problem. Chapter 3 extends the theory to treat renewable resources, with special attention to the problem of managing stocks for sustained yields in a common-property setting. Chapter 4 is an empirical counterpart to Chapters 2 and 3, a discussion of the behavior of extractive-resource costs and prices, and some other indicators of scarcity. It includes a review of recent findings on the substitutability of the more important exhaustible energy sources: oil, gas, and coal.

Chapters 5 and 6 deal with environmental issues. Chapter 5 makes the transition from extractive resources to in situ resources of a natural environment. The question considered here is how the ordinary efficiency analysis, or benefit–cost analysis, of an extractive-resource development project can be extended to take into account the environmental values that will be foreclosed, perhaps permanently, by the project. A theoretical discussion of this question is followed by an in-depth analysis of a specific (though, I believe, fairly typical) case of a proposed hydroelectric project in an attractive setting. Chapter 6 is a theoretical and empirical inquiry into the economics of pollution control. In the theoretical portion of the chapter we look first at the rather abstract problem of attaining efficiency in the presence of pollution externality, and then we consider the strengths and weaknesses of the various policy instruments proposed to control pollution, such as taxes, subsidies, marketable permits, and direct controls on technology or emissions. The empirical portion is concerned with how to measure the benefits and costs of control, with some relevant estimates taken from other studies.

Chapter 7, which I hope will be provocative, especially to those who are not economists, is essentially a defense of the economic approach to resource and environmental issues, or perhaps I should say a defense of my understanding of the approach.

This leads to the question of the book's intended audience. It is intended, first, for my fellow economists, both those actively researching, teaching, and consulting in the field and those looking for a concise introduction to at least some of the major themes and a guide to the literature. It is intended for students in economics, both graduate students and advanced undergraduates, as well as those in the related fields of resource management, conservation, geography, and public policy. The treatment of both resource issues and environmental issues in a relatively concise manner makes the book particularly appropriate for a one-semester course, but it can also be used in conjunction with other materials in a longer sequence. I hope that it will also prove useful to professionals in the field of resource and environmental management, as an indication of what economic analysis can contribute to the solutions of the very challenging problems they face.

A word of caution is appropriate here in regard to a point that has already been made in passing. Because the book is short, compared with the average textbook, and because it seeks to present both resource and environmental materials, it is inevitably selective. The questions and issues treated are, naturally enough, those I find particularly appealing, although I believe that most people working in the field will agree they are among the most interesting and most important. For what is left out, the footnotes and references can at least serve as guides; however, even here I do not claim that the coverage is exhaustive. Many excellent works, particularly those from outside the United States, will through no fault of their own not be cited in these pages.

Finally, I wish to acknowledge the helpful comments of a number of friends and colleagues regarding early drafts of individual chapters, as well as other assistance I have received in preparing this volume. I am grateful to Richard Zeckhauser for many stimulating suggestions spanning the material in all of the substantive chapters. Shanta Devarajan helped me with a searching critique of both the mathematics and the economics of the long theoretical chapter (Chapter 2). Anthony Scott provided a useful perspective on the literature in this area, along with some additional references, particularly those regarding studies of mineral taxation. I also gratefully acknowledge penetrating and helpful comments on Chapter 5 from John Krutilla, on Chapter 6 from William Baumol, Myrick Freeman, and Suzanne Scotchmer, and on material in several chapters from Gardner Brown.

Useful and constructive suggestions on the manner in which the material was to be presented were made by Cambridge University Press editors Colin Day and Phyllis Deane. Two anonymous reviewers of the first draft also provided helpful criticisms of both style and substance.

For impressive work in tracking down data and references I wish to thank Mari Wilson, librarian in the Energy and Resources Group of the University of California at Berkeley;

and for careful typing of the manuscript, as well as helpful questions and comments, I am grateful to Susan Buller and Patty Redifer. Glenda Earl ably researched the literature and prepared short summaries of recent (early 1978) contributions.

Although he took no part in the preparation of this book, Fred Peterson, my coauthor for two survey articles listed in the references, has greatly aided my understanding of these subjects.

I hope that the reading of this volume will prove as useful for others as preparing it has been for me.

ANTHONY C. FISHER

*Berkeley, California*
*March 1981*

# 1

## Introduction

### 1.1. Scope of the study

In recent years there has been a revival of interest in the concerns expressed by the early conservationist movement, primarily concern as to the adequacy of the natural-resource base in our advanced industrial economy. The early conservationists stressed the importance of extractive resources, in the words of Pinchot (1910, p. 123), "the five indispensably essential materials in our civilization . . . wood, water, coal, iron, and agricultural products." Today, of course, we are worrying a great deal about energy resources: oil, gas, uranium, renewables of all kinds, in addition to coal. In this sense our focus seems to have narrowed, but in another sense it has broadened to include what might be called in situ natural resources, such things as clean air, natural beauty, and other aspects of the environment that yield satisfaction directly rather than through some productive transformation.

However we interpret its focus, there is no question that there is renewed concern. It is no exaggeration to say that one can hardly pick up a newspaper without coming across several items dealing directly with one or another energy or environmental issue. For example, in looking through the *San Francisco Chronicle* for March 27, 1980 (not an unusual day, not an unusual paper), we find the following: "Angry San Francisco

1

Hearing on Lake Tahoe Plan" (p. 4), which deals with public reaction to a plan to try to control pollution in Lake Tahoe; "State Tests Show Gasohol Is Smoggy" (p. 5), which discusses the air pollution that will result from automobile engines that burn a mixture of gasoline and alcohol; "Pacific Gas and Electric Program: Interest-Free Loans to Conserve Energy" (p. 6), describing a program under which the local northern California utility, the Pacific Gas and Electric Company, will offer local residents loans for insulation and other energy-conserving investments; "Elk Hills Oil Too Costly for 3 Top Bidders" (p. 19), which describes the problems of oil companies that bid successfully for the right to extract oil from the federally owned Elk Hills petroleum reserve in California; "Gold Dredging Resumes in Yuba" (p. 30), describing plans to develop additional goldmining capacity in the mother-lode country of California.

In addition, a special supplement to the same newspaper carried a long article entitled "Energy in the 80's: Conservation is the Key." It described some of the difficulties faced by the United States in attempting to expand supplies of conventional energy resources, and it argued the cost advantages of conservation. Also in the supplement was a shorter piece reproduced from the *New York Times*: "Sharp Debate on Mining the Moon." This dealt with political opposition within the United States to a draft of a United Nations treaty concerning rules to govern the exploitation of mineral resources in space.

Again, all of these items represent no more than an average day's discussion of resource and environmental issues by a paper that has not, to my knowledge, won any awards for its coverage of these issues. On a better-than-average day one might expect to find front-page treatment of, say, an oil-pricing decision from the organization of petroleum-exporting countries (OPEC), a presidential proposal to subsidize the production of synthetic fuels (such as oil and gas from coal), and a major new research report linking disease of the human respiratory tract to sulfates and particulates in the air.

This book is about all of these issues; it is about our natural environment as a source of energy, as a source of other extractive resources, and as a source of life-support and amenity services. Perhaps it would be more accurate to say that it is about the economic theories and findings that bear on these issues. The newspaper items mentioned earlier are not discussed specifically in succeeding chapters, nor, for that matter, is much attention given to the details of the workings of resource industries, such as their market structures and the effects of specific taxes and regulations, including environmental regulations. But I do believe that a better understanding of the developments and controversies reported in that newspaper, as well as a better understanding of many similar issues, will follow from study of the more general principles and issues treated in this book.

What are these more general issues? Obviously there are many possible schemes for defining and organizing the issues in resource and environmental economics. With respect to extractive resources, the approach we shall take here is to ask two important questions, and in what follows we shall try to develop the tools and concepts needed to answer them: (1) Are resources limits to growth? (2) What is the optimal rate of resource use or depletion?

The first question concerns how rapidly our resources have been and are being used and the prospects for future shortfalls. This is the same question that troubled the early conservationists, and today it is the issue raised by those who fear that our now very much larger, and still expanding, global economy is in danger of outstripping the capacity of the earth and its resources. Although the question is an empirical one, it cannot be answered without considering some of the theoretical properties of the suggested indicators of resource scarcity, such as stocks of reserves, prices, and so on.

The second question is theoretical, concerning how rapidly our resources should be used. An answer clearly requires that we specify the nature of the resource as exhaustible or renewable, that we specify who makes the decision about the rate of use (competitive firm, monopoly, or public agency), and that we specify criteria for determining optimal use of each. Of special interest here are comparisons between the rates of depletion under different market structures and a "socially optimal" rate. For example, who will tend to deplete a given resource stock faster, a competitive industry or a monopoly? And how do these rates of depletion compare with a rate determined by a hypothetical planner seeking to allocate the resource efficiently over time?

With respect to the environment, the questions are similar: (1) What are the damages from pollution and other forms of environmental disruption? (2) What is the optimal degree of environmental protection? In trying to answer the first question, as economists we shall be concerned mainly with the problems of measuring and especially evaluating damages. An answer to the second question requires, obviously enough, a comparison of damages, or the benefits from environmental controls, with the costs of those controls. But because of severe practical difficulties in estimating benefits (which will be considered in due course, along with achievements in this field), economists have proposed a less ambitious alternative to benefit–cost analysis, namely cost-effectiveness analysis. This is best understood as a response to still another question: (3) What is the optimal method for achieving a desired degree of environmental protection? By "optimal" we mean simply the least cost, and the available methods include direct controls on pollution emissions, a tax on emissions, subsidies for the construction of waste-treatment facilities, and marketable pollution permits. The question then turns on the properties (in particular, the effects on control costs) of the different methods, or policy instruments, that can be used to bring about the desired degree of control.

These questions might, in fact, be viewed as extensions of the questions about resources. Because of the law of conservation of mass, the extraction, conversion, and use of resources inevitably involve the generation of residuals, or waste materials. These, in turn, affect air and water quality, so that questions about optimal rates of resource use take on an environmental dimension. Of course, it is often convenient to take a more restricted view in discussing specific issues.

### 1.2. **Plan of the study**

In Chapter 2 we shall take up the theory of exhaustible-resource depletion. The basic approach is to set up an appropriate objective for the resource owner or manager (e.g., to allocate the resource over time in such a way as to maximize its value), specify the constraints on his actions (e.g., that there is no more than a fixed and limited amount of the resource that can ever be produced), and determine the conditions that characterize the resulting depletion program.

A number of interesting extensions and policy issues can be handled in this format. We shall consider, in addition to the effects of different market structures on depletion, the effects of uncertainty about such factors as future demand and the size of the resource stock, as well as the special problems of intergenerational equity in allocating an exhaustible resource. In the section on market structures, the importance of OPEC is recognized in a discussion of pricing and output strategies for the international oil cartel.

Chapter 3 concerns renewable resources, such as biomass energy sources and the more traditional resources such as forests and fisheries. The approach taken is an extension of the theory developed to deal with the allocation of exhaustible resources. Once again, a decision maker is assumed to maximize the value of the resource subject to constraints. The difference in this case lies in the nature of the constraints. In particular, instead of a fixed resource stock that can only be depleted over time, the resource can be renewed by natural growth. This considerably changes the nature of the conditions that characterize optimal use.

As in the exhaustible-resource case, the theoretical apparatus can be used to consider some interesting issues. Biologists and resource managers have long advocated a harvest policy of "maximum sustainable yield," that is, managing the resource stock to produce the largest annual yield in perpetuity. We shall consider how this "biological optimum" compares with an economic optimum.

Another question is addressed: Under what circumstances might a renewable resource be exhausted? At first glance this may appear to be a contradiction, but we are all familiar with the plight of the whale and other endangered species. Although they are renewed by natural growth, species can be harvested to the point of extinction. An important influence on the potential for extinction turns out to be the pattern of property rights in the resource. It will be seen that the implications for stocks and yields in the long run are quite different when the resource is a common property, such as an ocean fishery, owned by no one and by everyone.

In Chapter 4 we shall return to the theme of resources as limits to growth. A review of the evidence will be presented, and the evidence will be interpreted with the aid of some of the concepts and models developed in Chapters 2 and 3. The properties and behavior over time of a number of alternative indicators of resource scarcity will be discussed, including reserves: production ratios, resource extraction costs, and prices. To determine the potential for substitution away from key exhaustible resources, especially in the energy sector, we shall review recent econometric and engineering-economic estimates of demand elasticities.

Chapters 5 and 6 take up in detail the environmental questions that to some extent parallel those considered for extractive resources. In Chapter 5 we make the transition from extractive resources to in situ resources of a natural environment. The major question here concerns alternative uses of the environment. Suppose a scenic wonder like the Grand Canyon can be developed to produce hydroelectric power. Should it be? To take another example, should any part of California's remaining virgin redwood forest be opened up to logging to meet the demands of the nation's housing industry? These are, to be sure, quite well-known resources that have already been accorded a certain degree of statutory protection. But there are literally thousands of other resources up for grabs in the United States alone. For example, the U.S. Forest Service is currently conducting an evaluation of remaining roadless areas in the national forests for possible inclusion in the wilderness system. What factors are relevant in making these decisions?

The notions of *irreversibility* and *uncertainty* in environmental decisions like the ones just cited are central to the discussion here. For example, development of the Grand Canyon for its energy values would be virtually impossible to reverse once the dams, lakes, generating equipment, and transmission lines were in place. How would this affect an analysis of the benefits and costs of such a project? And what about our inability to estimate with precision the environmental values affected by the project? Following a theoretical discussion of needed modifications in the traditional benefit–cost approach, we shall consider in detail an actual case: not the Grand Canyon, but Hell's Canyon in the Pacific Northwest. The object is to show how an analysis that can be useful in making a decision about developing a natural environment can be conducted even in the face of substantial uncertainty about the benefits precluded by the development.

A mix of theoretical and empirical materials also characterizes Chapter 6, which deals with the major environmental problem: pollution. The focus involves the three questions mentioned earlier: (1) What are the damages from pollution, the benefits from control? (2) What is the optimal level of control? (3) What methods can best achieve it?

We shall look first at questions 2 and 3, which involve the economic theory of pollution control. For question 2, the procedure is first to derive the conditions that characterize a socially efficient allocation in the presence of pollution externalities and then show how these conditions can be brought about through the imposition of a tax on emissions. After noting some qualifications, we turn to the less ambitious question 3, concerning how to achieve any desired degree of control at the least cost. Once again, a tax is shown to have this capacity, but again this is subject to important qualifications. These lead us to consider the comparative strengths and weaknesses of a number of frequently mentioned alternatives: direct controls on emissions, a subsidy for waste-treatment facilities, and a system of marketable pollution permits.

Whatever system of control is adopted, it is likely to work better (in the sense of moving the economy closer to efficiency in resource allocation) the more we know about the benefits and costs of control. This is the subject matter pertinent to question 1, to which we shall turn after investigation of the alternative control strategies. Approaches to benefit and cost estimations will be discussed at some length, with attention to the difficulties involved. Some sample findings will also be presented to give an idea of the magnitude of the problems faced and the appropriateness of existing and proposed controls.

Chapter 7, the concluding chapter, provides some reflections on the contributions of economics to an understanding of resource and environmental issues and to the formulation of policies.

Following the text is the list of references: books, journal articles, unpublished papers, and so on. The list is quite long, even though it is based on only the limited selection of topics and issues treated in the text; thus, many excellent works on related topics will not be cited there. Furthermore, the list is not exhaustive even for the areas covered. The references listed are those that have come to my attention and have proved useful in the preparation of this volume.

### 1.3. **A word about organization**

One purpose of this book is to provide a review of the literature dealing with natural resources and the environment.

To some degree this is accomplished by the reference list. The footnotes should serve as a guide to the references. Although the text contains some discussion of specific works, especially when they are relevant to the debate on a controversial issue, most such discussion is confined to the footnotes. Thus it is hoped that the literature review will not interfere with the main purpose of the book, which is to provide a self-contained development of selected questions and issues in resource and environmental economics.

# 2

## Exhaustible resources: the theory of optimal depletion

### 2.1. Introduction

Are our exhaustible energy resources being depleted too rapidly? Or are they perhaps being depleted too slowly as a consequence of efforts by producing nations and large corporations to restrict output and thus raise prices? Questions like these, which have been given new urgency by the energy crisis of recent years, lead quite naturally to an inquiry into what constitutes optimal use of exhaustible resources. A fairly standard approach in such an inquiry, and the one taken here, is first to derive the conditions that characterize socially efficient resource use and then determine to what extent these are also realized in a competitive equilibrium. In other words, does the fundamental theorem of welfare economics continue to hold in the context of exhaustible resources?

As the question about the large energy producers implies, all sorts of imperfections are known to interfere with the tendency of a system of competitive markets to allocate resources efficiently. Thus, even if it turns out that a competitive equilibrium is efficient, one still must consider the effects of relevant imperfections, or market failures. For example: What about monopoly? What about the environmental disruption that often accompanies the extraction, conversion, and use of exhaustible resources? Further, as will be argued later in this

10

chapter, there may be other kinds of market failures peculiar to these resources, involving such things as the uncertainty that surrounds their discovery and the long-lasting effects of current decisions about their use.

In the next chapter, patterns of efficient use of renewable resources will be studied by extending the theory to be developed presently to take account of natural renewal or growth. Different sets of questions and complications are peculiar to these renewable resources. We shall be looking, for example, at the case for maximum sustainable yield and at the kinds of conditions that can spell extinction for a resource.

As the mention of extinction suggests, the line between exhaustible and renewable can become blurred. Renewable resources can be exhausted, and exhaustible resources can, in a sense, be renewed through the discovery of new deposits or through technical advances that make it economically feasible to recover a resource from low-grade materials. But for the most part we shall keep to the convention that classifies resources as exhaustible or renewable depending on their rates of regeneration. Oil is exhaustible, because millions of years are required for its formation, whereas timber is renewable, growing to maturity within just a few decades.

## 2.2. **Plan of the chapter**

In the next section, some of the simplest and most intuitive results involved in the theory of depletion will be presented. Following this, in Section 2.4, they will be more formally derived, along with a number of extensions that, it is hoped, will embody a greater degree of realism. One key extension, for example, allows the costs of extraction to vary with cumulative extraction or with the size of the remaining resource stock. In particular, we shall assume that costs rise with cumulative extraction.

The mathematical method used in the more formal analysis is known as optimal control. However, the derivations are considerably simpler than this would suggest. The problem of optimal depletion is stated in an elementary calculus format, and key features of the solution are developed in this same format. As will be seen, these constitute both the specific optimal-depletion conditions and also, with minor substitutions, the more general optimal-control conditions. The reason it is important to have the latter is that they can then be applied directly in related problems. For example, we need not work through all of the intermediate steps to obtain a solution to the renewable-resource problem in Chapter 3. Instead, we simply state the optimal-control conditions, then make the substitutions appropriate to the renewable-resource case.

Somewhat less formally, the same approach is also useful in analyzing the imperfections and complications noted earlier: monopoly, cartel behavior, exploration, and questions of intergenerational equity in the use of exhaustible resources. Section 2.5 concerns monopoly and, in particular, the OPEC cartel. Section 2.6 deals with the effects of various kinds of uncertainty in resource markets. Section 2.7 treats exploration, an activity special to the resource sector. Externalities and other kinds of market failures associated with uncertainty and exploration are considered. However, for the most part, the effects of environmental externalities are not considered in this chapter; they are taken up in detail in Chapters 5 and 6. Intergenerational issues that seem to be prominently associated with the use of exhaustible resources are reviewed in Section 2.8.

### 2.3. Key results in the theory of optimal depletion: an informal introduction

There are essentially two conditions that must hold along an optimal-depletion path. These turn out to be the optimal-control conditions, but they can be understood much less formally as well.

How is an exhaustible resource different from an ordinary good or resource? Simply in that it is limited in quantity and is not producible. But this means that extraction and consump-

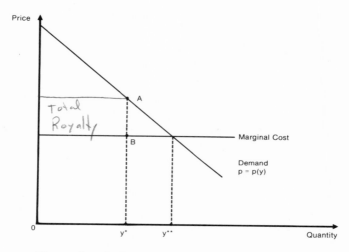

Figure 2.1. Relationship between marginal cost and price for an exhaustible resource.

tion of a unit today involves an *opportunity cost:* the value that might have been obtained at some future date. The opportunity cost must be taken into account in determining how to allocate the resource over time. In particular, instead of the usual efficiency condition, price = marginal (production) cost, we have price = marginal (production) cost + opportunity cost. This is the first condition of optimal depletion; as shown in Figure 2.1, it implies that less of the resource will be extracted today than if it were producible. Given the demand $p = p(y)$, where $p$ is price and $y$ is quantity, only $y^*$ units will be extracted by a planner or resource manager seeking to allocate extraction efficiently over time, leaving a positive difference (*AB* in Figure 2.1) between the price and the marginal cost of production or extraction.[1]

---

[1] This result was first described in a little-known article by Gray (1913). In a later and better-known work (1914) he clearly anticipated the second key result developed in the following text. Gray analyzed the pattern of depletion by a profit-maximizing mine owner, but as we shall demonstrate, under certain circumstances this will also be efficient.

The second condition of optimal depletion describes the behavior of the opportunity cost over time. But before getting into this, we should introduce a bit of terminology. The difference between price and marginal extraction cost is known by a number of different names in the resource-economics literature: user cost (from the opportunity cost to the user of taking a unit today), royalty, rent, net price, and marginal profit. We shall generally use the term *royalty,* although one should be familiar with the others. In Chapter 4, which concerns measures of resource scarcity, the term *rent* is used, mainly for historical reasons.

Now what can be said about the behavior of the royalty over time? Consider a unit of the resource, say a barrel of oil. What is the net social benefit from extracting the barrel today? Clearly it is the royalty, the difference between the price (or what consumers are willing to pay) and the cost of extraction. But that same barrel might also be expected to yield a royalty if extracted and consumed next year. At which of the two times should it be extracted to yield the greatest net benefit?

To help answer this question, let us work through a simple numerical example. Suppose that there are just 10 barrels of oil in the ground in total, that the (constant) marginal cost of extraction is $2 per barrel, that the demand in period $t$ ($t = 0$, 1) is given by the equation $p_t = 10 - y_t$, where $p$ is price and $y$ is extractive output, and that the rate of discount is $r = 0.10$. Now we can ask our question: What allocation of output over the two periods will yield the greatest net benefit from the oil? For simplicity, we assume just two periods, but the results we obtain can readily be extended. This is an approach that will be used frequently. For many purposes, a simple two-period example or model will do. Where it becomes important to determine the behavior of some variable such as output or price over many periods, an appropriate model will be formulated.

Net (social) benefit in a single period is customarily measured as the difference between what consumers are willing to pay for a good and what it costs to produce. In Figure

2.1 this is the area between $p(y)$ and MC from $y = 0$ to $y = y^*$.
Note again that the area, or benefit, is bounded by $y^*$, not $y^{**}$,
the output for which price = marginal cost. The net benefit
can also be represented analytically, according to the geomet-
ric interpretation of the integral of a curve as the area under
the curve. In this case the total willingness to pay is the
integral of the demand curve, and the total cost is the integral
of the marginal cost curve. The net benefit, or the difference
between willingness to pay and cost, can then be written as

$$\int_0^{y_0} (10 - y')dy' - \int_0^{y_0} 2dy'$$

or

$$\int_0^{y_0} [(10 - y') - 2]dy'$$

in the first period and

$$\int_0^{y_1} [(10 - y') - 2]dy'$$

in the second period, where $y_0$ and $y_1$ represent actual first-
and second-period outputs and $y'$ is a variable of integration.

Our objective is now to choose a level of output in each
period in such a way as to maximize the sum, over both
periods, of these benefits, taking care to multiply the second
period's benefit by the discount factor $1/(1 + r)$ to obtain a
present value. In symbols, the problem is

$$\underset{y_0, y_1}{\text{maximize}} \int_0^{y_0} [(10 - y') - 2]dy' + \int_0^{y_1} \frac{[(10 - y') - 2]dy'}{1 + 0.10}$$

subject to

$$y_0 + y_1 = 10$$

This is a constrained maximization problem, which we can
readily solve by setting up the Lagrangian expression

$$L = \int_0^{y_0} [(10 - y') - 2]dy' + \int_0^{y_1} \frac{[(10 - y') - 2]dy'}{1.1} \\ + \lambda(10 - y_0 - y_1)$$

where $\lambda$ is a Lagrange multiplier, differentiating with respect to $y_0$, $y_1$, and $\lambda$, and setting the results equal to zero. We obtain

$$(10 - y_0) - 2 - \lambda = 0 \qquad \frac{(10 - y_1) - 2}{1.1} - \lambda = 0$$

and

$$10 - y_0 - y_1 = 0$$

Solving for $y_0$, $y_1$, and $\lambda$, we find $y_0 = 5.14$ (approximately), $y_1 = 4.86$, and $\lambda = 2.86$. Substituting the values for $y_0$ and $y_1$ back into the demand equation, we find $p_0 = \$4.86$ and $p_1 = \$5.14$.

Now let us interpret these results. The royalty in period 0, the difference between price and marginal cost, is \$2.86. The royalty in period 1 is \$3.14, but notice that when discounted it comes to just \$2.86 (\$3.14/1.1). In other words, the present value of the royalty is the same for both periods; equivalently, the (undiscounted) royalty has grown by 10%, the rate of discount. This is, in fact, a fairly general result, even though we have obtained it in a simple numerical example. As we shall see, for the special case in which costs do not rise with cumulative extraction, the second condition of optimal depletion is that *the present value of the royalty must be the same in all periods* or, equivalently, *the undiscounted royalty must rise at the rate of interest.*[2]

There is an illuminating interpretation of the Lagrange multiplier, $\lambda$, here. Recall that the multiplier is a *shadow price:* the change in the (optimal) value of the objective function corresponding to a small change in the constraint. In this case we are talking about the increase in benefits that would result

[2] As indicated in footnote 1, this condition was obtained by Gray (1914) on the basis of a simple arithmetic example. For an exposition of Gray's reasoning here with a somewhat more modern flavor, see the work of Herfindahl (1955), and for a broader discussion of Gray's work, see the work of Crabbé (1980), which also contains an informative survey of related early contributions.

from having one more barrel of oil in the ground, or the decrease that would result from having one less. But this is just the opportunity cost of producing the barrel now, the royalty. Notice that because of the first-order conditions in our example this is indeed equal to the difference between price and marginal cost in the current period, or the present value of the difference in the next period.

All of this makes economic sense. Consider oil in the ground as a capital asset. How much of this asset must be held if the pattern of investment in the economy is to be efficient? Efficiency requires that there be no gain to be had in shifting from one asset to another, which in turn implies that the returns must be the same for all. Ordinarily the return includes a capital gain, plus a dividend, minus depreciation. However, for an exhaustible resource there is no dividend and also no depreciation. The return in this case must come entirely in the form of a capital gain or a rise in the value of the asset. But the value is just the difference between price and marginal cost, or the royalty. Thus extraction is apportioned among periods in such a way that the royalty rises at the (common) rate of interest.

The discussion to this point has been in terms of efficiency in allocating an exhaustible resource over time, but it should be intuitively clear that (as we shall prove later in this chapter) the same conditions must hold in a competitive equilibrium. As long as there are gains to be had in shifting a unit of extraction, or the pattern of investment in resources in the ground, there can be no equilibrium.

Now let us make explicit some additional simple points about the behavior of resource price and output over time. We have established that the royalty rises at the rate of interest. In symbols, this can be stated as

$$(p_1 - \text{MC}) = (p_0 - \text{MC}) (1 + r)$$

Then the equation for the time path of price is

$$p_1 = \text{MC} + (p_0 - \text{MC}) (1 + r)$$

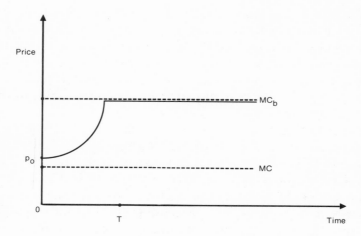

Figure 2.2. Time path of price and its relationship to resource and backstop costs.

Extending this to many periods, we have

$$p_t = \text{MC} + (p_0 - \text{MC})(1 + r)^t \tag{2.1}$$

Price draws away from marginal extraction cost, rising at a rate that approaches the rate of interest as the royalty component of price comes to dominate the extraction cost component. This is shown in Figure 2.2.

Does price rise indefinitely? Clearly in our numerical example it cannot rise above \$10 per barrel, because at that price the quantity demanded falls to zero. More generally, we may suppose that there will be a limit set by the price, or cost, of a substitute. For oil, the substitute, or "backstop," as it is sometimes called, could be coal, and ultimately perhaps nuclear fusion or some form of solar energy. The backstop is just a resource or a technology that can provide the same services as the oil (thermal units of energy), but at higher cost, and without risking exhaustion in any meaningful time frame.[3]

---

[3] The backstop terminology may have been introduced by Nordhaus (1973*b*) in his pioneering study of the efficient allocation of different energy resources over time. This study will be discussed

Of course, it may be that it will be impossible to substitute for some relatively minor uses of oil, in which case price could continue to rise, although even here a limit would be set by the value of the product or service using the oil.

Let us suppose that a backstop exists, say solar energy, that can provide energy at a (marginal) cost equivalent to $MC_b$ dollars per barrel of oil. Note that this is also the price, because with an unlimited resource stock there is no royalty. What we shall show is that the cost of the backstop not only sets an upper limit on the price of oil but also determines the initial price by determining the initial royalty to be added to the marginal cost of extraction.

At time $T$, the switch data from oil to the backstop, the price is given, from equation (2.1), by

$$p_T = MC + (p_0 - MC)(1 + r)^T$$

But we also have $p_T = MC_b$, so that

$$(p_0 - MC) = \frac{(MC_b - MC)}{(1 + r)^T}$$

In other words, the royalty at $t = 0$ $(p_0 - MC)$ is the difference between the cost of the backstop and the cost of oil, discounted back from the switch date. Substituting this expression for $p_0 - MC$ into equation (2.1), we obtain an equation in terms of the cost of the backstop (and the cost of oil) for the price of oil at any time $t < T$:

$$p_t = MC + \frac{(MC_b - MC)}{(1 + r)^{T-t}} \tag{2.2}$$

This is shown in Figure 2.2, where the royalty rises at rate $r$ to $MC_b - MC$ and the price rises to $MC_b$ at time $T$.

The model in the next section is essentially a much more general treatment of the same idea, namely that costs rise with

further in Section 4.4. Herfindahl's (1967) "cost limit" is an earlier expression of the backstop concept. Many examples are given by Goeller and Weinberg (1976) for energy and other resources.

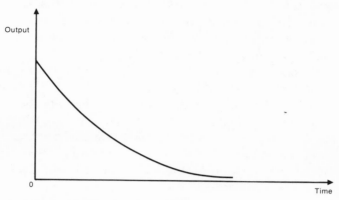

Figure 2.3. Time path of output.

cumulative extraction. There, instead of a single jump to a backstop, we shall consider the more realistic situation in which there are in effect many backstops, different qualities of the resource being extracted, each denoted by a different cost.

But first, what can we say about the behavior of output in the simple model in this section? Clearly, if demand is stable (and downward-sloping), as assumed in our example, and price is rising, then output must be falling, as shown in Figure 2.3. However, this is not a general result, because demand could well be rising over time as a consequence of rising income or improvements in the technology of using the resource. Output must, of course, ultimately fall as the resource approaches exhaustion.

At this point the reader familiar with the behavior of extractive-resource prices over time may wish to object. As will be shown in Chapter 4, many of these prices (appropriately deflated) have, in fact, tended to fall over a period of several decades ending in the early 1970s. But if this is true, the price path in Figure 2.3 must also represent a special case of some sort. There are indeed two important qualifications: that the amount of the resource available and the cost of extracting it be known. Clearly, discoveries of new deposits, as well as cost-reducing innovations, can affect the price of a resource. Subject to the conflicting pulls of depletion and discovery, price is observed to fluctuate, often about a downward trend. This is not inconsistent with the simple theory we have been developing. The theory describes an equilibrium path, one that will tend to be followed in the absence of shocks provided by unanticipated discoveries. The theory can also be extended to describe an equilibrium with resource stocks augmented by (costly) exploration. These possibilities will be considered in Section 2.7. There we shall show that, in general, they will reduce the rate of price appreciation and may even make it negative. The magnitude of the effect is, of course, an empirical matter to which we shall return in Chapter 4.

The easy identification of an efficient pattern of exhaustible-resource allocation with a competitive equilibrium also deserves some qualification at this point. There are at least two sources of difficulty. First, as with other goods or resources, externalities or, more generally, market failures can make an equilibrium inefficient. Two kinds of externalities seem particularly important in the case of extractive resources: spillovers associated with exploitation of a common pool (of oil or fish, to take frequently cited examples) by several different producers, and environmental disruption. The common-pool problem will be discussed further in Chapter 3, and environmental externalities will be considered in Chapters 5 and 6.

A second source of divergence between market-determined and efficient rates of depletion is the divergence between private and social rates of discount. We have already seen the crucial role played by the discount rate in determining resource price and output paths. If, as some economists and others have suggested, the appropriate social discount rate is below the rate used by private resource owners, there may be a tendency for resources to be used up too quickly in a market economy. The effect of discounting on depletion is further discussed in Section 2.6, and private versus social discount rates, along with related questions concerning the welfare of future generations, will be discussed in Section 2.8.[4]

There is perhaps one final point that should be made before we launch on a discussion of optimal depletion in the next section. By optimal depletion we mean efficient depletion, and by this we mean, as explained in connection with our numerical example, the pattern of depletion that maximizes the present value of net benefits from the resource. Now, when we make a decision on the basis of present value, we are, as in the example, discounting the benefits that accrue to future periods, or generations. The resulting effect on income distribution between the generations is the concern of Section 2.8. But there is another distributional issue as well, namely, the effect of exhaustible-resource use on the income distribution within a generation, or a period. Thus far we have spoken of net benefits from resource use, without specifying to whom the benefits (or the costs) accrue. Yet clearly all individuals do not share equally in the fruits of depletion. Some gain a little, others gain a lot, and still others may be hurt. Moreover, the gain or loss of a dollar of income may mean more to some than to others.

The concept of efficiency we shall be using (maximization of net benefits) does not address these distributional concerns. In our models a dollar is a dollar, no matter to whom it accrues. Benefits and costs are added algebraically, and the net result is all that matters. This concept of efficiency has been long established in welfare economics, especially in applied studies, as have objections to its use. Because none of this is in any way special to extractive or environmental resources, we shall have little to add to the discussion. However, the impacts of pollution-control policies on income distribution will be discussed briefly in Chapter 6. My personal

---

[4] A clear nontechnical discussion of these issues is provided by Solow (1974*a*). For a somewhat more technical review, at about the level of the discussion in this section, see the work of Heal (1977).

feeling is that efficiency is, or ought to be, an important consideration in the making of resource and environmental policy, but it need not be the only one. It is important to know how to use a resource efficiently, but neither the economist nor the policy maker is obliged to ignore distributional consequences.

### 2.4. A model of optimal depletion

We come now to the heart of this chapter, a derivation and extension of the results discussed to this point. We shall proceed by first obtaining the necessary conditions for efficient or optimal depletion and then showing how they can be realized in a competitive equilibrium.[5]

The major difference between the example in the last section and the model to be developed here lies in an emphasis on the resource stock. Whereas we previously assumed that extraction costs were not affected by the size of the remaining stock, we now assume that they are. This leads to a somewhat more general formulation of the problem of how to extract a resource over time to maximize net present value, and it importantly affects the solution.

Formally, we shall write the extraction costs for each of $n$ identical resource firms as a function of both the firm's output and the stock it holds. In symbols, $c = c(y_t, X_t)$, where $c$ is the (total) cost of extraction, $y_t$ is output in period $t$, and $X_t$ is the resource stock in $t$. Cost can be positively ($\partial c/\partial X > 0$) or negatively ($\partial c/\partial X < 0$) related to the stock [or not related

---

[5] We have already suggested the intuition behind this result. The first proof, using calculus-of-variations methods, is due to Hotelling (1931), who also noted some of the qualifications. Probably in part because it was too difficult, mathematically, to be accessible to many economists at the time, Hotelling's work was largely neglected until the recent burst of activity in this area. However, there were some indications of interest in the 1960s: a diagrammatic exposition of Hotelling's results (Herfindahl, 1967) and further mathematical analysis (Gordon, 1967; Cummings, 1969). Recent lucid demonstrations of the efficiency of a competitive equilibrium include those by Schulze (1974) and Weinstein and Zeckhauser (1975).

$(\partial c/\partial X = 0)$, as in the example in the last section], but normally we will assume that it is negatively related. That is, the smaller the remaining stock, the larger the cost of extracting a unit.

What is the justification for this? As Ricardo (1817) originally suggested, it seems plausible that the higher-quality (i.e., the lower-cost) deposits of an exhaustible resource will be worked first, just as the better agricultural land is cultivated first. Mill (1848) later pointed out that increasing costs can set in even as the deeper and thinner portions of a single deposit are worked. Either way, the cost will tend to rise as the stock is depleted. Thus, letting cost be a function of stock size seems to be a simple but general way of capturing both of these effects.

Although it is simple, this formulation implies something quite profound about exhaustible resources; namely, they are, in a sense, not exhaustible! What is exhaustible (neglecting discovery and technical change) is the amount available at modest cost. Depletion proceeds indefinitely, because ultimate Malthusian limits are never reached. On the other hand, Ricardian limits, in the form of increasing costs, can set in very early. At some point (again, influenced by discovery and technical change), perhaps where the resource will have to be recovered at very high cost from "average rock," presumably the economy switches to a substitute. Clearly, if no substitute exists, and if the cost of recovering the resource becomes prohibitive, the prospects for continued economic growth will be bleak, as the classical economists feared. The real question, as most students of the problem agree, is one of costs – of providing some sort of substitute or of continuing to recover the resource. Nothing in our model says that these costs will not become very high (or, for that matter, that they will). All of this will be discussed at greater length in Chapter 4 in relation to the evidence on resource scarcity.

Before introducing the other elements of the model, let us take note of another difference between costs as specified in the model and in the earlier example. In the example, all production might just as well have come from a single deposit.

We did not trouble to distinguish separate producers. Now we shall find it convenient to do so, not because this is needed to characterize optimal depletion but because it greatly facilitates the analysis of competitive depletion and its relationship to the optimum. In what follows we first suppose that many (identical) resource firms are under the control of a planner and determine the necessary conditions for a program of optimal depletion, the conditions that tell the planner how much of the resource is to be produced by each of the firms, and therefore in total, in each period. Following this, we suppose that the firms are independently managed and competitive and that they seek to maximize the present value of profits. If the resulting depletion path turns out to be the same as the planner's, we shall have shown that a competitive equilibrium is efficient, subject, of course, to the qualifications concerning potential market failure noted earlier.

Now let us pick up the description of the rest of the model. The measure of benefit, as in the example, is willingness to pay, given by the integral of the demand for the resource. In symbols, this is $\int_0^{ny_t} p(\zeta)d\zeta$, where $ny_t$ is consumption in period $t$, $p(ny_t)$ is demand in period $t$, and $\zeta$ is a variable of integration. The net benefit is just the difference between benefit and cost: $\int_0^{ny_t} p(\zeta)d\zeta - nc(y_t, X_t)$.

Because the essence of the depletion problem is that what is extracted and consumed in one period is not available in another, in making a decision about what to extract in any one period the planner must look to the effects on benefits and costs in other periods as well. Thus the planner's problem is to maximize the present value of the sum of benefits minus costs over all relevant periods. In symbols, this is

$$\underset{y_0,\dots,y_t,\dots,y_{T-1}}{\text{maximize}} \sum_{t=0}^{T} \frac{\int_0^{ny_t} p(\zeta)d\zeta - nc(y_t, X_t)}{(1 + r)^t} \tag{2.3}$$

There are, of course, constraints involving the resource stock available to each firm. Here we shall generalize a bit from the earlier example. There we specified $X_0 = 10$ and $X_T = X_2 = 0$. We now require (for each firm) only that $X_0 = \overline{X}_0$ and $X_T = \overline{X}_T$, where $\overline{X}_0$ and $\overline{X}_T$ are known numbers. The constraint on cumulative extraction by the firm becomes

$$\sum_{t=0}^{T-1} y_t = \overline{X}_0 - \overline{X}_T.$$

This can be written to provide additional information about the evolution of the resource stock through time. We know that the amount extracted from the stock in any period is just the difference in the amounts in the stock at the beginning and end of the period. That is, $y_0 = \overline{X}_0 - X_1, y_1 = X_1 - X_2, \ldots, y_t = X_t - X_{t+1}, \ldots, y_{T-1} = X_{T-1} - \overline{X}_T$. Summing both sides of these constraint equations, we get $\Sigma_{t=0}^{T-1} y_t = \overline{X}_0 - \overline{X}_T$. But let us display the additional information by writing the constraints as

$$y_t = X_t - X_{t+1} \quad (t = 0 \text{ to } t = T - 1 \text{ for each firm}) \quad (2.4)$$

We can now proceed to solve the constrained maximization problem by setting up a Lagrangian function, differentiating with respect to the $y_t$, the $X_t$, and the multipliers, and setting the resulting expressions equal to zero.[6] The Lagrangian is

$$L = \sum_{t=0}^{T} \frac{\int_0^{ny_t} p(\zeta)d\zeta - nc(y_t, X_t)}{(1 + r)^t} + n \sum_{t=0}^{T-1} \mu_t(X_t - X_{t+1} - y_t)$$
$$+ n\alpha(\overline{X}_0 - X_0) + n\beta(\overline{X}_T - X_T) \quad (2.5)$$

where the $\mu_t$, $\alpha$, and $\beta$ are Lagrange multipliers.

[6] The method of analysis here is based on the discussion of discrete-time optimal control provided by Varaiya (1972). A somewhat similar adaptation is that of Opaluch (1980). For more rigorous and more detailed derivations of optimal-control results and discussions of their role in economics, there are various sources. On an intermediate level there is the work of Almon (1967) and Dorfman (1969). More formal treatments include those by Intriligator (1971), Arrow and Kurz (1970), and Hadley and Kemp (1971). No doubt others have appeared since. An exposition of applications to natural-resource problems and environmental problems is provided by V. L. Smith (1977), but this does assume familiarity with the mathematical methods.

The necessary conditions for $y_t$ and $X_t$ are, respectively,

$$\frac{p(ny_t) - (\partial c/\partial y_t)}{(1 + r)^t} - \mu_t = 0 \quad (t = 0 \text{ to } t = T - 1) \tag{2.6}$$

and

$$-\frac{\partial c/\partial X_t}{(1 + r)^t} + \mu_t - \mu_{t-1} = 0 \quad (t = 1 \text{ to } t = T - 1) \tag{2.7}$$

Equation (2.6) is the first condition of optimal depletion. It says that, along an optimal path, the price of the resource $p(ny_t)$ is just equal to the marginal cost of extraction $\partial c/\partial y_t$ plus the (undiscounted) royalty $\mu_t(1 + r)^t$. Note that the Lagrange multiplier $\mu_t$ is interpreted as the royalty: the value, in terms of the (discounted) objective function (2.3), of a unit of the resource "in the ground."

Equation (2.7) is the second condition of optimal depletion that describes the behavior of the royalty over time. However, some manipulation is needed to get this in a form that is easily interpreted. Because $\mu_t$ is a discounted royalty, we can write it as $\mu_t = \lambda_t(1 + r)^{-t}$, where $\lambda_t$ is an undiscounted royalty. Then (2.7) becomes

$$-\frac{\partial c}{\partial X_t}(1 + r)^{-t} + \lambda_t(1 + r)^{-t} - \lambda_{t-1}(1 + r)^{-(t+1)} = 0$$

or, following a little further manipulation,

$$\lambda_t - \lambda_{t-1} = r\lambda_{t-1} + \frac{\partial c}{\partial X_t} \tag{2.8}$$

This is almost, but not quite, the statement of the second condition we seek. One further step is needed. The planner's problem has been formulated, to this point, in discrete time. Let us now rewrite it (or, rather, just the solution) in continuous time. There are two reasons for doing this. First, the optimal-depletion conditions and, more generally, the optimal-control conditions are normally stated in continuous time. Second, in part because of this, our subsequent analysis will be a good deal easier.

Suppose, then, we let the time periods become very short. Equation (2.6), the first condition, is essentially unaffected. However, equation (2.8) becomes

$$\frac{d\lambda_t}{dt} = r\lambda_t + \frac{\partial c}{\partial X_t} \qquad (2.9)$$

Let us see in what way this result is consistent with our earlier and less formal derivation of the second condition of optimal depletion and in what way it tells us something new.

### *Discussion and interpretation of results: the behavior of royalty, cost, and price*

Suppose, first, as in the earlier discussion, that the extraction cost is not affected by the size of the remaining stock of the resource; that is, suppose $\partial c / \partial X_t = 0$. Then equation (2.9) confirms that the rate of change in the royalty $(d\lambda_t / dt)/\lambda_t$ is just equal to the rate of interest $r$. If, in addition, the marginal cost of extraction $\partial c / \partial y_t$ is negligible, then from equation (2.6) we know that the royalty is equivalent to the price, and equation (2.9) tells us that the rate of price change $(dp/dt)/p$ is just equal to the rate of interest.

This is often cited as a fundamental result in the economics of exhaustible resources. Our analysis shows it to be a rather special case, but there may be circumstances in which it holds as a reasonable approximation, at least. Persian Gulf oil, for example, is extracted at a cost of 10¢ to 20¢ per barrel, certainly a negligible fraction of the selling price ($30–$40 per barrel, as of this writing). Moreover, the effect of cumulative depletion on extraction costs is probably negligible in the larger fields. Of course, price does not rise smoothly at the rate of interest, because OPEC decisions do not necessarily coincide with those that would be taken by a planner seeking to maximize consumer surpluses or those that would emerge from the workings of a competitive market.

Now, suppose that the extraction cost is affected by the size of the remaining stock; in particular, suppose that it is negatively affected ($\partial c/\partial X_t < 0$), as it is in a world in which depletion proceeds from better and more accessible deposits (or portions of deposits) to poorer and less accessible ones. In this case, equation (2.9) tells us that the rate of change in the royalty is less than the rate of interest.[7]

The wedge between these two quantities, $\partial c/\partial X_t$, can be interpreted as a kind of dividend to holding a unit of the resource in the stock. Remember that the return to investment generally includes both a capital gain and a dividend. We argued earlier that there is no dividend on investment in resources in the ground and that therefore the entire return must come in the form of a capital gain, the rise in the royalty. But when a reduction in the stock has the effect of increasing subsequent extraction costs, then holding the resource in the ground and not reducing the stock provides a dividend in the form of a cost saving. Thus we can rewrite equation (2.9) as $d\lambda_t/dt - \partial c/\partial X_t = r\lambda_t$, which says that the capital gain plus the dividend (remember that $\partial c/\partial X_t < 0$, so $-\partial c/\partial X_t > 0$) is equal to the interest cost of investing in resources in the ground, $r\lambda$.

An interesting intermediate case is that in which the extraction cost is not affected by stock size over an interval corresponding, say, to production from a deposit of constant quality, but rises when the deposit is exhausted and production shifts to a poorer deposit. In this case the royalty will rise at the rate of interest along the intensive margin, that is, as the richer deposit is being depleted ($\partial c/\partial X_t = 0 \rightarrow d\lambda/dt = r\lambda_t > 0$), and

---

[7] Although the rate of royalty or price increase is often related simply to the rate of interest, a more complicated condition, such as that given in equation (2.9), has been derived in a number of studies, including those of Cummings (1969), Schulze (1974), Weinstein and Zeckhauser (1975), Heal (1976), Solow and Wan (1976), Peterson and Fisher (1977), and Pindyck (1978*b*). Solow and Wan and Heal attributed the effect of depletion on costs to shifts among deposits. A more explicit treatment of the many-deposit case is provided by Weitzman (1976) and Hartwick (1978).

then fall at the extensive margin, that is, as production shifts to the poorer deposit. This generalizes the result obtained in the simple case considered in the last section, where the royalty rose at the rate of interest as a resource was mined at constant cost and then fell to zero as the switch was made to a backstop.

Of course, it is the resource price, not the royalty, in which we are normally interested and that we observe. What does our model imply about the behavior of prices over time? Rewriting equation (2.6) in terms of $\lambda_t$, not $\mu_t$, and differentiating with respect to time, we obtain

$$\frac{dp}{dt} = \frac{d(\partial c/\partial y_t)}{dt} + \frac{d\lambda_t}{dt} \qquad (2.10)$$

That is, the change in price depends, not surprisingly, on the change in extraction cost and the change in the royalty. The latter, as we have just concluded, is indeterminate, in general, although we can say whether it is rising or falling in important special cases. The cost change can also be further analyzed.

The first term on the right-hand side (RHS) of equation (2.10), $d(\partial c/\partial y_t)/dt$, is the total derivative of marginal extraction cost with respect to time. Suppressing the time subscripts, we have

$$\frac{d(\partial c/\partial y)}{dt} = \frac{\partial^2 c}{\partial y^2}\frac{dy}{dt} + \frac{\partial^2 c}{\partial X \partial y}\frac{dX}{dt} \qquad (2.10a)$$

and substituting $-y$ for $dX/dt$,

$$\frac{d(\partial c/\partial y)}{dt} = \frac{\partial^2 c}{\partial y^2}\frac{dy}{dt} - y\frac{\partial^2 c}{\partial X \partial y} \qquad (2.11)$$

In other words, the change in marginal extraction cost over time is due to the change in the amount extracted and the change in the stock. The first term on the RHS of equation (2.11) represents a movement along the marginal cost curve; the second reflects a shift of the curve. What is the net effect? There are numerous possibilities, special cases, depending mainly on the nature of the cost function. We can trace just a few.

If marginal cost is not affected by stock size, the second term on the RHS of equation (2.11) vanishes. Then, assuming that marginal cost as a function of output is increasing ($\partial^2 c/\partial y^2 > 0$), the net change over time will depend solely on the change in output. However, if marginal cost increases as the stock decreases ($\partial^2 c/\partial X \partial y < 0$), the second term on the RHS is positive. Still another plausible possibility is that marginal cost as a function of output is constant, for a given stock, so that the first term on the RHS vanishes and the change in cost is unambiguously positive.

Adding the generally indeterminate change in cost to the generally indeterminate change in the royalty obviously leaves us with a generally indeterminate change in price over time. But special cases, depending again on assumptions about costs, are of some interest. Suppose, for example, that costs are negligible. Then the equation for price change becomes

$$\frac{dp}{dt} = rp$$

the very special case just discussed in which the price rises at the rate of interest.

If extraction costs are not negligible, but also are not affected by the size of the stock, the price equation becomes

$$\frac{dp}{dt} = r\lambda = r\left(p - \frac{\partial c}{\partial y}\right)$$

Price rises more slowly, but at a rate that approaches the rate of interest as it draws away from extraction cost. This is essentially the case considered in the last section, with the difference that marginal cost as a function of output is now not assumed constant.

However, if this cost is constant for a given stock, but rises as the stock falls, the price equation will be [substituting equations (2.9) and (2.11) into equation (2.10)]

$$\frac{dp}{dt} = r\left(p - \frac{\partial c}{\partial y}\right) + \frac{\partial c}{\partial X} - y\frac{\partial^2 c}{\partial X \partial y}$$

This case is sufficiently general that the sign of $dp/dt$ is once more indeterminate. The first term on the RHS is positive, as is the third, but the second is negative. Finally, note that if we back off a bit and assume that the cost function can be written less generally as $c(y,X) = yc(X)$, the last two terms on the RHS cancel each other, leaving $dp/dt$ unambiguously positive.

Such a rich variety of results (and there are still other possibilities) is not easily summarized. However, if pressed, we should say that the price of an exhaustible resource will rise along an optimal depletion path, but not in any simple fashion. Later in this chapter we shall consider briefly how this conclusion is affected by the possibility of expanding the resource stock through exploration.

### The optimal-control conditions

Thus far we have derived the conditions for optimal depletion of an exhaustible resource. These are easily modified to yield more general optimal-control conditions. Let us do this, both because the optimal-control conditions are customarily stated in a way that makes them easy to remember and because we shall have occasion to use them later on.

The net benefit from depletion at any time is made up of two components: the current flow of benefits minus costs, $\int_0^{ny_t} p(\zeta)d\zeta - nc(y_t,X_t)$, and the impact on future flows caused by removal from the stock of lower-cost units of the resource. The value of this impact is just $\omega_t y_t$, the (undiscounted) value of a unit in the stock of each firm, $\omega_t$, multiplied by the number of units removed, $y_t$ (note that $\omega_t = n\lambda_t$). The net benefit from depletion at time $t$ can then be written as

$$H = \int_0^{ny_t} p(\zeta)d\zeta - nc(y_t, X_t) - \omega_t y_t \qquad (2.12)$$

where $H$ represents the Hamiltonian, as the expression is known.

Now notice that differentiating $H$ with respect to $y_t$ yields $p(ny_t) - \partial c/\partial y_t - \omega_t/n$, so that the first condition of optimal depletion, equation (2.6), can be rewritten simply as

$$\frac{\partial H}{\partial y_t} = 0 \qquad (2.13)$$

The interpretation is that the Hamiltonian measures the net effect of extraction, current benefits minus future losses. It is maximized by extracting the resource at a rate such that the net benefit from the marginal unit extracted is just balanced by the loss of the unit from the stock.

Turning now to the second condition, because $\partial H/\partial X_t = -n(\partial c/\partial X_t)$, we have

$$\frac{d\omega_t}{dt} = r\omega_t - \frac{\partial H}{\partial X_t} \qquad \text{or} \quad \frac{\partial H}{\partial X_t} = -\dot{\omega}_t + r\omega_t \qquad (2.14)$$

Alternatively, equation (2.9), in terms of $\lambda$, can be rewritten as

$$\frac{\partial \lambda_t}{dt} = r\lambda_t - \frac{\partial H/\partial X_t}{n}$$

Equations (2.13) and (2.14) are the optimal-control conditions, written in terms of the Hamiltonian, that correspond to the optimal-depletion conditions of our problem. A third condition can also be written in terms of the Hamiltonian. The constraint equation, in continuous time, is $dX_t/dt = -y_t$, or, equivalently,

$$\frac{dXt}{dt} = \frac{\partial H}{\partial \omega_t} \qquad (2.15)$$

The three optimal-control conditions are shown in Table 2.1, along with the corresponding optimal-depletion conditions and a complete statement of the depletion problem in continuous time. Notice that, in continuous time, the discount factor is $e^{-rt}$, not $(1 + r)^{-t}$. In the terminology of control theory, $y_t$ is the control variable, $X_t$ is the state variable, and $\omega_t$ is the (undiscounted) co-state or auxiliary variable, akin to a

Table 2.1. *A comparison of optimal-depletion and optimal-control conditions*

---

*The depletion problem*

$$\underset{\{y_t\}}{\text{maximize}} \int_0^T \left[ \int_0^{ny_t} p(\zeta)d\zeta - nc(y_t, X_t) \right] e^{-rt}dt$$

subject to

$$\frac{dX_t}{dt} = -y_t$$

$$X_0 = \overline{X}_0$$

$$X_T = \overline{X}_T$$

*Hamiltonian*

$$H = \int_0^{ny_t} p(\zeta)d\zeta - nc(y_t, X_t) - \omega_t y_t$$

| Optimal-depletion conditions | Optimal-control conditions |
|---|---|
| $p(ny_t) - \dfrac{\partial c}{\partial y_t} - \lambda_t = 0$ | $\dfrac{\partial H}{\partial y_t} = 0$ |
| $\dfrac{d\lambda_t}{dt} = r\lambda_t + \dfrac{\partial c}{\partial X_t}$ | $\dfrac{d\omega_t}{dt} = r\omega_t - \dfrac{\partial H}{\partial X_t}$ |
| $\dfrac{dX_t}{dt} = -y_t$ | $\dfrac{dX_t}{dt} = \dfrac{\partial H}{\partial \omega_t}$ |

---

Lagrange multiplier. In the Hamiltonian the co-state variable is attached to the constraint or transition equation describing the behavior of the state variable over time.

Now let us apply the general control conditions to the problem of competitive depletion.

### Competitive depletion

The difference between this and the preceding problem is that instead of a hypothetical planner seeking to maximize net social benefits from the resource, the decision maker here is a firm seeking to maximize profits. In the framework of the preceding problem, let us focus on one of the $n$ identical firms, now assumed to be acting independently. The firm is also assumed to be competitive, taking price $p = p(ny)$. The firm's problem, in symbols, is

$$\underset{\{y_t\}}{\text{maximize}} \int_0^T [py_t - c(y_t, X_t)]e^{-rt}dt \qquad (2.16)$$

subject to

$$\frac{dX_t}{dt} = -y_t$$

$$X_0 = \overline{X}_0$$

$$X_T = \overline{X}_T$$

The Hamiltonian for this problem is

$$H = py_t - c(y_t, X_t) - \rho_t y_t \qquad (2.17)$$

where $\rho_t$ is the co-state variable, and the necessary conditions are, from Table 2.1,

$$\frac{\partial H}{\partial y_t} = p - \frac{\partial c}{\partial y_t} - \rho_t = 0 \qquad (2.18)$$

and

$$\frac{d\rho_t}{dt} = r\rho_t - \frac{\partial H}{\partial X_t} = r\rho_t + \frac{\partial c}{\partial X_t} \qquad (2.19)$$

These are exactly equivalent to equations (2.6) and (2.9), if $\rho_t = \lambda_t$. Because the equations and the parameters are the same, the solution values of the variables must also be the same; in particular, $\rho_t = \lambda_t$. (Away from the solution, $\rho_t$ is not, in general, equal to $\lambda_t$.)

### Some qualifications, and a preview of the rest of the chapter

What we have shown is that the conditions that describe the profit-maximizing depletion path for a competitive producer are identical with the conditions that describe the socially optimal path, given a number of assumptions of varying degrees of plausibility. What happens when the assumptions do not hold is the subject of the remainder of this chapter. We shall be looking first at the problem of monopoly, where the resource firm is no longer a pricetaker, but recognizes that its production will affect the price of the resource. It seems obvious that this ought to change production decisions, and hence the depletion path. But how? Does the monopolist gobble up the resource too quickly, as compared with the competitive firm or the planner? Or does he sit back and hoard it, behaving in effect like a conservationist?

There is also the problem of externalities, such as pollution. We have assumed that the extraction-cost function facing the firm is the same as that facing the planner, but if extraction and related downstream activities entail external costs, this need not be so. Environmental externalities of various sorts will be discussed in Chapters 5 and 6.

Still another problem, to be treated later in this chapter, is uncertainty about future demand and supply of the resource. We have assumed that the planner knows future demand and that the firm knows future prices, in deriving depletion paths for each. What can we say about the situation in which these future magnitudes are not known? And how are prospects for expanding the known resource stock through exploration folded into the depletion decision?

Finally, we have seen the importance of the discount rate in determining the depletion profile, for both planner and firm. The optimality of the competitive equilibrium clearly depends on the discount rate being the same for both. If, as some economists and others have suggested, the market rate is "too high," royalty and price may tend to rise more rapidly, and depletion may proceed too quickly. Questions and issues related to the role of time in decisions about exhaustible-resource use will be treated in the concluding section of this chapter.

### 2.5. **Monopoly in resource markets**

How monopoly affects the rate of depletion is an important question, because monopoly episodes are not uncommon in the history of resource markets. Let us look first at the pure monopoly, an industry composed of a single producer. Following this, we shall consider some complications introduced by the relationships between the members of a *cartel,* an association of producers who band together to act as a monopolist. The current leading example of this sort of behavior is, of course, OPEC, the oil cartel.

The monopolist's problem can be stated, analytically, exactly as the competitive firm's problem in equation (2.16). The only difference is in the first condition of optimal depletion, equation (2.18), because the monopolist will take into account the influence of his output decision on price. This condition becomes

$$p + y_t \frac{dp}{dy_t} - \frac{\partial C}{\partial y_t} - \rho_t = 0 \tag{2.20}$$

The royalty, $\rho_t$, is then the difference between marginal revenue, $p + y_t(dp/dy_t)$, and marginal cost, $dc/dy_t$. Although the royalty behaves according to equation (2.19), price (and therefore output) will, in general, behave differently than in the competitive case. Whether the resource is depleted more or less rapidly by the monopolist depends on the nature of demand (the relationship between price and marginal revenue), especially its behavior over time. This is easily illustrated with the aid of some simple numerical examples.

We have already determined, in Section 2.3, the solution to a problem involving 10 barrels of oil to be optimally depleted over two periods, given demand, costs, and a discount rate. This is also, of course, the competitive solution. Now, how does the monopoly solution compare? The key is that marginal revenue less marginal cost must rise at the rate of interest (remember, in this example $\partial c/\partial X_t = 0$). That is, instead of equation (2.1), we have

$$MR_1 - MC = (MR_0 - MC)(1 + r)$$

and substituting for $MR_1$, $MR_0$, MC, and $r$,

$$10 - 2y_1 - 2 = (10 - 2y_0 - 2)(1 + 0.10)$$

This equation can be solved for $y_0$ and $y_1$ (because $y_0 + y_1 = 10$, we have two equations in two unknowns) to yield $y_0 = 4.95$ and $y_1 = 5.05$. These values compare with the competitive $y_0 = 5.14$ and $y_1 = 4.86$, indicating that the monopolist depletes the resource more slowly.

This is not a perfectly general result. However, it does follow as long as elasticity is decreasing, over quantities. The linear demand curve in our problem clearly falls in this class. But examples can be constructed that show the monopolist accelerating depletion, given a demand curve that exhibits increasing elasticity over some range of output.[8]

The same result, the monopolist accelerating depletion, can also occur as a consequence of changes in demand over time. For example, suppose demand becomes less elastic, shifting from $p_0 = 10 - y_0$ to $p_1 = 20 - 2y_1$. Then, proceeding as before, the competitive depletion path is $y_0 = 3.48$, $y_1 = 6.52$, and the monopoly path is $y_0 = 4.97$, $y_1 = 5.03$. This makes sense. The monopolist can restrict second-period output to take advantage of the less elastic demand.

There is a qualification here, however. If depletion is accelerated, as in the example, price may rise at a rate greater than the rate of interest, as in fact it does in the example. But it is not clear that such an equilibrium can be sustained in the face of the opportunity it creates for profitable arbitrage. Further, the necessary condition for accelerated depletion, elasticity falling over time, does not seem very likely. Instead, we might expect that demand will become increasingly elastic as substitutes become increasingly available. It is easily verified that increasing elasticity leads to slower depletion by a monopolist. The intuition in this case is that the monopolist restricts

---

[8] This was done by Lewis (1976), who also derived the general result that decreasing elasticity leads to slower depletion by a monopolist.

first-period output to take advantage of the (relatively) inelastic demand.

My impression, then, is that there is a tendency for monopoly to retard depletion in a model where a resource stock of uniform quality is exhausted in finite time, as in the examples just analyzed, and in much of the literature on this question.[9] To this, I would only add the conjecture that the tendency would be strengthened in a model where costs rise with cumulative depletion. Where costs do not rise and the resource is entirely depleted, competitive and monopoly depletion paths must cross. If the monopolist produces less (than the competitive industry) in the early periods, he must ultimately produce more. But my conjecture is that this need not happen where the resource is not exhausted, where very high cost units remain in the ground indefinitely. In such a case, cumulative production need not be the same under both regimes; in particular, it may be lower for the monopolist, who simply produces less in each period.[10]

*Intermediate market structures: the resource cartel*

Thus far we have been contrasting the polar cases of perfect competition and pure monopoly. What of intermediate market structures, in particular one or another form of oli-

---

[9] This was Hotelling's view, and it is supported by the results of more recent studies by Weinstein and Zeckhauser (1975), Kay and Mirrlees (1975), Dasgupta and Stiglitz (1975), Stiglitz (1976), and Sweeney (1977). A number of these studies obtained the result that monopoly and competitive depletion paths coincide if elasticity is constant over quantities and over time and if there are no extraction costs. This is easily illustrated in our numerical format, but we shall not bother to do so, because the result seems hardly more than a theoretical curiosity, given the stringent and unlikely conditions required. Assuming that the demand for a resource is a derived demand, Kamien and Schwartz (1977*a*,*b*) showed that constant (over quantities) elasticity depends on an aggregate production function that is Cobb-Douglas in form. Their analysis also allowed for general equilibrium effects. That is, the monopolist allows for the impact of his price on the incomes of those who demand the resource.

[10] A somewhat similar argument was made by Tullock (1979), but he put greater emphasis on the effect of changing demand elasticities.

gopoly? There are, of course, many different models of oligopoly behavior that are now being applied to exhaustible-resource industries. We shall not attempt a review of the literature here, other than to note an approach that has proved interesting in connection with the analysis of cartel, specifically OPEC, behavior.[11]

In this approach, the cartel, even acting as a unit, is not the only seller in the market. Some production comes from a "competitive fringe," small producers who take the price set by the cartel in each period. The cartel, in turn, takes account of fringe supply in setting price. With the additional (and crucial) assumption that fringe supply adjusts with a lag, a price path can be determined to maximize the present value of cartel profits.

This has been done for the OPEC cartel in a numerical simulation of the world oil market by Pindyck (1978*a*). The results, shown in Table 2.2, are quite different from those discussed thus far for a competitive industry or a monopoly, in that price change is not monotonic. The price initially jumps dramatically, to take advantage of the lag in fringe adjustment. It then falls, gradually (and modestly) over a period of about five years, and only after this time begins a slow and steady rise.

How well has the simulation tracked OPEC pricing decisions? OPEC did, in fact, jump the price of oil to around the predicted level, over $10 per barrel, but in 1974, not 1975. More significantly, price did fall, in real terms, over the next four to five years — especially if one takes into account the fall in the value of the dollar, in which oil prices are denominated, relative to other currencies. Moreover, early 1979 looked like the final turning point, with a modest price increase scheduled by OPEC. Up to this point, the agreement between theory and

---

[11] Contributions to the theory of resource cartels, generally with reference to OPEC, include those of Kalymon (1975), Blitzer, Meeraus, and Stoutjesdijk (1975), Schmalensee (1976), Salant (1976), Cremer and Weitzman (1976), Pindyck (1977*b*, 1978*a*), and Gilbert (1978*b*).

Table 2.2. *Optimal OPEC price path*

| Year | Price[a] |
|------|----------|
| 1975 | 14.08 |
| 1976 | 11.75 |
| 1977 | 10.70 |
| 1978 | 10.28 |
| 1979 | 10.19 |
| 1980 | 10.26 |
| 1985 | 11.28 |
| 1990 | 12.51 |
| 1995 | 13.80 |
| 2000 | 15.18 |
| 2005 | 16.72 |
| 2010 | 20.52 |

[a]1975 dollars, 10% discount rate.
*Source:* These figures are taken from a more detailed comprehensive table in the work of Pindyck (1978*a*).

simulation, on the one hand, and events, on the other, is striking.

By the middle of 1979, however, price had again jumped sharply. Why did the model suddenly fail? A general answer is that calling three key turning points, over a period of up to five years, is probably already more than one ought reasonably to expect of a model of such a complex process. In the more distant future, uncertainties multiply, institutions change, and so on. In the case at hand it seems fairly clear that the rapid price rise can be explained, at least in part, by the virtual halt in oil exports from Iran, which until 1979 was OPEC's second largest producer, after Saudi Arabia. The model, and for that matter economic theory, can perhaps be faulted for failing to predict the Islamic Revolution in Iran. A fairer conclusion, in my judgment, is that the model did reasonably well for a time, then ran into trouble because of events normally considered outside the realm of economics.

Note, by the way, the tendency of a dominant producer

initially to restrict output and raise price, just like a monopolist. To be sure, this represents another special case, but one that embodies a greater degree of realism than the simple two-period monopolies analyzed earlier.

Relationships between a dominant producer and the competitive fringe are of interest whether or not the producer also happens to be, like OPEC, a cartel. But there is a classic question concerning cartel behavior that has recently received an illuminating answer in another application to OPEC pricing and production decisions, an extension by Hnyilicza and Pindyck (1976) of Pindyck's model of a unified cartel.

The question is how the implied output restrictions (implied by the cartel's price increase) are to be allocated among the members. Cartels are generally believed to be unstable because of the difficulties they face in trying to resolve this question. Each member, especially each small member, has a powerful incentive to cheat, to sell more than his assigned share by slightly shaving price. It is clear that if all members (or even a substantial fraction) try to do this, the cartel will collapse. There has, in fact, been some scattered price shaving by OPEC members over the past several years. But the cartel has raised prices very substantially and has held together rather well, by and large. Why has it been so successful?

One reason, clearly, is the enormous incentive. Pindyck's simulation suggests a joint gain from cartelization in the neighborhood of $1 trillion, present value! Where this much money is at stake, ways may be found to overcome the counterincentive to cheat. Another reason is probably the Iranian cutback. This was fortuitous, but it has certainly helped solve the question, for the past two years at least.

What the study by Hnyilicza and Pindyck (1976) shows is that the dynamics in the exhaustible-resource case suggest a more general solution: rotate the cutbacks among the members. Specifically, for OPEC, members were classified in the study as either savers, with (relatively) low immediate cash needs and a low discount rate, or spenders, with high cash needs and a high discount rate. In a numerical simulation of pricing and saver and spender output decisions, discounted profits were increased for both groups (over the amounts they would receive under historically given output shares) by having the savers absorb the initial cutbacks.

There is some evidence that this solution has been adopted by OPEC. The model simulation called for no production from the savers, initially. Clearly this is not realistic. As these authors recognized, the temptation to cheat would be strong, because savers would risk the breaking up of the cartel before they would even begin to deplete their reserves. Further, the model appears not to take account of the costs of adjusting away from historical production levels. That is, the spenders might not be able to expand production as rapidly as they would need to in order to take up the slack caused by a complete shutdown by the savers. Nor, presumably, would the savers, for their part, welcome the idea of a complete, if temporary, shutdown, with very substantial investments in capacity for producing, transporting, and refining oil already in place. Yet the model does point in the right direction. Much, if not all, of the excess capacity in OPEC is in Saudi Arabia, the principal saver country. Despite ambitious domestic investment plans, the Saudis have, in effect, absorbed the cutbacks needed to sustain OPEC.

We began this section by observing that some degree of monopoly has characterized markets for different resources at different times. Let us close by considering why this is so. Specifically, what are the conditions required for a successful cartel? What can we learn from the experience of OPEC?

Two things stand out, I think. First, the cartel must control a substantial share of the supply of the resource. OPEC, with about two-thirds of the world's oil reserves and a similar fraction of (noncommunist) world oil production, clearly qualifies. By contrast, the less well known international council of copper-exporting countries (CIPEC) accounts for only about one-third of (noncommunist) world copper production, and as shown in Pindyck's original study, they can expect very modest gains from cartelization.

The comparison of OPEC and CIPEC well illustrates a second condition for a successful cartel: inelastic supply response from the competitive fringe. This is satisfied in the case of OPEC by the lag in fringe supply. In the short to medium run, non-OPEC petroleum supplies are not easily expanded, despite large price increases. Unfortunately for CIPEC, this is not true for copper. "Secondary" copper, produced from scrap, appears to be quite responsive to price in the short run.[12]

Both conditions (a large share of the market and inelastic fringe supply) seem likely to be associated with substantial gains to cartelization. And if, as in the case of OPEC, the joint gains are large enough, it seems that ways might be found to hold the cartel together. A fair conclusion, on the basis of this casual survey of the evidence, is that whether or not a resource cartel will be successful depends importantly on the relationship between cartel and fringe supply, and also perhaps on the cartel's ability to solve the problem of allocating cutbacks among its members. Oil may not be the only exhaustible resource subject to cartelization and a rapid increase in price, but as the experience of the copper producers suggests, the success of OPEC does not necessarily portend similar developments in other resource markets.

### 2.6. Uncertainty and depletion

Just as we have considered whether monopoly speeds up or slows down depletion, we can raise the same question about the effect of uncertainty. There are two easy answers, both probably wrong or, at least, incomplete. One is that in an Arrow-Debreu economy, in which markets exist for every commodity at every date in every state of the world, uncer-

---

[12] See the econometric study of the world copper market by Fisher, Cootner, and Baily (1972).

tainty will not affect the rate of depletion. The reason is that the resource owner not only knows current and future prices but also can insure himself against adverse events, such as unexpectedly running out.

The difficulty is, of course, that such a complete set of contingent commodity markets does not exist in any real economy. There are insurance markets and, especially in the resource sector, futures markets in which dated commodities are traded. But these markets are limited. It is not possible, for example, to buy or sell at a given price a barrel of oil in the year 2000 in the event that there is a revolution in Saudi Arabia. So the difficulty is that resource owners must form expectations about future prices and then act on these expectations in making decisions about how much of the resource to use at any time. Further, they probably have to bear at least some of the risk involved in such decisions. The question we shall be asking in the remainder of this section is this: How are depletion decisions affected by uncertainty in an economy characterized by incomplete futures and risk markets?

We have said that there is another easy answer to the question about the effect of uncertainty. It is that uncertainty is typically reflected, at least in economic models, in a higher discount rate. And our own models tell us that the higher the discount rate the higher the rate of price increase, and therefore the rate of depletion. This is certainly one possible result, but I believe that a complete answer to the question about the effect of uncertainty is more complicated. Uncertainty can arise in many different ways, involving resource demand or supply or both. The effect on the rate of depletion is not always captured simply by an increase in the discount rate. Further, the effect of a change in the discount rate is not clear-cut, once we take into account the possibility of expanding the resource stock through exploration and development of new deposits.

A formal analysis of the effects of the many different kinds of uncertainty is beyond the scope of this study. The model of

Section 2.4 could be extended to deal with one or two, perhaps, but this would involve the more advanced mathematical methods of stochastic control. Instead, our strategy will be to identify some key uncertainties in resource markets and then see what intuition and a little analysis, where intuition may not suffice, backed by references to the literature, suggest about the effects of each. Note that we are trying to answer a positive question about the behavior of resource owners. There is also a question whether or not that behavior continues to be consistent with allocative efficiency. This turns out to be more difficult in that it involves first determining what we mean by efficiency in these circumstances.

*Effects on depletion of different kinds of uncertainty*
        The conventional answer to the question about the effect of uncertainty (namely, that it is reflected in an increase in the discount rate, which in turn accelerates depletion) can be appropriate when the uncertainty is about demand for the resource. This sort of uncertainty might be assumed to be positively related to the distance in time from the depletion decision. The resource owner is likely to be less certain about demand 10 years from today than about demand 1 year from today. If he is risk-averse, depletion will be shifted toward the present, just as it would be if the discount rate were raised.[13]

But demand uncertainty can be time-related in a different way that can lead to just the opposite conclusion. Suppose the variation in returns from extraction is related only to the amount extracted in a given period. Price is random, but the random component is identically distributed in each period. We noted earlier that, ignoring uncertainty, and assuming that price is rising, unless demand is shifting out over time, output will be falling (Figure 2.3). Then the variation in returns, which is proportional to output, must also be falling. The

---

[13] For a rigorous derivation of this result, see the work of Koopmans (1974) and Weinstein and Zeckhauser (1975).

risk-averse resource owner will therefore shift extraction toward the future.[14]

Still another kind of uncertainty related to demand for the resource can be shown (here a little analysis will be required) to lead to the conventional result, a tilt toward the present. Suppose the resource is subject to the threat of expropriation. Or suppose there is a risk that the market might be lost because of the appearance of a lower-cost substitute (a cheaper backstop) at some future date. The uncertain event is then one that, when it occurs, will destroy the value of the resource to the owner. What is uncertain is the date. Let us assume that the owner wishes to maximize the expected present value of the resource. In other words, he is risk-neutral. The result we shall obtain clearly follows if he is risk-averse, but it does not depend on this.

Let the probability of disaster through expropriation or obsolescence at the end of period $t$ be $\pi_t$, $0 \le \pi_t \le 1$, $\Sigma_t \pi_t = 1$, and let the value obtained during the period be $v_t$, $t = 0$ or $1$. The expected present value is

$$\pi_0 v_0 + \pi_1 \left[ v_0 + \frac{v_1}{(1 + r)} \right]$$

where $r$ is the discount rate. This can be rewritten as

$$(\pi_0 + \pi_1)v_0 + \pi_1 \frac{v_1}{(1 + r)}$$

Because $\pi_0 + \pi_1 = 1$, and $\pi_1 \le 1$, taking account of the probability of disaster by maximizing expected value is simply equivalent to adding a new discount rate or effectively increasing the old one.[15] This, in turn, means that price must rise more rapidly, and depletion is accelerated.

Now, what about uncertainty on the supply side? This may

---

[14] For a rigorous derivation of this result, see the work of Lewis (1977).

[15] Heal (1975*a*) established this result in a discussion of the effect on depletion of the threat of expropriation. For further theoretical

Table 2.3. *Effects on depletion of different kinds of uncertainty*

| Kind of uncertainty | Effects on depletion |
| --- | --- |
| Uncertain demand for the resource, with degree of uncertainty related to distance in time from the depletion decision | Shifts depletion toward the present |
| Uncertain demand for the resource, with variation in expected returns related to quantity of output | Shifts depletion toward the future |
| Uncertainty regarding date of event that will destroy the value of the resource to the owner (e.g., expropriation, discovery of a cheaper substitute) | Shifts depletion toward the present |
| Uncertain size of resource stock | Shifts depletion toward the future |

be largely uncertainty about the outcome of exploratory activity, which we shall treat in Section 2.7. But suppose exploration is not made explicit, and the resource owner's problem is simply one of optimally depleting a stock of unknown size. What he is worried about, in this case, is running out unexpectedly. Our intuition tells us, correctly, that if the owner is risk-averse he will wish to slow depletion to husband the resource against the (unknown) day when it will run out.[16]

The different kinds of uncertainty we have considered and their hypothesized effects on depletion are summarized in Table 2.3. These informal results suggest that uncertainty does

analysis of the expropriation problem, see the work of Long (1975). For a wider-ranging discussion of the effects of uncertainty about the date of arrival of a new technology that will substitute for an exhaustible resource, see the work of Dasgupta and Heal (1974). This question was studied under alternative market arrangements for the resource and the substitute by Dasgupta and Stiglitz (1975).

[16] Theoretical analyses of the problem of optimal depletion of an uncertain stock have been provided by Kemp (1976), Gilbert (1978*a*), Hoel (1978*b*), and Loury (1978).

not necessarily speed up depletion and therefore is not always appropriately reflected in a higher discount rate.

### Discounting and depletion

There is, in addition, difficulty with the proposition that a higher discount rate, for whatever reason, will lead to more rapid depletion. Thus far we have ignored the effect of the discount rate on activities other than depletion of a known deposit. But a high discount rate is likely to restrict investment generally, and the exploration and development of new deposits of a resource specifically. Exhaustible resources have been likened to hardtack consumed by sailors stranded on a barren island. Alternatively, they might be viewed as capital, capable of accumulation through investment. The truth probably contains elements of both views, but to the extent that resources are like capital goods, we might conjecture that a rise in the discount rate would lead to more rapid depletion for an initial period, followed by a reduced rate as a consequence of restricted investment in exploration and development during the initial period. This pattern seems particularly likely when the resource is subject to expropriation. Depletion from known, producing mines or wells would be accelerated, but little effort would go into finding and developing new ones.[17]

### Instability in resource markets

We may not be able to say whether uncertainty, in general, leads to a slowing down or a speeding up of depletion – it depends on the nature of the uncertainty. But there is a presumption that it is likely to lead at least to instability in

---

[17] Koopmans (1973) put the question whether exhaustible resources resemble hardtack or capital. The argument that the discount rate, through its effect on investment generally, can be negatively related to the rate of depletion was made by Scott (1955*a*) in a pioneering study of natural-resource economics. The conjectured response to a rise in the discount rate (a rise in the rate of extraction, followed by a fall) was obtained in a simulation of the time paths of exploration, extraction, reserves, and prices for a mineral industry by Peterson (1978).

resource markets, with the consequence that depletion, whether too fast or too slow, may be inefficient.[18]

As we noted earlier, in the absence of a complete set of futures markets, resource owners must form expectations about future prices and then act on these expectations in making decisions about how much of the resource to extract at any time. It is easy to think of ways in which this can lead to instability. (What is at stake here is the existence, not just the stability, of an equilibrium.)

Suppose that for some reason the current price of the resource rises. One plausible way for expectations regarding future prices to be formed is from the behavior of current prices, perhaps from a distributed lag of current and past prices. Suppose a rise in the current price leads to a rise in the expected future price. But this, in turn, will lead to a further rise in the current price as resource owners decide to cut back on production and hold more of the resource in the ground to take advantage of the higher price expected in the future.

Does the second-round rise in the current price imply a further rise in the future price? There does appear to be a possibility that the cycle of changes is explosive, that an equilibrium price path does not exist. Clearly the possibility depends on what we might call the *elasticity of expectations*, the percentage change in expected future price divided by the percentage change in the current price. In particular, the existence of an equilibrium will depend on the behavior of the elasticity of expectations at the "corners" (i.e., where the expected future price is either very high or very low).

It is easy to see how the elasticity must behave in order to assure an equilibrium. We can illustrate with a simple two-period example. We make the following assumptions: the current price of a competitively owned resource, oil, is $10 per barrel; next year's expected price is $11; there are no costs of

[18] For discussions of instability and inefficiency in resource markets, see the work of Nordhaus (1973*b*), Solow (1974*a*), Stiglitz (1974*b*), Heal (1975*a*), and Mishan (1977).

production; the discount rate is 10%; the elasticity of expectations is 2. Now, as a consequence of a shift in demand, the current price jumps 10%, to $11. Then next year's expected price must increase by 20%, to $13.20. But this, in turn, means that the price of oil is expected to rise by more than the rate of discount (a 10% rise, from a base of $11, would imply an expected future price of just $12.10). Oil in the ground becomes an attractive investment, so that owners of oil resources cut back on current production – until the current price rises to $12, restoring equilibrium in the capital market (a 10% rise, from this point, would mean that oil would sell for the expected $13.20 after one year).

So the change in current price has induced a change in expected future price, which in turn has induced a further change in current price. But this is not the end of the story. The $12 current price is not an equilibrium, because the rise from $11 induces a further change in next year's expected price (from $13.20 to $15.58), which, again, leads to cutbacks in current production to bring about a capital-market equilibrium in which the current price of oil is $14.16 per barrel! By exactly the same reasoning, this increase leads to still a further increase in the expected future price, and so on, in an explosive cycle.

Now suppose that all the conditions of this example hold, except that the elasticity of expectations is just 1. In this case, the original 10% increase, from $10 to $11, triggers a 10% increase in the expected future price, to $12.10. But this is exactly the price implied by an oil price increase at a rate equal to the rate of discount (also 10%, in our example). No change in production plans is called for, and so there is no pressure on current price.

Equally simple calculations will verify that any elasticity of expectations greater than 1 will lead to the explosive cycle, whereas an elasticity of 1 or less will be consistent with equilibrium of the price path. In fact, an equilibrium will result provided that the elasticity eventually falls to 1. This is not an unreasonable requirement. Resource owners, assisted perhaps by information compiled by government agencies, might be assumed to hold expectations of future prices rooted in their knowledge of developments in the technology for producing the resource and the likely demand for it. Although there will still be uncertainty, bounds on future price might be set, at least.

This informal analysis is supported by some results from the much more abstract theory of temporary general equilibrium, in particular by one of the conditions for the existence of a temporary general equilibrium. Suppose that future prices (for all commodities) are not known, and agents must form expectations and act on them in making decisions about current consumption and production, exactly as we have assumed for exhaustible resources. Current or spot markets can clear, but because individual expectations about the future need not coincide, markets will reopen, and must clear again, and so on. One condition for the existence of a sequence of spot-market equilibria (temporary equilibria) is that each individual's expected future price lies within a closed bounded interval. But this is essentially what we are talking about in the resource case. Knowledge of demand and cost developments is likely to set bounds on expected future price.[19]

### *Uncertainty and inefficiency*

Given that an equilibrium exists, will it be efficient? The theory of temporary general equilibrium can shed some light on this question, too. The key result is that the sequence of temporary equilibria need not be Pareto-optimal. Fairly restrictive conditions on consumer preferences must be met to assure optimality. Of course, if an equilibrium does not exist, the question of optimality can hardly be raised.

The question can also be attacked more directly by speci-

---

[19] Temporary-general-equilibrium theory was developed in several studies by Grandmont (e.g., Grandmont, 1977).

fying, as in our analysis of depletion under certainty, objectives for planner and private resource owner and determining whether or not the resulting price and output paths coincide. The choice of objective is crucial, but not obvious in either case. In particular, what do we assume about attitudes toward risk and about markets for sharing or spreading risk?

There has long been a notion that social decisions might appropriately be made on the basis of a neutral attitude toward risk, even though individual members of society are risk-averse. This is one reason that some economists believe that the true social discount rate is below the rates observed in private capital markets. The private rates include a premium for the risk borne by the individual investor, and this ought to be disregarded in a public investment decision.[20] Recently this notion has been formulated precisely with respect to the choice of objective for a planner. There are conditions under which maximization simply of aggregate expected consumer surplus will be efficient, but these conditions are fairly restrictive. What is required is essentially that all of the stochastic variation in price originate on the supply side. If demand is also subject to random shifts, as a consequence of fluctuations either in income or in any of the factors affecting consumer preferences, expected consumer surplus will not be an appropriate measure of welfare.[21]

For the private resource owner, the situation is somewhat different. Maximization of an expected value (e.g., expected profits) will generally not be appropriate. Because a complete set of markets for shifting risk does not exist, the resource owner will presumably display some degree of risk aversion. Recent analyses of firm behavior under uncertainty have suggested that even in an economy with a stock market, which permits risk sharing and spreading, simple expected-value

---

[20] For arguments in support of this assertion, see the work of Samuelson (1964), Vickrey (1964), and Arrow and Lind (1970).
[21] For a formal derivation of these conditions, see the work of Rogerson (1980).

maximization by the firm's manager is not in the interest of risk-averse shareholders.[22]

A comparison of firm and plan objectives suggests at least the possibility of some differences in attitudes toward risk and ways of dealing with it. Where differences exist, presumably competitive depletion will veer away from the planner's optimum. Still, we need to be cautious in drawing conclusions here. The planner cannot in all cases (perhaps not even in most cases of interest) appropriately ignore the risk preferences of individuals. Where he cannot, both socially optimal depletion and competitive depletion may be affected in much the same way by uncertainty.

A more fruitful way of proceeding may be to search for types of risk that would be perceived differently by planner and firm. One obvious example is the risk of expropriation. As we have suggested, this would lead a private resource owner to speed up depletion. But such behavior would not be socially optimal, at least not from a global point of view. Note, however, that if the resource owner could insure himself against the risk of expropriation, the depletion decision would not be distorted.

Finally, in weighing the merits of market and government in managing an exhaustible resource, we should take note of the skeptical view of governmental behavior generally voiced by economists of the Chicago and Virginia schools. We have already abandoned the assumption of a complete set of competitive markets, leading to all the difficulties discussed earlier. But if we now similarly abandon the notion of a perfect planner, it is not clear, in my judgment, that the government will do any better. Apart from the question of the planner's motivation to behave in the way assumed in our models, to allocate the resource efficiently, there is the question of his ability to do so. Even if the problem is simply to maximize the expected value of consumer surplus, the planner will need to

---

[22] For a discussion and review of the literature on firm objectives under uncertainty, see the work of Leland (1973).

form expectations of future demands. It is not obvious that he will be more successful in this than private resource owners will be in forecasting future prices.

## 2.7. Exploration

We have suggested that changes in expected future price have a feedback effect on the current price of a resource. A rise in expected future price, for example, would lead suppliers to cut back on current production, implying a rise in current price. The effect of the discovery of new deposits of the resource can be understood as an example of the working of the same feedback mechanism.

Consider again the rising price path in Figure 2.2. We noted in the discussion accompanying the figure that the path will tend to be followed in the absence of shocks provided by discoveries of new deposits. Now let us consider what will happen to prices if new deposits are, in fact, discovered. Presumably the price expected in the future, when production from the new deposits becomes significant, will fall. This, in turn, will lead suppliers to expand current production, resulting in a fall in current price. So the smoothly rising path of Figure 2.2 must be modified, as in Figure 2.4. Each drop in the path represents the effect of a new discovery. Price can continue to rise smoothly between shocks, although the long-term trend is down, as in the case illustrated in the figure. For that matter, price might rise still more rapidly, between shocks, if resource owners are risk-averse and need a higher rate of appreciation in expected price to compensate for the risk of a sudden sharp fall.

Thus far we have been talking about unanticipated discoveries. But discovery, or exploration, can be modeled as a purposeful activity. The motivation for this is especially clear when, as in the model of Section 2.4, extraction costs rise as the stock of a resource is depleted. Exploration can be defined quite generally as an activity that increases the stock and thereby lowers extraction costs. Obviously, discovery of a new deposit will do

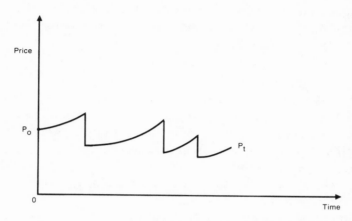

Figure 2.4. Time path of price with unanticipated discoveries.

this, but so can research and development of a new process that makes profitable production of the resource from materials formerly considered too poor in quality. Although we shall speak simply of exploration, it should be apparent that this can refer to a fairly wide range of behavior.[23]

Purposeful exploration can be included in the model of Sector 2.4. We shall carry out a simple exercise of this sort to obtain a couple of results that will prove useful in subsequent discussions of the long-term behavior of resource royalty, price, and output. There is just one difficulty here. We suggested earlier that uncertainty about the supply of a resource might be understood as uncertainty about the outcome of exploratory activity. Yet now we are proposing to include this activity in a deterministic model. Specifically, we shall assume there exists a function that relates costs to discoveries, just as another function relates costs to extractive output. This approach can be justified in two ways. First,

---

[23] Theoretical analyses that treat explicitly the effects of technical change on depletion include those of Dasgupta and Heal (1974), Dasgupta and Stiglitz (1975), and Kamien and Schwartz (1977*b*, 1978).

formally modeling the exploration uncertainty would involve the more advanced mathematical methods we have been trying to avoid. Second, and more important, in this particular case the sense of the results will not be affected by introducing uncertainty.

Uncertainty can, of course, affect the level of exploratory activity, just as it affects depletion. We have already noted one way in which this can happen in discussing firm behavior under uncertainty about the timing of expropriation. Uncertainty about the cost or outcome of exploration itself can obviously also be important. Further, uncertain exploration may be inefficient, just like uncertain depletion. Competitive firms may explore too little, or too much, or too rapidly, from a social point of view. We shall return briefly to these questions later.

The new element in the model of Section 2.4 is an exploration cost function for each firm, $\phi = \phi(z_t)$, where $z_t$ represents new finds, measured in units of the resource. The firm's problem is to maximize the present value of profits from the resource, where profits are net of the costs of both production and exploration. In symbols, this is

$$\underset{\{y_t\}, \{z_t\}}{\text{maximize}} \int_0^T [py_t - c(y_t, X_t) - \phi(z_t)]e^{-rt}dt \tag{2.21}$$

The constraint equation is also affected. The change in the resource stock is equal to the difference between discoveries and depletion. With no exploration, the stock was monotonically decreasing. Now it may actually increase, if more is found in any period than is used up. Something like this appears to have happened for many resources, as we shall show in Chapter 4. In symbols, the constraint equation is

$$\frac{dX_t}{dt} = z_t - y_t \tag{2.22}$$

The firm now has two variables to control, $y_t$ and $z_t$. In addition to extraction, $y_t$, it must decide on a target level of new finds, $z_t$. The new finds hold down extraction cost through their influence on the stock, $X_t$. On the other hand, they are not free; so the firm must balance the benefit of reduced extraction cost against the cost of exploration. There is an optimality condition for each control corresponding to the single condition of equation (2.18) in the case of no exploration. In fact, the condition for $y_t$ is just equation (2.18). The condition for $z_t$ is

$$-\frac{d\phi}{dz_t} + \rho_t = 0 \qquad (2.23)$$

where $\rho_t$ is again the co-state variable attached to the constraint equation (2.22).

This tells us that the royalty, or shadow price of a unit in the stock, is just equal to the cost of finding another to replace it, in a competitive equilibrium. Previously the royalty was interpreted as the benefit of having an additional unit in the stock. Where a unit can be added, the benefit is just balanced by the cost of adding it.

This is a useful result, because it provides an observable measure of the resource royalty. The royalty may be a particularly appropriate measure of scarcity, a leading indicator of future shortages and price rises and even of impending exhaustion. The difficulty is that, unlike other suggested measures of scarcity (reserve stocks, costs, and prices), it is not observable. But if the royalty is equated to the marginal cost of exploration, in a competitive equilibrium, we can examine data on exploration costs to shed some light on the behavior of the royalty. In fact, we shall do this in Chapter 4, with interesting results in the case of oil.

There is a complication that should be noted before we go on to discuss the effect of exploration on the behavior of price over time. The exploration cost function should probably include as an argument the sum of previous finds. Just as the cost of extraction is affected by cumulative extraction, we can assume that the cost of exploration is affected by cumulative finds. Altering the cost function in this fashion leads, as is easily verified, to an adjustment in equation (2.23). The royalty is now equated to an adjusted marginal exploration cost, where the adjustment is a term that can be interpreted as (minus) the shadow price of a unit added to the stock of cumulative finds.

It is difficult to say whether or not this is important, or even in what direction it cuts. If the better deposits are found first, the shadow price will be negative, and the royalty will exceed the unadjusted marginal exploration cost. If, on the other hand, the early finds provide information that will reduce the cost of future finds, the shadow price will be positive, at least initially. None of this is explicit in the model presented here, making even conjecture difficult. In any event, to the extent that the adjustment is important, the royalty will only be approximated by the marginal cost of exploration.[24]

Now let us see how the possibility of adding to the stock affects the price path. The key is what happens to extraction cost as the stock is expanded. In particular, we are interested in the sign of the second term on the RHS of equation (2.10a): $(\partial^2 c / \partial X \partial y) \, (dX/dt)$.

Without exploration, $dX/dt$ is just the change in the stock due to depletion $(dX/dt = -y)$ and is necessarily negative. If, as we have assumed, the marginal extraction cost increases as the stock decreases, and vice versa, $\partial^2 c / \partial X \partial y$ is also negative, so that $(\partial^2 c / \partial X \partial y) \, (dX/dt)$ is unambiguously positive. This is one of the factors pushing up price as the stock is depleted. With exploration, however, the effect of depletion on the stock is countered, at least in part. The change in the stock is equal to the number of units found less the number extracted: $dX/dt = z - y$. If the number found exceeds the number

---

[24] For a derivation of the adjustment to equation (2.23) and further discussion of the sign of the shadow price, see the work of Fisher (1977) and Pindyck (1978*b*). A result like the unadjusted equation (2.23) was also obtained by Brown and Field (1978). Pindyck further studied the behavior of price, output, and the level of exploration over time.

extracted $(z - y > 0)$, the change in the stock, $dX/dt$, is positive, and $(\partial^2 c/\partial X \partial y)$ $(dX/dt)$ is negative. A positive term in the equation for price change is accordingly replaced by a negative one; price rises more slowly, and may even fall. Note that the rise in price will be mitigated by any addition to the stock (i.e., by any positive $z$). Even if $z - y = dX/dt < 0$, the magnitude of this expression, and therefore of $(\partial^2 c/\partial X \partial y)$ $(dX/dt)$, is reduced.

We have said that technical change that has the effect of increasing the resource stock can be treated as exploration, in our analytical framework. This means that the effects on price just described can result from either of two causes: the introduction of a process that converts low-grade material into a usable resource, or the finding of a new deposit of the resource. But technical change need not be tied to expansion of the resource stock. It can be treated explicitly as an activity that lowers extraction costs. If technical change is time-related, then cost can be written as a function of time, explicitly, as well as of the rate of extraction and the size of the stock.

In this case there would need to be a third term on the RHS of equation (2.11) describing the change in marginal extraction cost over time, holding constant the rate of extraction and the size of the stock. The third term is the partial derivative of marginal extraction cost with respect to time, as opposed to the total derivative on the LHS of the equation. Because technical change reduces cost, the partial derivative $\partial(\partial c/\partial y)/\partial t$ is negative, further reducing the rate of price increase and perhaps even causing the price to fall.

### The shapes of price and output paths: evidence and conjecture

Let us try to pull all of this together to say something about the likely shape of the price path. Clearly, almost anything is possible, depending on the strengths of the competing influences on price: depletion, discovery, and technical change. Figures 2.5A and 2.5B describe two possibilities that

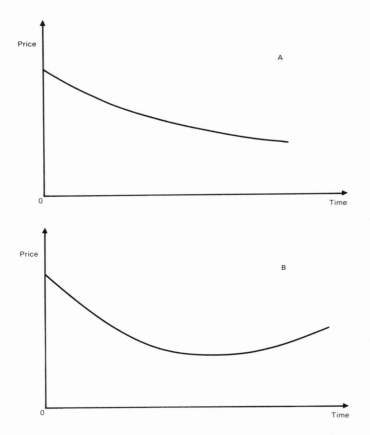

Figure 2.5. Influence of discovery and technical change on price. A: Optimistic version. B: Pessimistic version.

in my judgment are reasonable and roughly in accord with the empirical evidence to date on many exhaustible resources. In both cases, price is falling, initially. The interpretation is that a reduction in cost, due to new finds and technical innovations, dominates the rise in the royalty. Figure 2.5A describes a case in which this trend continues indefinitely, although it does level off.

Figure 2.5B, on the other hand, describes a case in which the trend is ultimately reversed. The explanation here is that the major finds have been made and that technical innovations cannot continue to reduce costs (by the same amount) indefinitely. Extraction costs, after all, cannot become negative.

As we shall demonstrate in Chapter 4, the evidence on resource prices could be consistent with either figure. Prices have generally fallen, over a period of many years, but there are hints that this could be changing, even in the absence of increases due to the formation of resource cartels. My guess (and that is all it is) is that Figure 2.5B will prove to be approximately correct, that the price path for most, if not all, exhaustible resources will be U-shaped. Of course, the bottom of the U could be fairly broad, as discoveries and innovations just compensate for depletion of known deposits of high-grade materials. A rise may be discernible for some resources in the middle and late 1970s, although not for others until perhaps some time in the next century.

There is an interesting implication for the behavior of the output of a resource over time here, if we can assume that demand is stable and downward-sloping. Figure 2.3 describes a case in which, as price rises monotonically, output falls monotonically. If, instead, price first falls and then rises, as in Figure 2.5B, output will first rise and then fall, describing an inverted U shape.

This is admittedly no more than a first approximation to an output path. Greater precision would require specific assumptions about the extraction cost function, about exploration, and about the rate of technical change. But it is interesting that the suggested path is consistent, at least in broad outline, with a well-known projection of output paths for a number of exhaustible resources based solely on geologic evidence.[25] The time path for one of these, domestic (U.S.) oil, is represented

[25] See the work of Hubbert (1969), the source for Figure 2.6. Hubbert's article appeared in a widely cited report by the National Academy of Sciences that assessed future prospects for a variety of exhaustible and renewable resources and human populations.

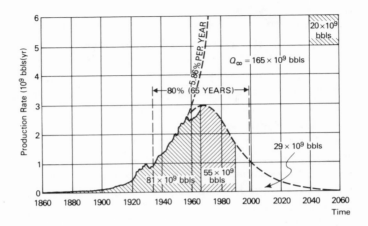

Figure 2.6. Time path of crude oil output in the United States, excluding Alaska. (From Hubbert, 1969, p. 183.)

in Figure 2.6. The projection (made in the late 1960s) puts the turning point at around 1970, which appears roughly consistent with the evidence to date. Our analytical framework can be interpreted as providing an explanation, based on economic behavior, of the evidence and the geologic projection.

### Uncertainty and information

The effect of uncertainty on exploration is just beginning to receive attention from theorists. Because there is not yet a substantial literature, and what there is is rather technical, we offer just a few informal remarks here.

One point to bear in mind is that uncertainty about the outcome of exploratory activity is likely to affect the rate of depletion as well. This is clear in a model like ours, where new finds hold down extraction costs. Recall that uncertainty about the size of the resource stock will tend to slow down depletion. If we do not know what we have left, it makes sense to proceed cautiously, to reduce the risk of suddenly running out. But if the uncertainty is not so much about the size of the stock at any time as about what remains to be found, then depletion need not be slowed. In this case there is a tendency for the uncertain exploratory activity to be restricted, whereas the rate of depletion may actually be increased.[26]

We have assumed that the motivation for undertaking any level of exploratory activity is to hold down extraction costs. But the problem of how to deplete an uncertain stock suggests another reason for exploring: to provide information about the size of the stock. One difference here is that there can be a benefit even from unsuccessful search. A dry hole, after all, provides information about how much oil there is in the ground, although not as much information as would a gusher.

More might be learned than just the size of a given oil field or mineral deposit. In discussing the shadow price of a unit of the resource added to the stock of cumulative finds, we noted that the price would be positive if a find provided information that reduced the cost of future finds. The idea is that the firm learns where and how to look in the future: in what region, in which geologic formation, using what search technique, and so on.

Nevertheless, exploration as an information-producing activity does appear subject to some rather interesting kinds of market failure. To the extent that the information produced by any one firm leaks out to others, it confers external benefits. A dramatic example of this is provided by the jump in the value of land adjacent to the tract where oil was discovered on the North Slope of Alaska in the late 1960s. Presumably the existence of external economies in the production of information leads to too little being produced. Each firm sits back and waits for the others to do the costly exploring.

A second, and possibly offsetting, kind of market failure stems from the common-property nature of discoveries.

---

[26] This and related questions were treated in a model of uncertain exploration that was similar in approach to the deterministic version in the text [Devarajan and Fisher (1980), and for a more comprehensive analysis, Devarajan (1980)]. Other models of uncertain exploration include those by Arrow and Chang (1978), Deshmukh and Pliska (1978), and Pindyck (1979).

Although this is no longer true for oil and gas, for the so-called hardrock minerals in the United States a kind of "rule of capture" prevails. According to the mining law of 1872, anyone is free to file a claim to the mineral rights (and in some cases the surface rights) of a publicly owned tract he can show may contain commercial deposits. This would presumably lead to excessive exploration, with each individual scrambling to preempt discoveries, with the attendant filing of claims, by others. Which effect, then, is dominant? Does the market produce too much information or too little? Probably a purely theoretical analysis cannot provide an answer, because this would seem to depend on empirical magnitudes.[27]

There is another way of characterizing the possibly offsetting market failures here. It seems likely that too little information is produced for the purpose of forecasting exhaustion, too much for the purpose of determining the value of mineral leases. Private producers presumably pay little attention to deposits that are too poor in quality to be exploited any time soon; yet it is information about these deposits that can shed light on the question whether or not, and when, we are likely to run out of the resource. On the other hand, mining firms and speculators trying to determine the value of potential oil or other mineral-bearing tracts in order to know how to bid on leases will tend to generate too much information.

[27] A formal analysis of the common-property problem will be presented in the discussion of renewable resources in Chapter 3. Both of the effects discussed here (information spillover leading to too little exploration, common-property discoveries leading to too much) were noted by Hotelling (1931), who worried about "wild rushes" to stake and exploit mineral claims, as well as unjustified windfalls to the beneficiaries of free information. More recently, both have been discussed by Gaffney (1967), Herfindahl and Kneese (1974), Peterson (1975), and Stiglitz (1975).

Uhler (1975) calculated the time path of petroleum exploration for a region in Alberta and found actual levels below optimal. The divergence was attributed to risk aversion, but it could also be explained by information spillover. This is not to say that attitudes toward risk are not relevant to the exploration decision. Grayson (1960) found small oil operators to be distinctly risk-averse, and both he and Kaufman (1963) developed decision rules for firms exploring in a risky environment.

Evidence of such behavior may be found in the drilling experience on the U.S. outer continental shelf. This area has been subjected to fifty times as many seismic measurements as the North Sea. Prospective bidders drill "line holes" bordering tracts. These help evaluate the tracts, but they contribute little to finding oil. The cost of finding a given amount of oil would clearly be less if holes were drilled "on structure," where the oil is most likely to be found.[28]

Perhaps the question is not whether the market generates too much or too little information about resources. Rather, does it generate the "right" information? It may be, for example, that too much effort goes into learning about the resource characteristics of tracts that are about to be leased, and not enough into learning about those that appear unlikely to be exploited any time soon. This is a question that deserves further study.[29]

Finally, let us note that although theoretical analyses of

[28] The excessive drilling could be explained in part by geologic factors. Problems of information gathering prior to lease sales have been studied by Hughart (1975), Leland (1975), Wilson (1975*b*), and Gaskins and Teisberg (1976).

[29] There is an extensive literature on mineral leasing that addresses a number of other questions. For example, does an increase in the number of bidders (at a lease auction) lead to an increase in the winning bid? It seems obvious that it should: The more bids there are, the more high bids there are. On the other hand, it has been suggested that the greater the number of bidders, the further they bid below their estimate of the value of the lease, because the further from the true value their estimate is likely to be if it is higher than everyone else's. For further discussion of this question, see the work of Rothkopf (1969), Capen, Clapp, and Campbell (1971), Oren and Williams (1975), Gaskins and Vann (1975), and Wilson (1975*a*).

There are also questions about the seller's strategy. Should bidding be sealed or open? Should the number of bids be controlled? Should bidding be on the bonus, a front-end payment, subject to a fixed share of revenues or profits? Or should the bidding be on the share, subject to a fixed bonus payment? The latter two questions were studied by Leland, Norgaard, and Pearson (1974). Other discussions of bidding strategies and leasing policies include those of Vickrey (1961), Mead (1967), Erickson (1970), Kalter, Stevens, and Bloom (1975), Kalter and Tyner (1975), and McGuire (1978), as well as the several studies in the volume edited by Crommelin and Thompson (1977).

uncertain exploration are relatively recent and few in number, the affinity between statistical inference and exploration has long been recognized. That is, exploration is considered as sampling from an incompletely known size distribution of deposits, where the distribution is generated by a stochastic geologic process. The work here represents an interesting blend of economics, statistics, and geology, but it lies outside the scope of this study.[30]

## 2.8. Equity and exhaustible resources: the intergenerational problem

Thus far, the criterion for judging rates of depletion (by a planner, by a competitive industry, by a monopolist) has been social efficiency.[31] But a question can, of course, be raised

---

[30] Exploration as a statistical sampling problem was considered by Allais (1957). Allais, Slichter (1959), and Uhler and Bradley (1970) analyzed size distributions and the stochastic process that generates them in order to evaluate specific mineral prospects. A detailed review of geostatistical techniques was provided by Harris (1975), with a number of applications. Harris (1965, 1966) also used multivariate statistical analysis to relate mineral occurrences to a variety of geologic variables. Other recent contributions to the statistical assessment of mineral prospects are found in the IIASA conference volume edited by Grenon (1976). For a survey of economic and statistical approaches to modeling exploration, see the work of Crabbé (1977).

[31] We have considered specifically the effects of monopoly and various forms of uncertainty. For further discussion of these and other potential sources of bias in the rate of depletion, such as one or another kind of taxation or government regulation, see the work of Kay and Mirrlees (1975) and Sweeney (1977).

With respect to the effects of taxation, there is a large early literature. Much of the early analysis of resource extraction appears to have been motivated by an interest in problems of taxation. See, in particular, the discussion in Scott's treatise (1955a), which contains several references to earlier contributions concerning mineral and forest taxes, and the studies in a volume edited by Gaffney (1967) dealing with the taxation of extractive resources. Both Gray (1914) and Hotelling (1931) also considered the effects of taxes on the rate of depletion.

More recently, applied studies of different kinds of (mainly energy) resource taxes and subsidies include (in alphabetical order) those by Adelman (1972), Agria (1969), Anderson and Spiegelman (1977), Brannon (1975), Cox (1976), Cox and Wright (1975), Davidson (1963), Epple (1976), Harberger (1955), Helli-

about the equity of any such rate, even if it is efficient. Suppose we lay aside the question of intratemporal equity, the question of who in the present generation benefits from a particular plan or market structure, on the grounds that it is not special to exhaustible resources and further that it is addressed at length in the main body of welfare economics. We are still confronted by the question of intertemporal equity. Although not associated exclusively with exhaustible resources, it does seem specially relevant.

Given a positive discount rate, it is possible that a depletion program that is efficient from the point of view of the present generation will leave little or nothing for some future generation. The ethical and welfare-theoretic issues raised by this possibility have been debated for a long time by economists and others, with no clear resolution. In this section we shall try to convey the flavor of the debate. The discussion is conveniently broken into two parts: social discounting and welfare criteria.

### On social discounting

The debate here concerns how to discount (and whether or not to discount) the utilities of future generations. The first shot is generally credited to Ramsey (1928), who in a well-known passage disapproved of discounting as "ethically indefensible," arising from a "weakness of the imagination."[32]

well (1976), Kahn (1960), Lovejoy and Homan (1967), MacAvoy and Pindyck (1975), McDonald (1963), Page (1977), and Steiner (1959). See also the theoretical analyses of Burness (1976) and Conrad (1980).

Aside from the effects of different taxes on the rate of depletion (e.g., a severance tax would tend to slow depletion, a depletion allowance would tend to speed it up), the following question was perhaps the most interesting question addressed in much of the early literature (it is still of concern): What is the effect of the tax on the exploitation of marginal resources? A "bad" tax would presumably be one that would lead to skimming only the best grades of a resource.

[32] Anthony Scott has pointed out that Ramsey "was anticipated by Sidgwick, and, I suspect, the whole barrel of Cambridge moral

Interestingly, Ramsey (1931) in a later work argued the opposing view in speaking of the need to apply perspective to time. Another well-known disapproval of discounting is that of Pigou (1932), who said that discounting "implies only that our telescopic faculty is defective."

Some modern theorists have taken the opposing side. Koopmans (1960) showed that acceptance of several seemingly noncontroversial postulates about the utility function for a consumption program over an infinite future logically leads to "impatience," or discounting. Less formally, Arrow and Kurz (1970) argued that because the revealed preferences of individuals are accepted in making other social choices, it is difficult to see why they should not be accepted in this case as well. However, a question then arises: Which individuals? In particular, why just those of the present generation? An answer has been provided by Marglin (1963). Present consumers are sovereign because it is "axiomatic that a democratic government reflects only the preferences of the individuals who are presently members of the body politic." Of course, this may not be totally satisfying to one who feels that lack of representation of the future is precisely the problem.

Although we have lumped Marglin in with the defenders of discounting, his work is usually considered to provide support for a somewhat different view: that the social discount rate, although not zero, is below the private rate. There is a vast literature dealing with the relationship between social and private rates of discount, usually in the context of evaluating public projects, such as the building of dams and highways, rather than deciding grand questions such as the fate of future generations.[33] However, Marglin's analysis is explicitly about the relationship between the generations.

philosophers and economists between 1885 and 1925. The debate by Mill and others on the burden of the debt was earlier still" (private correspondence).

[33] A review of this literature is beyond the scope of this study, but the following notes and references may be helpful. Early contributions,

The essential idea is that consumption by future generations is a public good to members of the present generation. That is, each of us derives some satisfaction from the prospect of a brilliant future for civilization. Yet the fact that you reap this satisfaction does not mean there is any less for me, and vice versa. Then we are all made better off by a collective decision to save and invest more than each of us acting individually would have done. This, in turn, implies, as Marglin showed, that the social discount rate is below the private rate.

An important additional point is that the appropriate policy, if one accepts this analysis, is not to discount public projects at a rate below that used by private investors. Clearly this would simply divert investment from high-yielding private projects to low-yielding public ones. Instead, interest rates should be driven down throughout the economy.[34]

Note, by the way, that this argument for a low social discount rate to help future generations is not rooted in considerations of equity. Only efficiency matters, provided we accept the idea that consumption by future generations is a public good to members of the present generation. Of course, one could still favor shifting consumption to the future (or, for that matter, away from it) solely on grounds of fairness. Recently a school of thought has arisen that challenges

at least in the United States, grew out of attempts to evaluate water-resources projects. Several landmark works in the late 1950s developed the welfare foundations of benefit–cost analysis for these projects, with some attention to determination of an appropriate discount rate; see the work of Krutilla and Eckstein (1958), Eckstein (1958), McKean (1958), Hirshleifer, DeHaven, and Milliman (1960), and the Harvard Water Resources Program (1962). Following this, a number of studies focusing specifically on the discount rate appeared in the journals. Notable contributions include those by Marglin (1963), Feldstein (1964), Hirshleifer (1965, 1966), Baumol (1968), Hirshleifer and Shapiro (1970), Arrow and Lind (1970), Sandmo and Dreze (1971), and Sandmo (1972).

[34] Where this is not possible, a second-best procedure has been suggested by Eckstein (1958). It avoids the inefficiency of a two-discount-rate system, but still favors alternatives with a benefit profile tilted toward the future.

conventional utilitarian efficiency analysis on just these grounds.

### On welfare criteria

Optimizing the rate of resource depletion means maximizing the present value of the resource, as we have formulated the problem. Of course, different decision makers will use different indicators of value. We assume that the private firm tries to maximize the present value of profits, that a planner will (ideally) maximize the present value of consumer and producer surpluses, and so on. Note, however, that even if the true social discount rate is below the private rate, the welfare criterion for the planner remains present-value maximization. Further, even a discount rate of zero would not change an important feature of the criterion: The value of the resource is determined by adding the values in different periods, or to different generations. It is this additive property, common to all of the approaches to depletion we have discussed thus far, that is challenged by a school of thought based on the "maximin" criterion suggested by Rawls (1971).

Suppose social welfare is determined by the welfare of the least-well-off member of society. Analytically, this translates into

$$W = \min(U_1, U_2, \ldots, U_n)$$

where $W$ represents social welfare, "min" stands for "the minimum of," and $U_i$ represents individual $i$'s utility, $i = 1, \ldots, n$. According to the maximin criterion, social welfare is maximized by maximizing the welfare of the least-well-off individual. Analytically,

$$\max W = \max[\min(U_1, U_2, \ldots, U_n)]$$

where "max" stands for "the maximum of." Thus the difference between maximin and conventional welfare criteria is that under maximin, social welfare is not additive. It is not determined by adding utilities, or surpluses, or anything else, across individuals.

Interestingly, Rawls intended that maximin apply only within a generation, which would make it largely irrelevant to the discussion here. It has since been extended to evaluate intergenerational programs, but a basic difficulty was noted by Solow (1974*b*).[35] He posed the problem of finding the largest sustainable level of consumption for a society, subject to constraints on capital accumulation and the availability of an exhaustible resource. The difficulty is that maximin requires a large initial capital stock. If it is small, the level of consumption will be low forever, because capital must not be accumulated by sacrificing the consumption of a generation that has little to begin with. Yet there is no reason that the initial capital stock should ever be large, in these circumstances.

A more optimistic view of accumulation under maximin was taken by Phelps and Riley (1978). The key difference is that they allowed the generations to overlap in order to mutually benefit from exchange. A generation that adds to the capital stock has a claim to more retirement consumption, provided by the labor of the next generation, which has, in turn, an obligation to work more in exchange for the added capital. Such a program can be supported, Phelps and Riley showed, by appropriate debt creation. Accumulation and growth are further encouraged if the early generations, whatever their endowment, have "ties of sentiment" to the later generations (i.e., derive utility from their consumption).

Certainly this is a less dismal view than that of Solow, but there is a catch. Phelps and Riley did not explicitly consider exhaustible resources. Put differently, they implicitly assumed substitutability of other factors, capital or labor, for resources.

This suggests a question on which we might appropriately close, because it brings us back to issues raised early in this chapter. The question concerns the substitutability of other factors for resources. Solow addressed this, too, and he showed in a two-factor model that a constant level of consumption can

---

[35] Maximin in an intergenerational setting was also studied by Arrow (1974), Dasgupta (1974), Hartwick (1977), and Calvo (1978).

be sustained indefinitely if any of the following conditions is satisfied: (1) the elasticity of substitution between resources and capital, the other factor, is greater than 1; (2) the elasticity is equal to 1 (the Cobb-Douglas case), and the share of capital is greater than that of resources; (3) there is (sustained) resource-augmenting technical change.[36,37]

That just one of these conditions should be satisfied does not seem unreasonable. But there may be a danger in drawing this conclusion from the evidence around us today. The real question, because we are talking about the indefinite future,

[36] See also Stiglitz (1974*a*). In the planning model of this chapter we have focused on the resource sector. But Solow and Stiglitz, along with a number of others, embedded resources in an aggregative growth model. The object was to determine the conditions needed to sustain growth, or just a constant level of consumption, with an exhaustible-resource input to production. As noted in the text, these conditions involve the degree of substitutability among resources and other inputs and the potential for resource-augmenting technical change. Other studies of optimal depletion in aggregative models include those of Anderson (1972), Vousden (1973), Banks (1974), Beckmann (1974), Stiglitz (1974*a*), Ingham and Simmons (1975), Sampson (1976), Suzuki (1976), Haurie and Hung (1977), Miller (1977), and Garg and Sweeney (1978). No doubt this list is not exhaustive, particularly with respect to contributions since 1977.

[37] Note that the possibility of recycling does not enter as an alternative. Although the availability of secondary or scrap copper prevents primary copper producers from duplicating the success of OPEC, as we argued earlier, recycling cannot extend the supply of a mineral indefinitely. Some dispersal in use is inevitable, and the laws of thermodynamics tell us that energy resources like oil, gas, and coal cannot be recycled at all.

If recycling does not offer an escape from exhaustion, it can at least affect prices and rates of depletion of virgin materials. Theoretical analyses that extend the models of optimal depletion to allow for recycling have been provided by d'Arge (1972), d'Arge and Kogiku (1973), Schulze (1974), and Weinstein and Zeckhauser (1974). They found, not surprisingly, that a competitive equilibrium with perfect futures markets, including one for scrap, will recycle efficiently. However, without a perfect scrap futures market, the scrap is likely to show up as an externality, with obvious implications for economic efficiency. Another problem is that existing (controlled) freight rates, tax policies, and other government regulations tend to discriminate against recycling and in favor of virgin materials, further depressing recycling below the efficient level. For a detailed discussion, see the work of F.A. Smith (1972) and Page (1977).

concerns what happens to the elasticity of substitution at the "corner." When a great deal of additional substitution of capital for resources has taken place, will the elasticity remain at or near 1 (assuming that is where it is today), or will it be sharply lower? And can resource-augmenting technical change be sustained indefinitely?

## 2.9. Concluding remarks

We are back to questions raised earlier about the nature of resources and depletion. When these questions were raised, it was to counter what I regard as an overly simple view, held by many noneconomists, to the effect that the economy is about to run out of many exhaustible resources and that running out of any one (especially if it is oil) will have a disastrous effect on human welfare. Now the questions should be taken to suggest caution in jumping to the opposite conclusion: that the possibility of exhaustion, and the consequences, need not be taken seriously.

All of this will be considered more systematically in Chapter 4. There we shall review the empirical evidence on measures of resource scarcity, including estimates of the substitutability of capital and labor for energy resources. However, because much of the concern for the adequacy of the resource base of advanced industrial economies centers on renewable resources and threats to their sustainability, in the next chapter we shall further develop the theory of optimal resource use to address the special features of renewable resources.

# 3

## Renewable resources: the theory of optimal use

### 3.1. Introduction

The line between exhaustible resources and renewable resources is not always clearly drawn. Exploration and technical change can, for a time at least, "renew" exhaustible resources by making possible production from new deposits and low-grade materials. Models that describe the effects of these activities on resource price and production paths were developed in Chapter 2.

Just as exhaustible resources can be renewed, renewable resources can be exhausted. In fact, as we noted in the concluding remarks to Chapter 2, much of the concern about resource exhaustion appears to involve renewable resources, endangered species ranging from the snail darter to the whale. As one prominent biological scientist put it:

> The worst thing that can happen—will happen [in the 1980s]—is not energy depletion, economic collapse, limited nuclear war, or conquest by a totalitarian government. As terrible as these catastrophes would be for us, they can be repaired within a few generations. The one process ongoing in the 1980s that will take millions of years to correct is the loss of genetic and species diversity by the destruction of natural hab-

itats. This is the folly our descendants are least likely to forgive us.[1]

A major purpose of this chapter is to try to shed some light on the reasons that even commercially valuable stocks of plants and animals can be threatened with extinction. It is clear enough how this can happen to a species that is not commercial. Destruction of habitat in the course of the economic development of a region is certainly a cost of development, but it is normally an external cost, not taken into account by the developers. Ways of internalizing these and other external environmental costs will be considered later in Chapters 5 and 6. But there is another question we might raise here: Under what circumstances might harvesting a commercial species to the point of extinction be rational?

Let us be clear on the limited sense in which the word "rational" is used to describe a pattern of use that results in the extinction of a species, the exhaustion of a renewable resource. In the first place, as just noted, any benefit from preserving a viable stock not captured by a commercial harvester (private or public; the Russian whaling industry is clearly a threat to several species of whales) is properly ignored, in a model that purports to explain or predict the harvester's behavior. Yet such benefit does exist. To cite just one example (we shall have more to say in Chapter 5), the conservation of genetic information embodied in an endangered species can lead to later discovery or development of commercially valuable medicinal or agricultural products. However, the full value will almost certainly not be captured by an individual who refrains from harvesting today.

A related point is that even when only currently known extractive values are at stake, if the resource is, like an ocean fishery, a common property not subject to clearly defined ownership rights, there will be a tendency toward overexploita-

---

[1] The quotation is from Wilson (1980). For further discussion, see the work of Ehrlich and Ehrlich (1981).

tion, with a correspondingly greater risk of extinction. Each firm, or for that matter each nation, exploiting the resource will have an incentive to take more sooner than it would if it owned the resource, or at least could control access. The common-property problem will be treated in Section 3.3. Let us emphasize here that to explain behavior in a common-property setting is not to endorse it. In fact, as we shall see, economists who have studied this problem typically recommend a management scheme that involves a clearer definition of ownership or control in order to protect the resource from overuse.

Thus far we have emphasized the potential for exhaustion of a renewable resource. But renewable resources are different from exhaustible resources by virtue of the fact that they are naturally regenerated on a time scale that is relevant to human exploitation. Catching a fish or cutting a tree does reduce the population of fish or trees in any period, but this is just temporary, unless the population has already been reduced to the point that any further losses will lead to extinction. Within relatively few periods natural growth will make good the loss in biomass due to the harvest. This is obviously not the case for an exhaustible resource like oil. Units remaining in the stock after others have been extracted do not grow, nor do they get together to form new units. So, although it is true that a renewable resource can be exhausted, it need not be. The conditions governing optimal use will normally reflect this fundamental distinction between exhaustible and renewable resources. In particular, a *steady state,* involving a sustained yield of the resource from a maintained stock, will normally be optimal.

The model developed in the next section will describe the properties of just such a steady state. In particular, we shall consider whether or not (and under what conditions) the optimal sustained yield is equivalent to the maximum sustainable yield often recommended by biologists and resource managers. In Section 3.3 the problem of extinction will be taken up in an analysis of the effect of a common-property regime on patterns of use.

In setting up the model we shall most often refer to a fishery when in need of an example of a renewable resource. Much of the renewable-resource literature to date has been about fisheries, and these also illustrate very well the common-property problem.[2] But animal populations and forests are likewise renewable resources, in that they can be renewed by natural growth on a time scale that is brief in comparison with that required to produce exhaustible resources like oil and coal. The model we shall develop, though motivated by problems of fisheries management, will be sufficiently abstract to apply (usually) to other kinds of renewable resources as well.[3] Of course, this comes at a cost. In order to apply the model to the management of an actual resource, features special to the

[2] The pioneering work was by Gordon (1954) and Scott (1955*b*), who were primarily concerned with the difficulties for socially efficient management caused by the common-property characteristics of a fishery. Models paying more attention to the natural growth law or population dynamics of the exploited resource appear to have been developed first by Schaefer (1954, 1957) and Beverton and Holt (1957).

[3] There have been numerous applications of a similar type of optimizing model to other resources, a few of which will be noted here. Cummings (1971) and Burt (1964, 1967, 1970) studied the management of groundwater stocks. Brown and Hammack (1972, 1973) and Hammack and Brown (1974) developed schemes for (optimally) increasing populations of migratory waterfowl and preserving their wetlands nesting grounds. V. L. Smith (1975) explained prehistoric animal extinction. Beddington, Watts, and Wright (1975) calculated optimal harvesting rates for red deer. Spence (1973) analyzed overexploitation of the blue whale, and Wilen (1976) of the northern Pacific fur seal. An interesting application to solar power generation in Israel was provided by Hochman and Zilberman (1980).

There have been several studies of optimal forest management, including those of Gaffney (1960), Goundry (1960), Jungenfelt (1975), Samuelson (1976), Howe (1976), and Berck (1979*b*). In fact, the forestry problem has a much longer history, going back at least to the work of Faustman in 1849. The literature is described in detail, with additional references, in Samuelson's bibliographic notes.

resource, such as the form of the natural growth law or of the harvest cost function, will have to be introduced.

## 3.2. A model of optimal use

Let us begin with what is special to a fishery or other renewable resource: the natural growth law. In fact, the rest of the model is much the same as the one developed for exhaustible resources. The usual assumption about the form of the growth law, which we shall follow here, is that growth is a function simply of the size of the resource stock.[4] But the relationship is not monotonic. It is assumed that the increment to the stock, in any period, first rises with the size of the stock, and then falls. The reason for a turning point is that the natural environment has a "carrying capacity" for the resource, a maximum population it can sustain. As the population or stock approaches this point, growth necessarily slows, ultimately to zero.

The growth curve $g(X)$, where $X$, as before, represents the resource stock, looks something like the curve in Figure 3.1. One root is at $X = X_c$, the carrying capacity. The other is at $X = 0$, indicating that no growth can occur once the stock has

[4] Although growth as a function of stock size is the usual assumption in bioeconomic models, following Schaefer, it has been suggested that this is too simple. Beverton and Holt (1957) and, more recently, Hannesson (1975) and Clark (1976), studied age structure as well as stock size, and Talbot (1975) argued for the further inclusion of competition and symbiosis with other species and stochastic variations in the environment. Hannesson cited evidence that the recruitment of young fish is, for many species, determined by environmental variations affecting survival of eggs and larvae.

No doubt these complicating factors are relevant in some cases, but as Gordon pointed out, most can be embodied in the environmental carrying capacity, $X_c$. This is the approach also taken by Hall (1977) in a note on natural growth laws and production function. He specified carrying capacity as a function of the relevant natural factors, including temperature, pollution levels, and so on. This expression was then substituted for the simple $X_c$ (in our notation), leading to correspondingly more complicated and more realistic production and cost functions. For our purposes, all of this will remain implicit, and we shall continue to specify growth as a function of stock size.

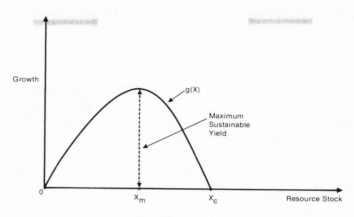

Figure 3.1. Biological growth law.

been totally depleted. Note that it is also possible for growth to cease before this point. Suppose, for example, that remaining members of the population (whales might be an example) are widely scattered. Then growth can cease (indeed, can become negative) even though the stock is not totally depleted. Another interesting point is $X_m$, where growth is maximum. This is the stock corresponding to the maximum harvest or yield that can be sustained indefinitely, the familiar "maximum sustainable yield" (MSY).

The growth of the stock can also be represented as in Figure 3.2. This shows cumulative growth, or the size of the stock, as a function of time. Because we have assumed that growth starts out very modestly, when the stock is still small, then rises, and then falls, the cumulative curve in Figure 3.2 takes the general logistic shape, with at first successively larger increments, then successively smaller. As growth eventually peters out, the stock approaches its maximum, $X_c$.[5]

---

[5] Such a logistic growth law, first developed and applied to many natural populations by Lotka (1924), has been criticized as overly simple. Beverton and Holt (1957), Zellner (1970), Southey (1972), and Clark (1976) suggested alternatives.

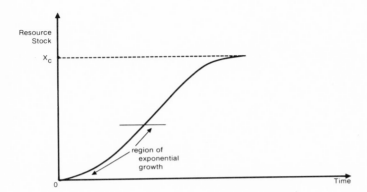

Figure 3.2. Stock size as a function of time.

This, then, is the natural setting. On it we now impose a human agent seeking to maximize the value of the resource. We could, as in Chapter 2, begin with a planner seeking to maximize the present value of the social surplus from the resource and then show that the same pattern of use would emerge from competitive exploitation, assuming that each firm enjoys a clear property right in its stock of the resource. However, let us take this result for granted and investigate a more interesting question. How is the pattern of use affected when the firm does not own or control the resource it is harvesting, that is, when the resource is a common property? We shall treat first the case of the sole owner, the firm that does enjoy a clear property right. For this case we might imagine each firm fishing from its own lake, just as in an earlier example each firm depleted its own mine. Then we shall consider what happens when the firms all fish from the same lake or ocean, that is, when the resource is a common property.

The problem for the sole owner can be stated formally as

$$\text{maximize}_{\{y_t\}} \int_0^T [p \, y_t - c(y_t, X_t)] \, e^{-rt} dt \tag{3.1}$$

subject to the constraint

$$\frac{dX_t}{dt} = g(X) - y_t \tag{3.2}$$

Again, $p$ is the resource price (taken by the owner), $c(y_t, X_t)$ is the cost of extraction, $y_t$ is the flow of extraction at time $t$, and $X_t$ is the remaining stock.[6,7]

The Hamiltonian for this problem is

$$H = py_t - c(y_t, X_t) + \rho_t[g(X) - y_t] \tag{3.3}$$

where $\rho_t$ is, as before, the co-state variable attached to the constraint. Differentiating with respect to the control variable $y_t$ and setting the result equal to zero, we obtain

$$\frac{\partial H}{\partial y_t} = p - \frac{\partial c}{\partial y_t} - \rho_t = 0 \tag{3.4}$$

exactly as in the exhaustible-resource case.

The expression describing the rate of change of the royalty $\rho$, is complicated by the presence of the growth function; $\rho$ evolves according to

$$\begin{aligned}
\frac{d\rho_t}{dt} &= r\rho_t - \frac{\partial H}{\partial X_t} \\
&= r\rho_t + \frac{\partial c}{\partial X_t} - \rho_t \frac{dg}{dX_t}
\end{aligned} \tag{3.5}$$

[6] As in Chapter 2, we ignore corner solutions. For a more formal analysis, see Clark's volume (1976) on mathematical bioeconomics. At the other end of the spectrum, an entirely diagrammatic treatment was provided by McInerney (1976) and Shaw (1977). Scherer (1976) used a discrete-time linear programming model, Crutchfield and Zellner (1962) used the calculus of variations, and Burt and Cummings (1970) used discrete-time nonlinear programming. For an extension of the model of Burt and Cummings to issues of technical change and regional development, see the work of Rausser (1974).

[7] Most fisheries models specify a production function, with the control variable being "effort," an index of labor and capital inputs. We shall, instead, continue to work with a cost function, with the control variable being the rate of extraction. For a similar

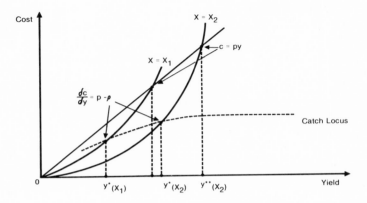

Figure 3.3. Derivation of catch locus.

The new element here is the last term on the RHS: $\rho_t(dg/dX_t)$. This can be interpreted as an additional "dividend" from holding a unit of the resource in the stock, the value of the extra growth that results.

The dynamics can be further analyzed, but in the absence of changes in demand or input supply conditions, the time path in renewable-resource models normally remains at or near the "turnpike" or steady state.[8] In the steady state, the rates of change of $X$ and $\rho$ must be zero, and of course the maximizing condition, equation (3.4), must continue to hold. The interesting question is how to determine the optimal steady-state values of the stock and flow variables, $X$ and $y$.

exposition using production functions and effort, see the work of Peterson and Fisher (1977). The Peterson-Fisher model is, in turn, similar to one developed by Brown (1974). Cost functions are employed in the renewable-resource and fisheries models of V. L. Smith (1968, 1969).

[8] See the work of Plourde (1970); for a discussion of similarities to capital theory, see the work of Clark and Munro (1975). In the remainder of this chapter we shall focus on the steady state, but note again the work of Hannesson (1975) and Clark (1976), which suggests that if age structure is incorporated, periodic fishing (every few years, for instance) may be optimal. This is discussed further in a survey by Butlin (1975) of recent contributions to the fisheries literature.

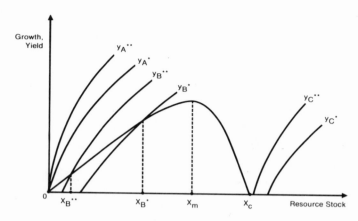

Figure 3.4. Equilibrium stocks and yields.

We can do this, relatively informally, with the aid of a couple of diagrams. These also show how a steady state can fail to exist, or, in other words, how the resource can be exhausted. Let us represent cost as a function of yield for each level of stock, as in Figure 3.3. There is an optimal yield for each stock, given by equation (3.4) and shown in the figure. The optimal yield for $X = X_1$ is $y = y^*(X_1)$, and so on. The locus of $X$ and $y$ values obtained in this fraction is sometimes called the "catch locus" in fisheries models.[9]

In Figure 3.4, three different catch loci, $y_A{}^*$, $y_B{}^*$, and $y_C{}^*$, corresponding to different assumptions about cost or demand, are plotted along with the growth function $g(X)$. The steady state, for each catch locus, is where it intersects the growth function. Here the stock is in equilibrium, because $dX_t/dt = g(X) - y_t = 0$.

The dependence of optimal stocks and flows on cost and demand is easily understood in this framework. From Figure 3.3 it is clear that the optimal yield for a given stock is lower as

---

[9] The diagrams and the terminology are taken from the work of Gould (1972), although he studied only the common-property case, in which the royalty or user cost of depletion is not taken into account.

marginal cost is higher or price is lower or both. Thus catch locus $y_C^*$ reflects the fact that fish are increasingly hard to catch or are not very highly valued or both. In this extreme case the optimal steady-state stock is just $X_c$, the population in the absence of commercial exploitation.

The opposite extreme (exploitation to the point of exhaustion) is represented by catch locus $y_A^*$. Here the fish are easy to catch even as the stock dwindles or they are highly valued or both. The species becomes extinct because the optimal yield, given by $y_A^*$, exceeds natural growth, given by $g(X)$, at all levels of stock. So extinction can occur even under sole ownership – again, ignoring the public-good aspects of preservation.[10] Still, as we shall see, extinction is more likely if the resource is a common property, as are many actual fisheries.

An intermediate and much more typical case (some harvesting, but not to the point of extinction) is represented by catch locus $y_B^*$. As long as the catch locus crosses the growth curve from below, yields and growth rates will correct any deviation from equilibrium: $y \gtreqless g(X)$ if and only if $X \lesseqgtr X_B^*$.

Notice that in none of the cases illustrated is the MSY optimal. This is perhaps surprising in view of the fact that the MSY is persistently recommended by biologists and others involved in resource management (and also for other renewable resources such as forests).[11] A closer look at the optimality conditions, equations (3.4) and (3.5), can explain the general nonoptimality of the MSY. The discount rate, largely neglected thus far, turns out to be crucial.

Suppose there is no discounting (i.e., $r = 0$) and also no increase in cost caused by depletion (i.e., $\partial c / \partial X_t = 0$). Then, from equation (3.5), because $d\rho_t / dt = 0$ in the steady state, $dg/dX = 0$. But $dg/dX = 0$ only at $X = X_m$, the MSY stock. In this special case the MSY coincides with the economic optimum. It makes sense to pick the stock that gives the

[10] This result is developed rigorously by Quirk and Smith (1970), Clark (1973, 1976), Neher (1974), and Clark and Munro (1976).
[11] It is embodied, for example, in the Multiple Use and Sustained Yield Act of 1960 for U.S. National Forests.

highest yield in perpetuity. Moving to the right in Figure 3.4 would yield a cost saving if cost increased with depletion, but by assumption it does not. Moving to the left, some extra fish could be caught temporarily by depleting the stock, but this would mean fewer available indefinitely into the future – a bad bargain with a zero discount rate.

Another interesting case arises when $r > 0$ and $\partial c / \partial X_t = 0$. From equation (3.5), $dg/dX = r > 0$. The equilibrium is to the left of $X_m$; in other words, the steady-state stock is below that corresponding to the MSY. The stock is optimally drawn down because future losses are discounted and there is no cost penalty for temporarily increasing the harvest. This corresponds, in a sense, to the exhaustible-resource case. However, instead of a unit of the stock growing in value at a rate just equal to the rate of return on an alternative asset, we have the stock growing physically at that rate (remember, in the steady state $d\rho_t / dt = 0$). Economists presumably have this case in mind when criticizing MSY.[12] However, note that it does depend on the absence of a stock effect on costs.

When this effect is present (i.e., when $\partial c / \partial X_t < 0$ and $r > 0$), from equation (3.5) we have $dg/dX = r + (\partial c / \partial X_t) / \rho_t \gtreqless 0$ as $r \gtreqless |(\partial c / \partial X_t)/\rho_t|$. Thus in the general case it is not possible to say whether the optimal steady-state stock is above or below the MSY stock.

### 3.3 The common-property problem

We have shown that extinction can result even from optimal exploitation of a renewable resource by a sole owner. However, as intuition would suggest, extinction is more likely when the resource is, like many fisheries, a common property. The basic idea is that when firms can enter freely and no cooperative agreements have been reached, each ignores the user cost ($\rho$ in our model) of extracting a unit today, as well as

---

[12] For a readable critique along these lines of MSY in forestry, see the work of Hirshleifer (1974) and also a number of the other chapters in the volume edited by Dowdle (1974).

any diseconomies of crowding (the difference between marginal and average costs, $\partial c/\partial y_t$ and $c/y_t$, respectively, in our model). All profit from the stock is competed away, and the industry equilibrium occurs when $py_t - c = 0$.[13] This zero-profit condition is graphed as the linear relationship $c = py_t$ in Figure 3.3. The catch locus is found by taking the intersection of total revenue, $py_t$, and total cost, $c$, for each stock. Common-property catch loci are plotted in Figure 3.4 for the same three cases as before: $y_A^{**}$, $y_B^{**}$, and $y_C^{**}$.

For a given stock, yields will typically be higher in a common-property regime, as shown in Figure 3.3. The intersection of the straight line $py_t$ with the cost curve $c$ for a given stock lies to the right of the point at which $\partial c/\partial y_t = p - \rho_t$. But the excessive yields may not be sustained in the long run, as illustrated in Figure 3.4 by the more typical case $B$, where the common-property yield is below the optimal yield. The explanation is, of course, that the stock does not remain the same. Stocks are generally lower in a common-property regime, as illustrated in Figure 3.4, and this will also tend to result in lower yields eventually.

Although common-property stocks are always lower in our model, it has been suggested that some species of fish, or trees, may need pruning. Freely entering competitors may do less pruning than is optimal, leaving excessive stocks.[14] Normally, however, with the common-property catch locus to the left of the sole owner's catch locus, stocks are driven down, and extinction is made more likely.

[13] The early economic analysis of this case was by Gordon (1954) and Scott (1955*b*). Later studies of aspects of the common-property problem in fisheries include those of Crutchfield (1964), Turvey (1964), Christy and Scott (1965), Scott (1970), Plourde (1971), Christy (1975), Clark (1976), and Hoel (1978*a*). Cheung (1970) described a model in which freely entering fishing firms drive profits to zero only in the limit, where their number approaches infinity. The necessary conditions for extinction of a common-property renewable resource were rigorously derived by Berck (1979*a*).

[14] This point was made by Southey (1972), who suggested that salmon may be a species that needs pruning.

Overexploitation of a common-property resource can be combated in various ways. The simplest is to define property rights in the resource and rely on the self-interest of the owner. Recent moves by several coastal states to extend their economic jurisdiction to 200 miles from their coastlines, more than an order of magnitude beyond previous limits, are examples of this approach to the management of fishery resources. Of course, the individual boats, whatever their origin, must still be constrained to behave as the new "owners" of the resource wish. One obvious way to do this (obvious to economists, at least) is a per unit tax on the resource (e.g., a tax per ton of fish landed). From equation (3.4) we know that, in an optimal regime, price equals marginal extraction cost plus royalty. In the unrestricted common-property regime, price equals average cost. A two-part tax is then called for, with one part equal to the royalty, $p_t$, and the other equal to the difference between marginal and average extraction costs, $\partial c / \partial y_t - c/y_t$, assuring that users take account of future losses and current crowding, respectively.[15]

Not surprisingly, most of the fishery conservation controls actually adopted have not been of this type. Although they sometimes succeed in raising stocks and yields, they do not attack the root problem, the common-property character of the resource. One form of control is imposing technical inefficiencies, such as restrictions on the kind of fishing gear that can be used. Another form of control is to directly limit the total catch. The typical result here is an expansion of fishing inputs, such as more and larger vessels, as each fishing firm or nation scrambles to get a larger share of the quota for itself. This, in turn, results in a shorter harvest season (in the case of yellowfin tuna in the eastern Pacific, now just 3 months, down from 9 or 10 months before the quota was imposed). Capital and labor are idled, or they move elsewhere and place addi-

[15] Alternatively, as in the work of Brown (1974), the tax can be set on effort (e.g., a boat tax). V. L. Smith (1969) suggested a tax that corrects for the externalities of net mesh size as well. Clark (1976) analyzed the dynamic response of a fishery to various tax policies.

tional pressures on already depleted stocks, as has happened in the case of tuna.[16]

The problems of regulating common-property fisheries have led to international conflict, as in the recent "cod war" between Britain and Iceland and the continuing disputes over tuna, salmon, and whales. Numerous international conferences have been convened to address these problems.[17]

## 3.4 Concluding remarks

This concludes our discussion of certain aspects of the pure theory of exhaustible- and renewable-resource use. In fact, the theory has not been all that pure; on a number of occasions we have referred in passing to empirical issues. The next chapter will take up in a more systematic way what most people would regard as the major empirical issue: the adequacy of the natural resource base to sustain growth, or even a continued high level of activity, in advanced industrial economies like that of the United States.

[16] See the work of Christy (1975).
[17] For more on conflicts, conferences, and regulations involving ocean fisheries, see the work of Turvey and Wiseman (1957), Hamlisch (1962), OECD (1972), and Christy (1975).

# 4

## Resource scarcity: are resources limits to growth?

### 4.1. Introduction

It is probably fair to say that the question in the title has triggered much of the recent interest in natural resources by economists and others. In Chapters 2 and 3 we derived conditions that must be satisfied by optimal programs of resource use under different market or institutional arrangements. We were specially interested in the relationship between market-determined use and socially efficient use. This chapter concerns the evidence on actual rates of use, to date, as well as future prospects. In short: Are we running out of resources? And does it matter?

A conventional view (or, at least, one we often hear expressed) is that the questions are meaningless, because they have no policy implications. The U.S. economy might, according to this view, be facing greatly depleted stocks of some resources, much higher resource costs and prices, and a consequent slowing of growth; yet no intervention by government would be warranted in the absence of clearly demonstrated market failure.

My own view is somewhat different. If, as discussed in Chapter 2, the welfare of future generations is a public good, members of the present generation might be made better off by government intervention to promote conservation and reduce the anticipated drag on growth. For that matter, the government might intervene to promote intergenerational equity even if the market were allocating resources efficiently from the standpoint of the present generation. We certainly do not need to resolve these issues here. We raise them only to suggest that an inquiry into the prospects for resource exhaustion need not be without interest.

Now, what can economics contribute to the debate over the Malthusian or neo-Malthusian view of the world urged by those who, like the authors of *The Limits to Growth* (Meadows et al., 1972), see resources as just that – limits to growth. Two distinct approaches have been taken. One, discussed in Chapter 2, studies the conditions under which it is theoretically possible for an economy to sustain a constant or growing per capita income with an exhaustible-resource input to production. Not surprisingly, the degree of substitutability between the resource and other inputs is important, as is the possibility of resource-augmenting technical change.

The second approach, largely empirical and associated with Resources for the Future (RFF), has looked at measures of resource scarcity and their behavior over time. For example, stocks of reserves of key minerals have been estimated and compared with current and projected future consumption. In perhaps the most influential of the early RFF studies (Barnett and Morse, 1963), the costs and prices of extractive resources were tracked over several decades.

In this chapter we shall be concerned mainly with these empirical studies and what they tell us about scarcity. This means, of course, some discussion of findings (the reserves:production ratio for crude oil, how costs and prices of energy minerals have changed over time, and so on), but also, and importantly, it means a critical evaluation of the alternative scarcity measures.

A further question of interest is the forecasted future behavior of these measures. The early studies of resource adequacy tended to equate demand with current consumption or informally projected future consumption. Cumulative consumption over a planning horizon (25 to 50 years) was then compared with reserve estimates to pinpoint future shortages and price rises. No doubt this is a useful first step in assessing the adequacy of known or discoverable stocks of a resource. But recent econometric studies of the demand for energy and engineering-economic studies of supply have allowed us to forecast future price and output in this sector with greater precision, or at least to forecast the prices and outputs that will follow from certain assumptions about technological developments and government policies. We shall also review the results of these studies, paying particular attention to what they tell us about prospects for the substitution of one fuel for another and substitution of labor and capital for all fuels.

The plan of the chapter is as follows. In the next section, some data on physical measures of scarcity, such as reserves, will be presented and critically evaluated. This leads to the introduction, in Section 4.3, of economic measures such as cost and price. The major findings concerning trends in the cost and price of extractive-resource output will be summarized. The properties of these measures and another measure mentioned earlier (the resource royalty, or rent, as it is often known in discussions of scarcity) will be discussed in light of the theory of Chapter 2. The techniques and results for estimation of energy demand and supply will be reviewed in Section 4.4.

### 4.2. Physical measures of scarcity
#### *Reserves*
Reserves are perhaps the most widely cited indicators of scarcity of specific extractive resources, such as oil. For example, current estimates place world oil resources at about 600 to 700 billion barrels.[1] Because it is difficult to say

---

[1] See, for example, the work of Richardson (1975), who discussed estimates from a number of sources.

Table 4.1. *World oil reserves*

| Date | Reserves (million metric tons) | Years of supply (reserves/production) |
|------|-------------------------------|---------------------------------------|
| 1947 | 9,478 | 22 |
| 1950 | 11,810 | 22 |
| 1955 | 25,969 | 33 |
| 1960 | 40,788 | 37 |
| 1965 | 47,687 | 30 |
| 1971 | 85,442 | 34 |
| 1972 | 91,376 ≈ 670 billion barrels | 35 |

*Source: Oil: World Statistics,* Institute of Petroleum Information, cited by Robinson (1975).

whether this is a lot or a little, reserves are often compared with a measure of depletion, such as annual production or consumption of the resource in question. Table 4.1, adapted from Robinson's survey (1975) of the availability of major energy commodities, presents an interesting picture for oil. It appeared that, as of 1972, oil reserves were sufficient for only 35 years at the 1972 rate of depletion. In fact, the situation was then and is now even more serious, because the rate of depletion has been increasing. The message is clear: Oil is a limit to growth.

Before we accept this conclusion, we had better look at the rest of the information contained in Table 4.1. Note that the reserves:production ratio has remained nearly constant since 1955, and it actually increased between 1947 and 1955. One observation of particular interest concerns 1950. At that time it appeared that the world had sufficient oil to last exactly 22 years. Why didn't everything grind to a halt in 1972, the world economy having reached a "limit to growth"? The reason we single out this observation is that 1972 was, by cruel coincidence, the date of publication of *The Limits to Growth.* But we, and the authors, are still around to debate the merits of the work. What happened?

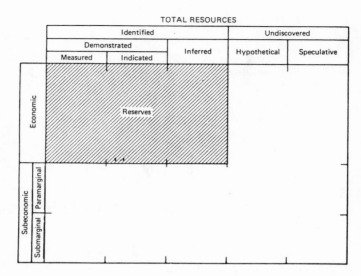

Figure 4.1. U.S. Bureau of Mines/U.S. Geological Survey mineral and coal resource and reserve categories. (From U.S. Department of the Interior news release, "New Mineral and Coal Resource Terminology Adopted," May 26, 1976.)

The answer lies in the definition of reserves. In what has come to be fairly standard usage, at least by the concerned government agencies and others in the United States, reserves are defined as the known amounts of a mineral that can be profitably produced at current prices using current technology.[2] The relationship between reserves and other measures of resource stocks is easily grasped with the aid of the "McKelvey diagram" used by the U.S. Geological Survey and the U.S. Bureau of Mines (Figure 4.1). Clearly, when discoveries are made or processes for extracting and converting resources more cheaply are developed, reserves increase. The influence of discoveries is obvious; the influence of technical change is

[2] Detailed discussions of this terminology, along with quantitative estimates, were provided by McKelvey (1972), by several of the chapters in the volume edited by Brobst and Pratt (1973), by Schanz (1975), and by Brobst (1979).

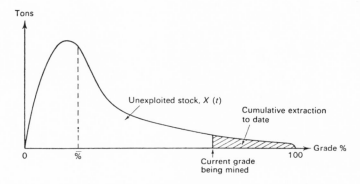

Figure 4.2. Tonnage–grade distribution for a mineral.

perhaps less so. Numerous studies have documented the ways in which technical change, in effect, augments reserves. One dramatic example is the tenfold increase, from 1907 to 1957, in services rendered by a ton of coal because of reductions in the energy required for mining, transport, and electricity generation and transmission.[3]

Just as new knowledge can lead to an increase in reserves, so can a change in economic conditions. When input prices fall, or when the resource-product price rises, more of the resource base qualifies as a reserve. The tonnage–grade relationship, which indicates the amounts available at different grades, can be used to construct a kind of cost curve for a mineral. An idealized tonnage–grade distribution is shown in Figure 4.2; a cost curve for uranium deposits is shown in Figure 4.3. Does the economy move smoothly along a tonnage–grade curve in the manner suggested? Surprises (new discoveries) obviously preclude exploitation of the best remaining deposits at all times. But monotonicity appears generally reasonable, as

[3] The example is taken from the work of Howe (1979), a good reference to this and other issues surrounding the measurement of scarcity. For a detailed discussion of possibilities for expanding reserves of copper and other metals, see the work of Radetzki (1975).

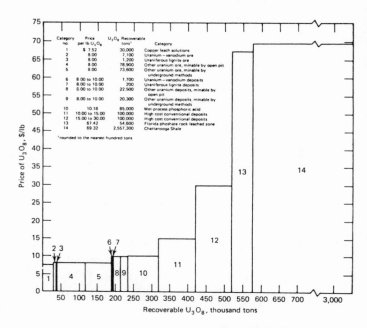

Figure 4.3. Availability diagram for uranium (expressed as $U_3O_8$). (From Bieniewski, Persse, and Brauch, 1971, p. 14.)

shown in studies of major energy resources like oil and uranium.[4]

Actual tonnage–grade distributions can be more complicated than the one in Figure 4.2 in at least a couple of ways. First, they can be multivariate; deposit size and depth and other quality characteristics can be important. For example, taconite has properties that make it more valuable than ores having higher iron content, such as paint rock. Second, the distribution need not be unimodal, with increasing quantities at lower grades. It has been suggested that copper, for exam-

---

[4] On oil, see the work of Hubbert (1969) and Steele (1974). On uranium, see the work of Lieberman (1976). For a study of coal depletion, including a discussion of cumulative costs of extraction, see the work of Zimmerman (1977).

ple, is less plentiful at grades just below those currently being mined, thus producing a bump on the tail of the distribution.[5]

To return to the reserves:production ratios of Table 4.1, it is now obvious why they are misleading indicators of scarcity. There is a lot of other material in the ground (or in the sea or the air) in addition to what at any time qualifies as reserves. This suggests that a more inclusive measure of physical stocks might be desirable. After all, if one is worried about some ultimate or Malthusian limits, what is wanted is a measure of what might ultimately be recovered. We shall consider this presently, but first we note one other matter regarding the interpretation of reserve statistics.

From 1955 to 1972 the ratio of oil reserves to production remained very nearly constant. Similar empirical regularities have been observed for other resources.[6] What is the explanation? Consider the reserves held by a mining firm as an inventory. Clearly the firm should hold a nonzero inventory, because it takes time to discover a resource deposit and develop it for production. Moreover, the outcome of the discovery process is uncertain. On the other hand, it doesn't pay to invest too much in exploration now. Exploration and development of additions to the reserve base can be costly, and the present value of costs is reduced by deferring them. We might even

[5] See the work of Singer, Cox, and Drew (1975). A discussion of bimodal distributions as a general feature of geochemically scarce elements was provided by Brobst (1979). Tonnage–grade information for lead and zinc was provided by Brooks (1967). The size distribution of petroleum reservoirs was estimated by Kaufman (1963). For further discussion of the geostatistical literature, see the work of Harris (1975) and the other studies noted in Chapter 2.

[6] See the work of Fischman and Landsberg (1972) for a discussion of reserves and projected consumption for various nonfuel minerals. This article is one of several addressing the resource and environmental consequences of economic and population growth in the United States over the period 1970–2020 written for the Commission on Population Growth and the American Future. A useful source of information about stocks of extractive and environmental resources and the natural processes that generate them is the work of Ehrlich, Ehrlich, and Holdren (1977).

Table 4.2. *Physical measures of availability of selected minerals*

| Mineral | Reserves/ consumption | Crustal abundance/ consumption | Ultimately[a] recoverable resources/ consumption |
|---|---|---|---|
| Copper | 45 | $242 \times 10^6$ | 340 |
| Iron | 117 | $1,815 \times 10^6$ | 2,657 |
| Phosphorus | 481 | $870 \times 10^6$ | 1,601 |
| Molybdenum | 65 | $422 \times 10^6$ | 630 |
| Lead | 10 | $85 \times 10^6$ | 162 |
| Zinc | 21 | $409 \times 10^6$ | 618 |
| Uranium | 50 | $1,855 \times 10^6$ | 8,455 |
| Aluminum | 23 | $38,500 \times 10^6$ | 68,066 |

[a]0.01% of total availability to a depth of 1 km.
*Source:* USGS, cited by Nordhaus (1974).

conjecture that if the determinants of the optimal inventory of reserves are not changing, any fluctuations observed in reserves:production ratios are due simply to "lumpiness" in the discovery process.

### Crustal abundance and other measures

If reserves, the known amounts of a mineral that can be profitably recovered at current prices, represent one extreme on the resource spectrum, crustal abundance represents the other. This is the material that exists in minute concentrations in the "average rock" of the earth's crust. To get some idea of how these amounts compare with reserves, Nordhaus (1974) calculated reserves:annual-consumption ratios and crustal-abundance:annual-consumption ratios for a number of key minerals. Some of his data are presented in Table 4.2.

The differences in the two ratios are striking. Supplies of the "scarcest" resource, lead, appear sufficient for just 10 years if we consult the reserve ratio, but for 85 million years if we look to crustal abundance. This is certainly an ultimate figure, and if it accurately represents resource availability there is no apparent reason for concern. But just as reserve estimates are misleading as indicators of availability, so is crustal abundance. As Jevons (1865) pointed out a long time ago, cost barriers (especially the energy required to convert very low grade materials) will in most cases prevent the mining of average rock. The environmental costs associated with moving and disposing of the very large tonnages of residuals generated by each ton of mineral produced could also be substantial. In the case of lead, for example, 77,000 tons of material will be required to produce a ton of the metal, even assuming 100% recovery.[7]

Two things are suggested by these figures. First, a measure intermediate between reserves and crustal abundance would be more accurate than either as a guide to availability. Second, such physical measures alone are not adequate; they must be supplemented by economic measures, such as the cost of obtaining the resource.

Taking the first point, Where can the line reasonably be drawn for ultimately recoverable resources? Brobst (1979) proposed the "mineralogical threshold," which represents a concentration between 0.01% and 0.1%. Below 0.01% a metal element occurs only in the atomic structure of silicate minerals, not in minerals of its own. Conversion of a silicate structure would be very expensive because of the immense amounts of materials that would have to be processed and the difficulty of separating the desired metal. For copper, the threshold is estimated to be about 0.1%, and it is further estimated that no more than 0.01% of the copper in the earth's crust will be found at this concentration. Thus, 0.01% of crustal abundance might be considered as the ultimately

---

[7] The computation behind this figure was carried out by Brobst (1979), based on a study of the abundance of chemical elements in the earth's crust by Lee and Chao (1970).

Table 4.3. *Unit costs of extractive outputs, United States*

| Date | All extractive | Agriculture | Minerals | Forest products |
|------|----------------|-------------|----------|-----------------|
| 1870–1900 | 134[a] | 132 | 210 | 59 |
| 1929 | 100 | 100 | 100 | 100 |
| 1957 | 60 | 61 | 47 | 90 |

[a]1929 = 100.
*Source:* Barnett and Morse (1963).

recoverable resource. In Table 4.2 this figure has been applied to all of the resources listed, to a depth of one kilometer, including copper. The resulting ratio is obviously no more than a crude approximation, at best, providing another reason to examine economic measures of scarcity.

### 4.3 **Economic measures of scarcity**
*Cost*

Both classical (Ricardo) and neoclassical (Jevons) economists have viewed the increasing costs associated with depletion as a limit to growth. Certainly resources have been extensively depleted over the last century and more. How have costs behaved? Probably the most widely known and most influential work here is that of Barnett and Morse (1963), who constructed indexes of the real costs of various categories of extractive output over the industrial history of the United States.

A summary of results is given in Table 4.3. Surprisingly, costs appear to have fallen, not risen, for extractive output as a whole, agriculture and minerals. Only the relatively unimportant forestry sector shows signs of increasing costs over the entire period (1870–1957), and all of the increases came in the first half of the period, with a slight decline over the second half. Data for fisheries are poorer and are presented only in diagrammatic form, but they tend to show a definite decline in harvest costs.[8]

Does this mean that resources are depleted in order of increasing quality, contrary to the views of Ricardo and Jevons, and also the views of modern theorists? No, or at least, not deliberately. Recall that exploration and technical change can lead to a decrease in extraction costs. Barnett and Morse interpreted their findings as being due primarily to technical change and to a lesser extent to economies of scale. There is ample empirical evidence of technical progress in the minerals sector, the one exhibiting the most dramatic decline in costs. Machines have replaced men and animals, and decreasing grades of ore have been processed. Further, technical change is often accompanied by the substitution of capital and labor for resources, and substitution of one resource or product for another.[9]

In the face of this evidence, a resource pessimist might still argue that the picture has changed since 1957, the last year covered by Barnett and Morse. The argument would be wrong, though, at least for the period through the early 1970s. A recent update by Johnson and Bell (1978) found no major changes. In fact, the decline in costs appears to have accelerated in the years 1958–70 for both agriculture and minerals.[10]

Still, the pessimist might argue that all of this proves nothing about the future. We could be coming to the end of a

[8] These findings are supported by those of Herfindahl (1959, 1961) for copper and other minerals. In a related study, Barger and Schurr (1944) observed a rise in mining productivity that exceeded that in manufacturing over the period 1899–1939.

[9] Earlier we noted the example of technical change in the coal industry. For further discussion, see the work of Peirce (1974). For a discussion of the cost-reducing effects of technology in oil drilling, see the work of Norgaard (1975), and for the influence of discovery and technical change on copper prices and production, see the work of Radetzki (1975). Substitution possibilities were documented by Rosenberg (1973) and by Humphrey and Moroney (1975).

[10] The existence of a time trend in costs was established and estimated by means of statistical regression analysis that formalizes as well as updates the work of Barnett and Morse (1963).

"resource plateau," to the end of a period of technical change that has kept us on a plateau for many decades. Cost would not indicate this. I think this is a legitimate argument. The question then becomes this: Is there a measure that signals impending exhaustion of a resource, even in the face of technical advances that may keep down costs?

### Price

The answer is suggested by the theory of Chapter 2: Yes, there is a measure that anticipates future scarcity. In fact, there are two: resource price and resource royalty, or rent. The rent is the shadow price of a unit of the resource in the stock, the amount by which the present value of the stock is reduced when the unit is removed. If one is interested in scarcity of the "pure" resource, unmixed with human labor or other productive factors, rent appears to be an appropriate measure. If, on the other hand, one is interested in the sum of sacrifices made to obtain a unit of the resource, then price, which includes both cost and rent, is relevant.

Because rent is ordinarily not observable, most of the empirical work in this area has focused on price. Another landmark RFF study, by Potter and Christy (1962), developed annual time series for prices, output, employment, and trade in natural-resource commodities over the period 1870–1957 in the United States. The output and employment series were used by Barnett and Morse to construct their cost estimates. The price series, deflated by an index for nonextractive goods, was used as an alternative to cost.

No econometric tests were performed by either set of authors, but Barnett and Morse displayed the (deflated) price data in charts like that of Figure 4.4. Visual inspection suggests no obvious overall trend for extractive resources as a whole. This is also true for agriculture and fisheries, separately. A modest decline appears in mineral prices, and there is an equally modest rise in forest-product prices. These trends are roughly consistent with those for costs, but because costs fell

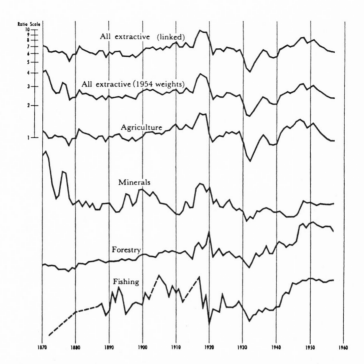

Figure 4.4. Trends in unit prices of extractive products relative to nonextractive products in the United States, 1870–1957. (From Barnett and Morse, 1963, p. 210.)

more rapidly, there is at least a suggestion that rents rose over the period.

Strong support for the finding of no price rise is offered in a more recent study by Nordhaus (1974) of the prices of several minerals over the period 1900–70. These price series, presented in Table 4.4, in fact exhibit a very marked decline in all cases, with only one, copper, showing signs of reversal over the most recent decade.

Nordhaus's statistics seem to lead to a still stronger rejection of the increasing-scarcity hypothesis. However, they may need to be modified. Brown and Field (1978) argued that the

Table 4.4. *Relationships between prices of important minerals and costs of labor*

|  | 1900 | 1920 | 1940 | 1950 | 1960 | 1970 |
|---|---|---|---|---|---|---|
| Coal | 459[a] | 451 | 189 | 208 | 111 | 100 |
| Copper | 785 | 226 | 121 | 99 | 82 | 100 |
| Iron | 620 | 287 | 144 | 112 | 120 | 100 |
| Phosphorus | — | — | — | 130 | 120 | 100 |
| Molybdenum | — | — | — | 142 | 108 | 100 |
| Lead | 788 | 388 | 204 | 228 | 114 | 100 |
| Zinc | 794 | 400 | 272 | 256 | 126 | 100 |
| Sulfur | — | — | — | 215 | 145 | 100 |
| Aluminum | 3,150 | 859 | 287 | 166 | 134 | 100 |
| Gold | — | — | 595 | 258 | 143 | 100 |
| Crude petroleum | 1,034 | 726 | 198 | 213 | 135 | 100 |

Dashes indicate no data.
[a]1970 = 100. Each value is the price per ton of the mineral divided by the hourly wage rate in manufacturing.
*Source:* Data are from "Historical Statistics, Long Term Economic Growth," *Statistical Abstract of the United States*, cited by Nordhaus (1974).

choice of price deflator, or numeraire, the hourly wage rate in manufacturing, leads to biased results. Clearly, nominal prices need to be deflated, but a more appropriate deflator would be a quality-adjusted wage rate that would reflect the value of labor of constant quality, just as the numerator reflects the value of a mineral of constant quality. The use of a constant-quality wage rate dampens the relative mineral price decrease by about 25%. Alternatively, the use of the price of capital as numeraire results in relative price increases over the period 1920–50 for 4 of Nordhaus's 11 minerals (coal, phosphorus, lead, and zinc), and smaller decreases for the others.

So we have, according to one interpretation, at least, an indication of turning points in some price series, even before 1950. This indication is strengthened by a couple of recent studies. Manthy (1978) extended the Potter-Christy price and other time series to 1972, and V. K. Smith (1979a) found on

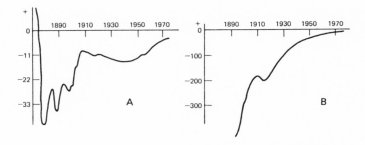

Figure 4.5. Behavior of price-trend coefficients over time. A: Metals. B: Fuels. (From Smith, V. K., 1979*a*.)

the basis of these data that the rate of decline in mineral prices was itself declining.

Smith's econometric tests were complex, but one in particular was rather striking and deserves explanation. Suppose price follows a simple time trend, as in

$$p_t = a + bt \tag{4.1}$$

where $a$ and $b$ are parameters that can be estimated from a time series on prices. Suppose this is done a number of different times, from a time series having a different end point in each case. For example, $a$ and $b$ can be estimated from data for 1870–90, then again from data for 1870–91, and so on, up to 1870–1972. Now, if the estimated $b$ is negative in all cases, then price is clearly declining over time. But if the estimated $b$ is also getting larger (falling in absolute value) as additional years of data are introduced, then the counter-scarcity effect is weakening. This is precisely what Smith found, as shown in Figures 4.5A and 4.5B. The estimated trend coefficient $b$ is plotted against the data end points for metals (Figure 4.5A) and fuels (Figure 4.5B). The fluctuations, especially in the case of metals, suggest the absence of a single linear trend (in a separate test Smith indeed found evidence of several trends); but laying these aside, it is clear that the estimated $b$ is large and negative over the early years and is approaching zero by 1972.

Table 4.5. *Real prices of selected important nonfuel minerals, 1969–79*[a]

| Mineral | 1969 | 1979 |
|---|---|---|
| Copper | $.45/lb | $.40/lb |
| Iron | $10.09/ton of ore (51.5%) | $10.61/ton |
| Phosphate rock | $5.23/short ton | $8.20/metric ton |
| Molybdenum | $1.62/lb | $3.24/lb |
| Lead | $.14/lb | $.23/lb |
| Zinc | $.14/lb | $.16/lb |
| Sulfur | $25.40/long ton | $24.74/metric ton |
| Aluminum (ingot) | $25.5/lb | $25.9/lb |
| Gold | $38.98/oz | $131.26/oz[b] |

[a]Deflated by producer price index; 1967 = 100.
[b]First half of 1979.
*Source:* U.S. Bureau of Mines, *Mineral Commodity Summaries, 1980,* and *Commodity Data Summaries, 1974,* and *Statistical Abstract of the United States* (1979).

An interesting question arises: What has happened to prices since 1972? We know what happened to oil and other energy prices, although a substantial part of the post-1973 increase is surely due to the market power of the energy producers. We have put together some data on the prices of key nonfuel minerals from 1969 to 1979, precisely the ones reported by Nordhaus. If a tendency to increasing scarcity, as measured by price, was threatening to emerge at the beginning of the period, we might expect some clear evidence of increases over the period.

The results are displayed in Table 4.5. The dominant impression is indeed one of substantial increases in most prices, even after they are deflated by the Producer Price Index, which itself rose sharply over the period. It is interesting that copper, the one mineral that registered a price increase in Nordhaus's data, registers a decrease here, in fact the strongest decrease, and one of just two (sulfur being the other).

Phosphorus, lead, and zinc all show substantial increases, confirming the trend noted by Brown and Field. In addition, sharp increases are shown by molybdenum and gold, and mild increases are shown by iron and aluminum.

How can we make sense of these numbers? Some evidence, based mainly on earlier data, suggests a decline in the real prices of exhaustible resources over a period of many decades. On the other hand, newer evidence, more sketchy, suggests that the decline may have come to an end and is, in fact, beginning to reverse. So price, at least for many exhaustible resources, appears to be following a U-shaped path. Recall that this is just what we hypothesized, based on the theory developed in Chapter 2. Price first falls, as discoveries and technical change reduce royalties and costs. But after a while, discoveries are harder to come by, and costs cannot be reduced indefinitely. Price then levels off and ultimately begins to rise.

One more piece of evidence that would bear on the existence of a turning point is the behavior of rent. We have said that this is not directly observable, but it may be possible to develop some indirect evidence. To this we now turn.

### Rent

Because rent is the difference between price and (marginal) extraction cost, if price has been fairly steady, and perhaps rising, while cost has been declining, certainly one possible explanation is that rent has been rising. The difficulty with drawing a firm conclusion here is that other factors, such as market imperfections and government regulation, may also have contributed to the observed price behavior. This is, of course, a difficulty in interpreting the price series as well, to which we shall return in the next section. Moreover, the extraction cost figures are average costs, not marginal.

Let us take another tack. Mention of discovery and technical change as explanations for the observed price behavior suggests an indirect way of estimating rent. Recall that to a first approximation, exploration will be carried to the point that the cost of finding an additional unit is equated to the benefit from finding it, the rent. Exploration cost is, in principle, observable, and it can be used to estimate rent.

Further, there may be an advantage in trying to get at rent in this fashion. The current market price of a resource, as we have just noted, is subject to a variety of distortions. Current energy prices, for example, are affected by both producer combinations and government controls. Rent is also subject to distortion, because it depends on expected future prices. But future prices might be less affected by the current crop of imperfections and controls, to the extent these are regarded as transitory. In addition, if marginal exploration costs are constant over the relevant range, price distortions will not affect the estimate of rent.

We have developed estimates of exploration costs for oil and gas in the United States; they will be presented along with estimates for Canada. Table 4.6 shows average real exploration costs per equivalent barrel of oil discovered for the years 1946–71 in the United States. The fairly low values are due to an adjustment of reported discoveries, in each year, to reflect ultimately recoverable reserves. Still, the trend is clear. Costs rose from just under 57¢ per barrel in 1946 to $1.38 in 1971, an average annual increase of 5.7%.[11]

Lest these results be interpreted too literally, it is important to emphasize their limitations. First, as for extraction costs, they refer to average costs, whereas the theoretical analysis was in terms of marginal costs, although note that this is not a problem if marginal costs are constant and coincide with average. Second, exploration costs are likely to be no more than an approximation to rent. But even if the estimates are biased, the trends are surely suggestive.

So, even before the events of the early 1970s, rising exploration cost was pointing in the direction of increasing scarcity of domestic (U.S.) oil. This was clearly opposed to the indications

[11] For evidence on a related magnitude (the costs of drilling a successful well) in the United States from 1939 to 1968, see the work of Norgaard (1975).

Table 4.6 *Average real exploration costs for U.S. oil and gas, 1946–71*

| Year | Cost[a] |
|------|------|
| 1946 | 0.568 |
| 1947 | 0.527 |
| 1948 | 0.291 |
| 1949 | 0.323 |
| 1950 | 0.497 |
| 1951 | 0.748 |
| 1952 | 0.827 |
| 1953 | 0.692 |
| 1954 | 0.628 |
| 1955 | 1.036 |
| 1956 | 0.789 |
| 1957 | 0.653 |
| 1958 | 0.950 |
| 1959 | 1.449 |
| 1960 | 1.213 |
| 1961 | 1.509 |
| 1962 | 0.98 |
| 1963 | 1.35 |
| 1964 | 1.26 |
| 1965 | 0.98 |
| 1966 | 1.65 |
| 1967 | 1.39 |
| 1968 | 0.14 |
| 1969 | 1.78 |
| 1970 | 1.24 |
| 1971 | 1.38 |

[a] Dollars per equivalent barrel of oil discovered (average 1947–9 dollars). To combine oil and gas discoveries, physical units were aggregated on the basis of market value.
*Source:* Devarajan and Fisher (1980), adapted from Merklein and Howell (1973).

from conventional measures. Extraction costs and prices for exhaustible resources generally were steady or falling, prior to 1970, and this was true also for oil. Table 4.7 shows, for example, that U.S. crude oil prices remained fairly stable over the period 1950–70. In light of the more recent experience, it

Table 4.7. *U.S. crude oil price per barrel*

| Year | Price per barrel[a] |
|------|---------------------|
| 1950 | 2.43 |
| 1951 | 2.20 |
| 1952 | 2.27 |
| 1953 | 2.43 |
| 1954 | 2.52 |
| 1955 | 2.50 |
| 1956 | 2.44 |
| 1957 | 2.63 |
| 1958 | 2.52 |
| 1959 | 2.42 |
| 1960 | 2.41 |
| 1961 | 2.42 |
| 1962 | 2.42 |
| 1963 | 2.42 |
| 1964 | 2.41 |
| 1965 | 2.35 |
| 1966 | 2.29 |
| 1967 | 2.32 |
| 1968 | 2.28 |
| 1969 | 2.30 |
| 1970 | 2.28 |
| 1971 | 2.32 |

[a]Prices in average 1947–9 dollars.
*Source:* American Petroleum Institute, *Petroleum Facts and Figures,* cited by Devarajan and Fisher (1980).

appears that exploration costs may have played the role of a "leading indicator" of scarcity, for one important resource at least. No doubt a substantial part of the subsequent oil price increase can be explained by the monopoly power of OPEC, but even this depends in part on the apparent inability of the United States to expand production, or perhaps even to sustain it at the level of the early 1970s.

Another piece of evidence on oil and gas exploration costs also points in the direction of increasing scarcity. Uhler (1975) estimated marginal exploration cost functions for the Cana-

Table 4.8. *Marginal exploration costs for oil and gas in Alberta, 1972–8*

| | Oil, cost per barrel | | Gas, cost per thousand cubic feet | |
|---|---|---|---|---|
| | Total oil in place ($) | Recoverable oil in place (0.3 recovery factor) ($) | Total ($) | Recoverable (0.7 recovery factor) ($) |
| 1972 | 0.28 | 0.93 | 0.0376 | 0.0537 |
| 1978 | 0.72 | 2.40 | 0.1320 | 0.1885 |

*Source:* Uhler (1976).

dian province of Alberta from 1971 data and forecasted costs for 1972–8. The results are presented in Table 4.8. The rises are quite striking, an approximate tripling over a rather short period.

### Qualifications

The evidence on resource scarcity that we have been discussing comes from historical cost and price series, which are subject to distortion. Let us consider, briefly, the implications of the more important sources of distortion, the market imperfections and government regulations that can affect costs and especially prices.

An obvious imperfection, since the success of OPEC, is the resource cartel. Although the influence of a cartel or monopoly on the price and output of an exhaustible resource cannot be determined theoretically in the general case, we have concluded that there is some presumption that price is raised and output restricted during an initial phase. The experience of OPEC is certainly consistent with this. The jump in oil prices almost certainly tells us more about the current market power of the organization of producing nations than it does about the impending exhaustion of global oil resources, although note, again, that OPEC's success in raising prices in the short term does depend in part on the inability of the competitive fringe to expand production at anything like historical costs.

To infer something about scarcity from price trends, observations that reflect significant monopoly rents should ideally be either eliminated or adjusted. Although the analyst must become knowledgeable about the institutional structure of the industry in question, this does not seem an insuperable barrier. Herfindahl (1959), in an early study of copper costs and prices, corrected observations tainted by collusive episodes and found no discernible trend in the resulting "competitive" price series.

Another obvious imperfection is the existence of environmental externalities. The direction of the resulting distortions of historical cost and price series seems clear. At least some part of the observed decline is, by hypothesis, due to the increasingly heavy demands placed on unpriced environmental resources like air and water. If the environmental damages are fully reflected in market costs and prices, presumably the decline will be more modest.[12]

The foregoing conclusion seems to be true for at least the period covered in the early studies. However, recent environmental policy has resulted in reductions in certain types of pollution, with some increase in production costs and prices. If the value of damages avoided exceeds the increase in costs, then the full social costs of extractive-resource use will rise by less than the direct production costs, or prices, and may even fall. Moreover, it seems plausible that the same kinds of cost-reducing innovations that have long been important in the

[12] This is a major theme of an introductory essay by Smith and Krutilla in a volume edited by V. K. Smith (1979*b*) featuring reconsiderations by a number of people of the Barnett-Morse results. Other contributions that deal with the environmental question are those of Brown and Field, Fisher, and Barnett. The papers by Brown and Field and Fisher are versions of papers already referenced.

extractive sector can play a role in protecting the environment.[13] Still, it seems fair to say that the costs and prices of extractive output have until recently not reflected environmental damage and that this damage has increased over the periods studied. Accordingly, historical cost and price series (until roughly 1970, at least) have been biased downward.

The costs and prices of extractive output are influenced by a variety of government controls as well: direct controls on price and production and indirect controls via fiscal instruments such as taxes and subsidies. The net effect on trends is not clear.

The oil and gas price controls of recent years obviously have imparted a downward bias to these price series. And extractive industries generally appear to have received increasingly favorable tax treatment over the years, causing a further downward bias in observed price series.[14] On the other hand, price supports have probably kept agricultural prices from falling further in this century. Similarly, most production controls probably have pushed up prices, as in the cases of agricultural acreage restrictions and oil import quotas.

It seems that what is required here, as with market imperfections such as monopoly, is a careful study of the history of distortions in the industry in question in order to adjust or eliminate tainted observations.

### 4.4. Demand and supply: empirical results

Resource prices are generated by the interaction between demand and supply. Thus to better understand and predict price movements, some knowledge of the underlying demand and supply relationships will be helpful. In this section we shall briefly review the main lines of evidence developed by recent econometric and other studies. The largest body of work

[13] Barnett (1979) made this point, with examples, in a discussion of extensions and qualifications to his earlier work that appeared in the V. K. Smith volume (1979*b*).

[14] For a discussion of the effects of changing tax laws on extractive industries, see the work of Page (1977).

concerns the demand for energy. We shall also look at some efforts to model and estimate energy supply and the interaction between demand and supply.

At the outset it should be said that I am not optimistic about the prospects for predicting energy and other resource price movements on the basis of the economic and econometric models we shall be discussing. There are too many influences on prices that are not endogenous to the models. For example, future energy prices depend on, among other things, the outcome of research on advanced energy-conversion systems such as solar photovoltaic cells and fusion reactors. In this sense we agree with the critics (and there are many) of such models. Certainly a model can be misleading if one attempts to use it as a crystal ball. But models can be helpful in a more modest role, as computing tools. Although a model cannot predict the outcome of a research program, or for that matter the outcome of the latest political flap in the Middle East, it can be used to determine the effects of assumed outcomes on economic variables, such as the prices and outputs of different energy forms. For example, if we assume technical progress that will continue to reduce the cost of photovoltaic electricity by $X\%$ per year for the next 10–15 years, no significant disruption in oil supplies from the Middle East over the same period, and a variety of other things such as the rate at which domestic oil price controls are phased out, it ought to be possible to determine from the relationships in a model the course of energy prices and the degree of penetration of the U.S. electricity market by photovoltaics. The important point is that these predictions (which are in any case uncertain and are appropriately stated in probabilistic terms) are conditional on assumptions about events exogenous to the model. If understood in this way, a model can, in my judgment, make a contribution to our knowledge of the implications that various technological and political developments will have for economic variables like energy prices.

There is another way in which some of the models we shall

discuss can be useful. The models of energy use and demand, in particular, can tell us a good deal about possibilities for conserving energy. For example, if energy prices are rising sharply, the ease with which labor, capital, and materials can be substituted surely indicates something about prospects for continued economic growth, just as would accurate forecasts of future energy prices.

### Energy demand, substitution, and conservation

The first thing to note about the demand studies is that their results are not easy to characterize, because scope and treatment have varied widely. Most have involved some degree of disaggregation: different "cuts" at demand. For example, there have been studies of residential demand for electricity and studies of industrial demand for electricity. There have been studies of demand for various primary fuels, like oil, coal, and natural gas. Some of the studies have been based on time-series data for the United States and others on data from U.S. states or regions or a mix of other countries. Not surprisingly, there is no magic number – say an agreed point estimate of demand price elasticity for "energy." Also, and more important, not all of the elasticity estimates reflect the kind of long-run adjustment we are interested in.

A second thing that ought to be noted is the innovation in method that these studies represent. There has been a long and continuing tradition of studies of consumption of energy (and other resources) over time in the United States and in other countries.[15] What is new here is the application of econometric

---

[15] Many of the early studies, at least in the United States, were associated with Resources for the Future (RFF) or its predecessor, the president's Materials Policy Commission. The commission's report, issued in five volumes in 1952, projected resource consumption and supplies over the next 25 years. The early RFF studies tended to follow this approach. Notable here are a study of past and projected future consumptions (to 1975) of energy resources in the United States (Schurr and Netschert, 1960) and a more comprehensive and more ambitious (to 2000) set of projections for energy and other resources (Landsberg, Fischman and Fisher,

methods, often highly sophisticated, to the estimation of structural demand relationships.[16]

Comparative results from a number of studies are presented in Tables 4.9, 4.10, and 4.11, adapted mostly from the work of Pindyck. Table 4.9 shows price elasticities for energy in the aggregate, and by fuel type (including electricity), for industrial demand. As expected, elasticity is less for all energy than for the separate fuels. But there is also substantial variation in the estimates for each. Looking at the aggregate, we find most estimates within the range of −0.3 to −0.6, with a couple somewhat larger, around −0.8. However, these differences appear to be explained largely by whether the estimates are based on time series for a single country (in which case they can be interpreted as short-run) or on a cross section of several countries (in which case they can be interpreted as a long-run adjustment to persistent price differences).

Table 4.10 shows aggregate energy and primary-source price elasticities for residential demand. The variation is somewhat greater here and is not readily explained. Still, a general conclusion to the effect that residential demand is

1963). The "demand" for specific resources was projected in these and other studies on the basis of patterns and trends in use by different sectors of the economy. In other words, a sort of informal input-output method was used. More recently, this approach has been extended and formalized with the aid of a dynamic input-output model in work done largely by RFF for the U.S. Commission on Population Growth and the American Future. A commission volume edited by Ridker (1972) includes projections for both nonfuel minerals and forest resources (Fischman and Landsberg) and energy resources (Darmstadter). Other recent RFF activity in this area includes a massive compilation of statistics on energy use (Darmstadter, Teitelbaum, and Polach, 1971) and an analysis of international differences (Darmstadter, Dunkerley, and Alterman, 1977). An influential non-RFF study of differences in the energy budgets of the United States and Sweden is that of Schipper and Lichtenberg (1976).

[16] Discussion of these methods is beyond the scope of this volume. A detailed discussion can be found in the reports by Pindyck (1976, 1977a, 1978c). For a narrower focus on the issues involved in estimating electricity demand, see the work of Taylor (1975) and McFadden, Puig, and Kirshner (1977). All four studies also contain many additional references.

Table 4.9. *Estimates of industrial energy-demand elasticities*

| Country | Estimate | Source |
|---|---|---|
| *Aggregate energy* | | |
| United States | −0.49 | Berndt and Wood (1975) |
| United States (two-digit industries) | −0.66 to −2.56 | Halvorsen and Ford (1978) |
| Canada | −0.36 | Fuss and Waverman (1975) |
| Canada | −0.49 | Fuss (1977) |
| The Netherlands | −0.90 | Magnus (1975) |
| 9 industrialized | −0.80 | Griffin and Gregory (1976) |
| 7 industrialized | −0.52 | Nordhaus (1976b) |
| 10 industrialized | −0.80 | Pindyck (1977a) |
| *Fuels* | | |
| United States | Electricity, −0.66; oil, −2.75; gas, −1.30; coal, −1.46 | Halvorsen (1976) |
| United States | Electricity, short run, −0.14; electricity, long run, −1.20 | Mount, Chapman, and Tyrrell (1973) |
| United States | Electricity, short run, −0.06; electricity, long run, −0.52 | Griffin (1974c) |
| United States | Electricity, −0.92; oil, −2.82; gas, −1.47; coal, −1.52 | Halvorsen (1976) |
| Canada | Electricity, −0.74; oil, −1.30; gas, −1.30; coal, −0.48 | Fuss (1977) |
| 10 industrialized | Electricity, −0.08 to −0.16; oil, −0.22 to −1.17; gas, −0.41 to −2.34; coal, −1.29 to −2.24 | Pindyck (1977a) |

*Source:* Pindyck (1977a).

Table 4.10. *Estimates of residential energy-demand elasticities*

| Country | Estimate | Source |
|---|---|---|
| United States | Short run, −0.12; long run, −0.50 | Joskow and Baughman (1976) |
| United States | Short run, −0.16; long run, −0.63 | Baughman and Joskow (1974) |
| United States | Short run, −0.50; long run, −1.70 | Nordhaus (1976b) |
| West Germany | Short run, −0.35; long run, −0.78 | Nordhaus (1976b) |
| Italy | Short run, −0.63; long run, −1.30 | Nordhaus (1976b) |
| The Netherlands | Short run, −0.42; long run, −1.30 | Nordhaus (1976b) |
| United Kingdom | Short run, −0.38; long run, −0.42 | Nordhaus (1976b) |
| United States | −0.28 | Nelson (1975) |
| United States | −0.40 | Jorgenson (1974) |
| Canada | −0.33 to −0.56 | Fuss and Waverman (1975) |
| Norway | −0.30 | Rødseth and Strøm (1976) |
| 6 industrialized | −0.71 | Nordhaus (1976b) |
| 20 OECD | −0.42 | Adams and Griffin (1974) |

*Source:* Pindyck (1976).

responsive to price, perhaps more responsive even than industrial demand, is clearly supported by the evidence. This may come as a surprise to those (noneconomists) who argue for energy rationing or other direct controls on the grounds that consumer behavior in this sector is not affected by market forces.[17]

The estimated industry demands can be used to calculate elasticities of substitution between energy and other inputs to production (Table 4.11). Once again, the results appear mixed with respect to energy substitution, and again the disagreement may be largely explained by the nature of the data. For cases in which we can be confident that we have identified long-run relationships from international cross sections, energy and capital are rather good substitutes; it is interesting that they have elasticities in the neighborhood of the critical value of 1 (critical for the possibility of sustaining production in the absence of further technical change).

Time-series data from a single country lead to the mixed results noted, with energy and capital in some cases appearing as complements. Another reason for this (in addition to the lack of time for adjustment) may be found in the behavior of relative factor prices over the period studied, roughly the two decades before 1970. Energy prices were low and falling, even in nominal terms, whereas labor costs were rising. Not surprisingly, firms substituted energy-using capital equipment for labor (note the positive elasticity of substitution between energy and labor in all cases).

Despite the mixed time-series results, examples of substitution possibilities of capital for energy are increasingly well known and presumably will account for substantial energy savings over the next several decades, assuming that energy prices remain high by historical standards. A substantial body of work is beginning to emerge in support of this proposition.

[17] For an example of this sort of argument, not uncommon in the U.S. energy-policy community, see the work of Henderson (1978).

Table 4.11. *Estimates of factor-substitution elasticities*

| Country | Estimate | Source |
|---|---|---|
| United States | $\sigma_{KE} = -3.25; \sigma_{LE} = 0.64$ | Berndt and Wood (1975) |
| United States (two-digit industries) | $\sigma_{KE} = -1.03$ to $2.02; \sigma_{LE} = 0.48$ to $2.88$ (production workers) | Halvorsen and Ford (1978) |
| Canada | $\sigma_{KE} = 0.42; \sigma_{LE} = 1.70$ | Fuss and Waverman (1975) |
| The Netherlands | $\sigma_{KE} = -4.50; \sigma_{LE} = 3.80$ | Magnus (1975) |
| 9 industrialized | $\sigma_{KE} = 1.02$ to $1.07; \sigma_{LE} = 0.72$ to $0.87$ | Griffin and Gregory (1976) |

*Source:* Pindyck (1977*a*).

Because historical time series are not especially relevant to the new substitution possibilities, engineering-economic analyses of particular production processes have been made. The idea is to try to determine the shape of the production indifference curve, or isoquant, between energy and one or another factor of production, usually some form of capital. Then, based on assumptions about energy and other factor prices, a least-cost combination can be selected. One example of this approach is the analysis of energy use in buildings. Such analyses have suggested the potential for substantial cost savings from the substitution of various kinds of building-shell insulation for the energy normally used in heating and cooling.

This is illustrated in Table 4.12, which describes annual energy savings (in millions of Btu), the cost of the energy-saving investment, and the rate of return on that investment for a typical single-family home in California. We must be careful here not to fall into the "Btu-theory-of-value" trap. Not all energy savings are desirable from the standpoint of economic efficiency. Other factors must be considered, and other resources are also scarce. But as the numbers in Table 4.12 suggest, there is apparently considerable opportunity for cost-effective conservation in the residential sector in California, and presumably elsewhere as well.[18]

---

[18] For a detailed discussion of sector-by-sector energy-saving possibilities, see the report of the (U.S.) National Academy of Sciences Committee on Nuclear and Alternative Energy Systems (CON-AES, 1979*a*). This is essentially an engineering analysis of the possibilities for substitution based on known technologies and an assumed price path. The results, which indicate a potential for very substantial substitution without sacrifice in growth, are consistent with projections made on the basis of the econometric estimates of long-run demand elasticities. See also the work of Long and Schipper (1978). An approach that combines disaggregated engineering and economic analyses is found in the work of Thompson and his associates (Calloway and Thompson, 1976; Thompson et al., 1976). From a (linear) programming model of production for an industry, they derived energy and other resource demands as functions of changes in factor prices and constraints, including environmental constraints.

Table 4.12. *California residential-sector retrofit*

| Option | Cost and savings per unit | | | |
| --- | --- | --- | --- | --- |
| | 1. Cost ($) | 2. Annual energy savings (MBtu/yr) | 3a. Cost savings (col. 1/ col. 2) ($/MBtu/yr) | 3b. Annual return on investment (%) |
| *Natural gas* | | | | |
| Cold-water laundry | 0 | 5 | — | — |
| Shower flow restrictor | 2 | 3.5 | 0.6 | 270 |
| Insulate water heater | 6 | 2.5 | 2.4 | 63 |
| Nighttime thermostat set back 70° to 55° (average overall housing) | 50 | 21 | 2.4 | 63 |
| The following three measures are assumed to be performed in sequence before night-temperature setback | | | | |
| Retrofit attic insulation (R-19) (single-family unit only) | 275 | 30 | 9 | 16 |
| Retrofit wall insulation (R-11) | | | | |
| Single-family house | 450 | 29 | 15.5 | 10 |
| Multifamily unit | 250 | 22 | 11.5 | 13 |
| Storm window | | | | |
| Single-family house | 440 | 12 | 37 | 4 |
| Multifamily unit | 250 | 8 | 31 | 5 |
| *Electricity* | | | | |
| Cold-water laundry | 0 | 11 | — | — |

| | | | | |
|---|---|---|---|---|
| Shower flow restrictor | 2 | 8.25 | 0.24 | 1,350 |
| Insulate water heater | 6 | 3.5 | 1.70 | 190 |
| Nighttime thermostat (set back 70° to 55°) | 50 | 24 | 2 | 160 |
| Insulate freezer | 25 | 4 | 6.25 | 50 |
| Storm windows | | | | |
|   Single-family house, Northern California | 440 | 39 | 11.3 | 29 |
|   Single-family house, Southern California | | 23 | 19.1 | 17 |
|   Multifamily unit, Northern California | 250 | 21 | 11.9 | 27 |
|   Multifamily unit, Southern California | | 11 | 22.7 | 14 |
| Kitchen fluorescent lamps | 30 | 2.65 | 11.3 | 29 |
| Solar hot water | 1,000 | 41 | 24.4 | 13 |
| Retrofit attic insulation (single-family house only) | | | | |
|   R-O to R-19, North | 350 | 107 | 3.25 | 101 |
|   South | 350 | 69 | 5 | 65 |
|   R-11 to R-19, North | 150 | 14 | 10.7 | 31 |
|   South | 150 | 9 | 16.7 | 20 |
| Retrofit wall insulation (Single-family house) | | | | |
|   North | 500 | 85 | 5.9 | 56 |
|   South | | 57 | 8.8 | 37 |
| Multifamily house | 250 | | | |
|   North | | 58 | 4.3 | 76 |
|   South | | 33 | 7.6 | 43 |

*Source:* Rosenfeld (1977).

## Supply and market equilibrium

With the exceptions just noted, energy demand has generally been estimated from historical data on prices and quantities. Although there have been econometric studies of cost and production functions, especially for electricity generation, the supply side in large models of energy in the economy has not been based on statistical estimation.[19] Instead, the supply problem is typically posed as one of sequencing energy sources to meet an assumed pattern of end uses over time, at the least cost. Then an optimization process (in practice, linear programming) is used to determine the least-cost solution, based on inputs of engineering information about the costs of alternative sources.[20]

A somewhat more ambitious approach has also been taken. Instead of simply assuming the pattern of end uses, this approach poses the supply problem as one of sequencing energy sources to maximize the sum of consumer and producer surpluses over time. Recall that this is just what we did in the theoretical analysis in Chapter 2. There the object was to sequence the extraction of a resource to maximize the sum of surpluses. In both situations the cost of obtaining a given output is minimized, but output is not given for any period. Instead, it is chosen, along with the inputs, to maximize an appropriate index of welfare.[21]

---

[19] For an extensive survey of econometric studies of electricity supply, see the work of Cowing and Smith (1978).

[20] This is the approach taken in perhaps the earliest of the published energy economy models, that of Nordhaus (1973*b*). For further discussion, see the report of the CONAES Modeling Resource Group (1978), and for a survey and comparison of models, see the work of Richels and Weyant (1979). Numerous earlier studies by economists used engineering information to estimate oil and gas supplies and costs. See, for example, the work of Netschert (1958), Fisher (1964), Bradley (1967), Norgaard (1975), and MacAvoy and Pindyck (1975). Kuller and Cummings (1974) incorporated decline rates in a theoretical model of optimal development and depletion of oil reservoirs. For further discussion of work in this area, see the volume on mineral modeling edited by Vogely (1976).

[21] An early energy economy model that takes this approach is that of

The energy modeling approaches just discussed (cost minimization and surplus maximization) have in common the simulation of a competitive market equilibrium by means of optimization. As we showed in Chapter 2, there is a certain legitimacy to this. But as we also showed, or at least asserted, a variety of market imperfections and government regulations can cause difficulties. Still another modeling approach is geared to take account of these. Costs are again minimized, and demand is again statistically estimated, but market-clearing prices and outputs are determined by means of an iterative procedure. Market imperfections, price controls, and so on can be built in. Of course, the resulting solution need not correspond to a welfare optimum.[22]

### 4.5 Concluding remarks

Estimates of reserve stocks and extraction costs alike suggest that in an economic sense resources have not been growing more scarce. Discoveries of new deposits, technical changes in mining, processing, and transporting, and perhaps scale economies and substitution have combined to offset the effects of depletion of known high-quality resources.

But the evidence from prices and rents, the leading indicators of scarcity, is less reassuring. Prices have been fairly stable over the decades preceding 1970, although the choice of a deflator appears to determine whether the trend is up or down for some resources. Econometric tests suggest that even if real

Manne (1976). For a listing and discussion of others, see the survey by Richels and Weyant (1979).

[22] The leading (early) example of this type of computational general-equilibrium model is perhaps the one developed by the U.S. Federal Energy Administration (1976). The demand side here is represented in much greater detail than in, for example, the Manne (1976) model. It includes a macroeconometric model along with interindustry and consumer demand models to generate energy demand curves, in much the same fashion as did Hudson and Jorgenson (1974). Another pioneering effort in this area was the Stanford Research Institute model described by Cazalet (1977). Again, for further listing and discussion of models, see the report of the CONAES Modeling Resource Group (1978) and the survey by Richels and Weyant (1979).

prices have fallen during this period, the rate of decline is moderating. A further hint of a turning point comes from evidence of rising real prices for a number of key mineral resources, in addition to energy resources, over the 1970s. Some fragmentary evidence on rents, estimated from oil and gas exploration costs, also points in the direction of increasing scarcity. So we may be approaching a historical turning point (indeed, we may have reached it) at which the resource base, after having effectively expanded for many decades, will begin to shrink. This need not be alarming provided that relatively abundant resources can be substituted for relatively scarce ones, that other factors can be substituted for resources, and that goods and services not intensive in resources can be substituted for those that are. The evidence concerning possibilities for substitution (assuming sufficient lead time) is encouraging, with an important qualification. The production and consumption of extractive resources tend to involve relatively heavy use of environmental resources. It is not clear to what extent these can be substituted away from, without at the same time adversely affecting conventional measures of economic welfare. In the next two chapters we shall consider a number of questions involving the source, nature, and control of various environmental disruptions.

# 5

## Natural resources and natural environments

### 5.1. Introduction: the transition from extractive to in situ resources

In the discussion of the theory of optimal depletion in Chapter 2 we noted (and formalized) two ideas from Mill (1848) that have a contemporary ring: (1) Extraction costs will increase as mineral deposits are depleted, owing to the need to sink shafts deeper, and so on. (2) The increase will be mitigated by discovery and technical change. Mill had another modern idea: that a stock of land was valuable not only for what could be extracted from it but also for the opportunities it provided for experiencing natural beauty and solitude.[1]

Whether this had any influence on resource policy is not clear, but Mill's treatise had been through several editions by the time the national park system was established in the United States (1872), and preservation of natural beauty in wilderness environments was a minor goal of the early conservation movement (1890–1920). But the theme was not, to my knowledge, picked up by the economics profession until very much later. Instead, environmental disruption was first analyzed as a static externality, following the work of Pigou

[1] For an interesting discussion of this and other views of the classical economists on resource scarcity, see the work of Barnett and Morse (1963). Although it is mainly empirical, the book contains a wide-ranging survey of approaches to scarcity.

(1932) and his examples of sparks from railway engines, factory smoke, and the like. By the 1950s, several economists were developing elements of the modern theory of externalities, but in the process they were losing sight of Pigou's environmental examples.[2] Only in the early 1960s was the Pigouvian approach applied in a systematic fashion to the problem of dealing with water pollution, and later air pollution.[3] More recently still, Mill's somewhat different concern for the preservation of natural environments has been embodied in several studies extending the traditional benefit–cost analysis of water-resource projects.[4]

This chapter will deal with the preservation of natural environments, or, not to prejudge the issue, with the allocation of in situ environmental resources. Suppose that the proposed site for a planned development project, such as a dam for hydroelectric power or an open-pit mine for molybdenum (to take two examples that have recently received attention in the literature), can also yield value in its natural state. How should this affect the benefit–cost analysis of the project? Further, what special problems are posed by the prospect that the in situ resource cannot be reproduced once it has been lost or destroyed in the process of development? The strong concern felt by many for the fate of threatened environments and their indigenous species presumably reflects a perception that loss

[2] Scitovsky's distinction (1954) between "pecuniary" and "technological" externalities dates from this period, as does the distinction made by Meade (1952) and Bator (1958) between "unpaid factor" and "public good" technological externalities. But the examples used to illustrate these concepts were mostly examples of external economies in production, occasionally of external diseconomies in production. They largely ignored the direct interaction between one or many producers, on the one hand, and large numbers of consumers, on the other, that characterizes air and water pollution and other forms of environmental disruption today.

[3] Credit for this achievement probably is due to economists in the water-resources program at RFF, notably Kneese (1962, 1964).

[4] This line of research stems from Krutilla's reconsideration of the traditional concerns of conservation, followed by further theoretical and applied studies associated mainly with the RFF program in natural environments, as will be discussed later.

will be irreversible. Assuming that this is true, what changes in project investment rules are called for? Questions can also be asked about the implications of uncertainty. Knowledge of the values to be attached to long-lived extramarket consequences is bound to become unreliable as one looks further into the future. Again, how can this be dealt with analytically? The first part of this chapter will treat these and related questions. The second part will describe methods and results for an empirical application. The next chapter will take up the analysis of pollution externalities, in the tradition of Pigou.

## 5.2. Irreversibility in economics and in environmental processes

Because the assumption that conversion of a natural environment is irreversible drives the theorems on optimal investment that we shall discuss, it ought to be explored in some detail.[5] Of course, one might take the view that any investment is irreversible, in the sense that time does not move backward. On the other hand, an economist's view might be that the consequences of any decision, including a decision to develop a natural environment, are reversible given sufficient input of labor and capital. My feeling is that neither view is helpful in determining how to use the resources of a natural environment. Meaningful distinctions can be made between uses that are reversible and those that, for all practical purposes, are not.[6]

Consider, for example, the use of resources that represent an accident of geologic processes – the geysers in Yellowstone National Park. These can serve either as a source of geothermal energy for the production of electricity or as a basis for

[5] Krutilla (1967) first addressed this question in a systematic fashion. The more detailed discussion that follows is based on a discussion in a comprehensive volume on the work of the RFF natural-environments program (Krutilla and Fisher, 1975). A similar discussion, but with special reference to long-lived water pollution, may be found in the work of Fisher and Krutilla (1974).

[6] For a different viewpoint, see the work of Cummings and Norton (1974).

tourism and related recreational activities and scientific activities. It is true that Yellowstone National Park represents a serious commitment to preservation of the natural features, but should the continued growth of the U.S. economy depend on its being reoriented to another use, no technical constraint would prevent this.

If these geothermal resources should be allocated to energy production, on the other hand, the consequences to the environment would be virtually impossible to reverse. Construction of plants to generate electric power by use of this geothermal steam, along with the associated switchyards, transmission towers, and so on, would result in an adverse modification of the scenic environment in the park for a considerable period of time, if not permanently. The mining of the superheated water would, in sufficient time, reduce subsurface pressures, eliminate the geyser phenomenon, and thus remove the reason for the establishment of the area as a national park. Any attempt to "restore" the area following depletion of the geothermal resources would be technically impossible.[7]

Is this an unusual special case? Probably not. Consider some of the complications that attend the development of a water-storage reservoir in an ecologically fragile area. Correcting an ill-advised decision to construct a dam involves more than dismantling the structure when its existence begins to incur environmental costs that exceed the returns from development. Supersaturation of the reservoir banks at full-pool elevations

---

[7] Withdrawal of steam for electric power production implies a withdrawal rate of superheated water exceeding the natural discharge and thus exceeding the aquifer's recharge rate. This would result in mining of the heated waters, which would cause the geyser action to stop. Cessation of any geothermal energy operations would not automatically restore the geyser action; many years would be required to replenish the water in the reservoir and to restore the heat energy of the system. Reestablishment or replacement of the geyser and spring vents would probably require hundreds of years. Many hundreds or thousands of years were required to form the vents and cones originally; they disintegrate rapidly when exposed to steam and acid gases, if not maintained by continuous deposition of silica from flowing springs and geysers.

may result in sloughing and landslides into the reservoir during drawdown. Moreover, if streams of high turbidity are impounded, one must allow for storage space in the reservoir to trap the sediments. Dismantling such a structure at some future time would, in many instances, leave the impoundment area with an abiotic base entirely different from the base that existed under the original conditions.

Mining projects also pose problems, especially in high mountain or arctic environments. Removal of the primitive vegetal cover to expose mineral earth can lead to increased absorption of solar heat, which in turn affects unstable soil relationships in areas of permafrost, with resultant thawing, erosion, and gullying.

Perhaps most important, as suggested in the introduction to Chapter 3, the biological environment can be adversely and irreversibly affected. An obvious example is the loss of an entire species and the genetic information it contains, should its essential habitat be destroyed. Even if species survival is not at issue, biological impacts can be very difficult to reverse over any time span that is meaningful for human societies. The clear-cutting of a climax species is equivalent to removing the results of an ecological succession that may represent centuries of natural processes. The removed climax species may be succeeded by various seral species in a procession of changing plant and animal communities, culminating in the original ecological relationships only after the lapse of a great deal of time. In the climates typical of some parts of the eastern United States, several generations may be sufficient to produce at least a superficial resemblance to the original conditions. But it is unlikely that even there the original faunal communities could be reestablished. For example, the woods bison, the eastern race of elk, and the caribou, along with the predator populations that in part made up the wilderness ecosystems, were features of the original wilderness that are now permanently lost. In the arid and semiarid west, in the higher elevations in alpine settings in the western mountains of the United States, and in many subarctic and arctic Alaskan life zones, perturbations to the ecology would take centuries to correct.

But might it not be technically possible, with sufficient input of conventional factors of production, to short-circuit these very slow natural processes in some cases? We have thus far considered a number of cases in which this would not be possible. Others that involve relatively ordinary landscapes in humid or subhumid zones may be candidates for some form of artificial restoration. But in evaluating any such restoration one must also take account of the preferences of users. No matter how skillfully Disneyland simulates an environment, devoted Sierra Clubbers may not be satisfied. This is not intended as a criticism of Disneyland or of the Sierra Club. Authenticity in a natural environment is, to some, a valued attribute, just as authenticity in a work of art is to others. And in assessing the value of a resource or a painting there is no obvious reason to overlook the preferences of the "purists."[8]

Suppose it is accepted that, to a first approximation, the economic development of a natural environment that is in some way remarkable will be irreversible. Are we really saying anything more than we have already said about exhaustible extractive resources? In my judgment we are. The in situ resources of the environment may be "more exhaustible" than conventional exhaustible resources.

Consider an open-pit mine in a scenic area. The final consumer of the mine's output is presumably indifferent to the source. Although depletion of a particular deposit is irreversible, this may not matter much if other deposits can be made available. Moreover, because the mineral output will tend to enter production as an intermediate good, lower-grade deposits

[8] The preferences of wilderness recreationists have been studied extensively by Stankey (1972) and others. Their results have suggested the existence of a substantial number of people who value highly the attribute of authenticity in an environment. Moreover, the prospect is that this number will grow, because such preferences appear to be positively correlated with income and education levels.

or even other minerals could easily substitute (think of aluminum for copper). In fact, as we have seen, technical change in the extractive and logistic-support industries has made possible the production of mineral commodities at generally declining relative supply prices, at least until quite recently. But technology can do little to reproduce the results of the particular patterns of geomorphology, weathering, and ecological succession found in the scenic environment in which the mineral deposit occurs. The amenity services of the environment tend to enter directly the utility functions of consumers, with no intervening production technology. When there are perceived differences between this environment and others, as in general there will be, perfect substitution (in consumption) is not possible, and loss of a particular environment may matter, at least to some.

## 5.3. Evaluating irreversible investments

To economists, the important question about irreversibility is this: What are the implications for resource allocation? If the in situ resources of an environment are declining in value relative to the extractive resources, then clearly irreversibility poses no special problem. An optimal investment program will call for conversion at a rate dictated by the changing relative values. Unfortunately, just the reverse is likely to be true. Unique natural environments are in many cases likely to appreciate in value relative to goods and services they might yield if developed. Then the restriction on reversibility matters, because value would be increased by going back to an earlier, less developed state.

The situation is represented in a broad aggregative fashion in Figure 5.1.[9] A production-possibilities curve having the usual concavity properties describes the trade-off between services of the in situ resources of natural environments $E$ and

---

[9] The discussion here draws on the seminal contribution of Krutilla (1967). Like the original, it is rather informal. For a more rigorous exposition that also deals with the richer and more realistic three-good case, see the work of V. K. Smith (1974).

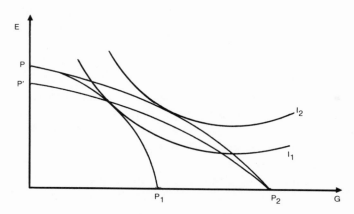

Figure 5.1. Production possibilities and preferences for produced goods and environmental amenities.

produced goods $G$ in an economy. The curve $PP_1$ gives this relationship for period 1, and the curve $PP_2$ gives it for period 2. $PP_2$ is flatter, reflecting the increased output of $G$ (but not $E$) made possible by technical progress. Curve $P'P_2$ is still flatter, reflecting the economy's inability to yield the period 1 level of $E$ because of irreversible conversion of some part of the natural environment in the process of producing period 1's $G$.

In order to say something about the relative values of the two goods, let us indicate $I_1$ and $I_2$ as community indifference curves for periods 1 and 2, respectively. Note that, even if tastes do not change from one period to the next, so that $I_2$ is roughly parallel to $I_1$, the slope at the new tangency point is flatter. If tastes do shift in favor of the environment, as some evidence (see footnote 8) suggests, the slope is still flatter; in other words, the relative price ratio $P_G/P_E$ is still lower. The point is not that consumption of $E$ is increased relative to $G$ (in fact, just the reverse occurs), but that the relative value of $E$ is increased.

The argument about technical change, relative values, and irreversibility then goes something like this. Technical change is asymmetric. It results in expanded capacity to produce ordinary goods and services, but not natural environments. As long as consumer preferences do not shift sufficiently in favor of the ordinary goods (and we have evidence that they are likely to shift in the opposite direction), the supply shift implies an increase in the relative value of the in situ resources. This is pertinent to the assessment of any proposed conversion of the resources (the construction of a large dam, say, or an open-pit mine). Because the value of the in situ resources may be increasing relative to that of the water, power, or minerals produced by the development project, and development is irreversible, we might reasonably expect project investment criteria to be somewhat conservative. A couple of theoretical exercises will establish this more precisely.

### Investment in a certain world

It might seem natural simply to extend the model of optimal depletion presented in Chapter 2 to take account of environmental costs. These could be related to the rate of depletion or the size of the stock or both. But recall that costs are already functions of both. It is easy to verify that adding an environmental component will increase (social) costs of depletion in each period, in turn resulting in a reduction in the optimal rate of depletion.[10] But this result does not, in my judgment, fully capture the effects of irreversibility, perhaps because these have more to do with the development of an area for extractive production than with the subsequent rate of extraction.

A model that focuses on the former has been constructed in the natural-environment program of the RFF group. The results are quite intuitive, and therefore simply described, but they are formally derived only with some difficulty.[11] Starting

[10] For a rigorous demonstration of this result, see the studies of optimal depletion with environmental costs by Anderson (1972) and Vousden (1973).

[11] See the work of Fisher, Krutilla, and Cicchetti (1972) and Krutilla and Fisher (1975). The methods used are based on Arrow's analysis (1968) of a formally similar problem of optimal capital accumulation with irreversible investment.

with the assumption that development is irreversible, one key result is that if there is a period of time over which it is anticipated that the benefits from development net of environmental costs will be declining, then development is optimally cut off some time before the start of that period. Further, if these benefits are always declining, for the reasons indicated, this "reduced" development is optimally undertaken at the initial point in time, if at all.

The intuition behind these results is clear. As long as development is irreversible, some account must be taken of the behavior of future costs and benefits. If these are changing in the way we have assumed, the optimal level of development is decreasing, over an interval of time that may stretch to the planning horizon. Then some near-term losses from having too little development are absorbed in order to avoid later losses from too much development. Further, in the case in which benefits are always declining, either no further development is appropriate or further development is undertaken at the initial point in time, when conditions are most favorable. Note that the same project assessed at a later date may look better than the alternative of no project. But the point is that it would have been even better to have undertaken it sooner.

This conclusion could, of course, be upset by changes in the behaviors of the cost and benefit streams. In the model we have been discussing, this is not possible. Expectations about benefits from both of the alternative uses of the environment are assumed not to change with the passage of time. Yet, clearly, people do learn. Prior probability distributions are revised in the light of new information. Such a situation is captured in another model that will be described next. As it turns out, the result we shall obtain will provide a further rationale for a conservative development strategy.

### Investment in an uncertain world

Suppose I may wish to visit the Grand Canyon at some time in the future. Would I be willing to pay anything to ensure the future availability of the canyon, in other words, to retain the option of visiting? There is, of course, my consumer surplus from the visit. But is the value of the option just expected consumer surplus? Suppose I am risk-averse. Then I would be willing to pay a premium in addition to the expected return. One line of analysis in the literature on option value holds that this premium is, in fact, option value – the difference between (a) what I am willing to pay for the option of consuming (at a predetermined nondiscriminatory price) in the future and (b) my expected consumer surplus.[12]

There are, however, a couple of difficulties. In the first place, preservation can also bring risks (to others, if not to me): the risk of flood, for example, or of power failure. The net option value of preserving a wilderness environment could then be negative.[13] Further, it is not clear that a social choice should display aversion to risk, even though the affected individuals do. Two arguments have been advanced in support of this view. First, if the government undertakes a great many investment projects, risks may be pooled. Second, if the net returns to a single investment are spread over a great many individuals, so are the risks. In either case, the risk premium disappears.[14]

Suppose we accept the view that a social choice about the

[12] Weisbrod (1964) was probably the first to suggest that when the demand for a publicly provided good is uncertain, there may be value in retaining the option to consume, apart from conventional consumer's surplus. Following some controversy in the literature, Zeckhauser (1970) and Cicchetti and Freeman (1971) demonstrated the point in the text: that option value can be identified with a risk premium over and above expected consumer's surplus. For an attempt to measure the option value of preserving water quality in a recreation area, see the work of Greenley, Walsh, and Young (1981).

[13] For an argument along these lines, see the work of Schmalensee (1972) and Henry (1974*b*).

[14] The first view (many projects → risk pooling) is associated with Samuelson (1964) and Vickrey (1964); the second (many investors → risk spreading) is associated with Arrow and Lind (1970). The Samuelson and Vickrey references are to informal discussions in American Economic Association proceedings. Arrow and Lind provided formal proofs of their propositions. A more recent study by James (1975) considered, also formally, the conditions under which one view or the other is correct.

economic development of a natural environment should be risk-neutral, or that, even if it is not, there are risks on both sides. How then can we establish the existence of an option value of preserving the environment? It turns out that the asymmetry of the alternatives (one is irreversible, the other is not) is crucial. Recall that we are assuming that the passage of time results in new information about the benefits of each. But this new information can be taken into account only to the extent that development has not already taken place. Once it has, information that suggests it would be a mistake cannot affect the outcome. Accordingly, there is some value in refraining from an irreversible action that otherwise looks profitable. This, at any rate, is the interpretation of a result we shall now obtain.[15]

Let $S_1$ be the fraction of an area to be developed in the first of two periods and $S_2$ the fraction to be developed in the second. Let $\pi_1$ be the benefit net of all costs, including environmental ones, from developing all of the area in the first period; $\pi_2$ is the corresponding (discounted) second-period benefit. Assume that $\pi_1$ is known at the start of the first period and that $\pi_2$ is a random variable with a known distribution: $\pi_2 = \alpha < 0$, with probability $q$; $\pi_2 = \beta > 0$, with probability $1 - q$ and expected value $E(\pi_2) > 0$. The decision problem is how to choose $S_1$ to maximize the expected value of the area if any development in the first period is irreversible.

We consider two cases. First, no further information about $\pi_2$ will be forthcoming before the start of the second period. This is, of course, equivalent to the case discussed earlier. Because $E(\pi_2) > 0, S_2 = 1 - S_1$, no matter what value is chosen for $S_1$. Put differently, because $E(\pi_2)$, the expected return in period 2, is not affected by the choice of $S_1$, only $\pi_1$, the return in period 1, should determine that choice. The decision rule is simple: $S_1 = 0$ if $\pi_1 < 0$ and $S_1 = 1$ if $\pi_1 > 0$.

Now let us consider the case in which new information

[15] The original analysis on which the following discussion is based is due to Arrow and Fisher (1974) and Henry (1974*a*, 1974*b*).

about $\pi_2$ is received at the start of the second period. In particular, assume that $\pi_2$ will be known with certainty, just as $\pi_1$ was known at the start of the first period. This is clearly a special case of the Bayesian procedure in which new information leads to revision of a prior probability distribution. In this case, it is learned that either $q = 0$ or $q = 1$. If $q = 0$, $\pi_2 = \beta$ and $S_2 = 1 - S_1$. If $q = 1$, $\pi_2 = \alpha$ and $S_2 = 0$.

The expected value of the area at the start of the first period, when the choice of $S_1$ must be made, is then

$$\pi_1 S_1 + q\alpha S_1 + (1 - q)\beta = (\pi_1 + q\alpha)S_1 + (1 - q)\beta \qquad (5.1)$$

Because this expression is linear in $S_1$, the decision rule is again of the "bang-bang" type: $S_1 = 0$ or $S_1 = 1$. But in this case, $S_1 = 1$ only if $\pi_1 > -q\alpha > 0$.

This is clearly more conservative than the rule we obtained when no new information was to be made available. Now, first-period benefits must exceed some positive number, whereas in the earlier case it was required only that they exceed zero. The positive number $(-q\alpha)$ in our example may be considered the value of preserving an option to use the environment as second-period demand dictates. Once again, it is the combination of irreversible development in the first period and improving information about demand in the second period that produces this result. Finally, note that we have not shown that just because a decision is irreversible it should not be taken. But it does carry an additional cost, alternatively viewed as a benefit to preserving an option.

## 5.4. **An empirical application**

We have just discussed a situation in which knowledge of future benefits from alternative uses of a natural environment was uncertain. Still, we assumed that the distribution of benefits was known. However, when we come to consider an actual development project, it will be seen that it may be difficult even to form an expectation of some of the values involved, especially the environmental values that would be sacrificed. How, then, is it possible to do an applied study, a benefit–cost analysis of a resource-development project in a natural environment?

The answer is that probably it is not possible to do a complete analysis, one that captures all of the values at stake. But what I would like to suggest here is that even a fragmentary analysis of some of the more accessible values can be helpful in guiding a decision about the fate of an environment, when set in the theoretical framework just outlined. It may prove instructive, for this purpose, to consider a case in depth. The idea is to draw a lesson generally applicable to research strategy: how to use limited research resources to produce limited information that nevertheless can be of assistance to a concerned decision maker. More cannot be claimed for any benefit–cost analysis. Theoretical welfare economics and political reality alike tell us that efficiency, in the sense of the gains exceeding the losses, is not the sole criterion for judging a project.    But it is surely one criterion that most people, including theoretical welfare economists and practical politicians, would agree is important, and it is the criterion our discipline is uniquely qualified to assess.

### The Hell's Canyon hydroelectric project

The case we shall consider concerns the construction of one or more large dams for generating electricity (and incidentally some flood control and recreation) along the Hell's Canyon reach of the Snake River, a part of the Columbia River system of the Pacific Northwest. I have selected this case because it seems representative, because it illustrates a number of the themes developed in the discussion thus far, and because it has received considerable attention in the literature and in the political arena.[16] I shall try first to provide some of

---

[16] The most complete discussion of the economics of Hell's Canyon is found in the volume by Krutilla and Fisher (1975), especially Chapters 5 and 6. The discussion here is based closely on that material. Earlier treatments appeared in articles by Krutilla and Cicchetti (1972) and Fisher, Krutilla, and Cicchetti (1972). Some

the background, then indicate the research strategy and some key results, and finally consider the robustness of the results, in particular how they might be affected by recent events in energy markets.

*Setting*

The lower Snake River, forming the boundary between northeastern Oregon and west central Idaho, passes through about 200 miles of a geologic formation known as Hell's Canyon. With the Seven Devils Peaks of Idaho rising on the east and the Wallowa Mountains of Oregon on the west, the Snake River in this reach is one of the most scenic streams to be found anywhere and is in an extraordinary natural environment (Leopold, 1969). At the same time, because of the volume of water flowing in the reach, its narrowness, the steepness of the canyon sides, and the excellent foundation conditions, there are numerous attractive sites for the development of hydroelectric and related water-storage facilities. The incompatibility between economic development of this reach of river for power and its preservation in an undisturbed state has sparked a controversy that has involved governmental agencies, courts, electric utilities, and citizens' organizations.

The Hell's Canyon reach of the Snake came under consideration for hydroelectric power development in some studies of the Columbia River and its tributaries conducted by the U.S. Army Corps of Engineers in the 1940s. During the 1950s the Federal Power Commission (FPC) licensed three sites in the

of the legal and political aspects are noted in the text that follows. Other cases treated in Krutilla and Fisher are the following: the conflict among molybdenum mining, livestock grazing, and outdoor recreation in the White Cloud peaks area of Idaho (Chapter 7); the conflict between developed recreation and wilderness recreation in California's Mineral King Valley (Chapter 8); the conflict between agricultural use and waterfowl nesting in the prairie wetlands area of the United States and Canada (Chapter 9, based on a study by Brown and Hammack, 1973); the conflict between a trans-Alaskan pipeline and a trans-Canadian pipeline for moving oil from the North Slope of Alaska (Chapter 10, based on a study by Cicchetti, 1972).

upper reaches of the canyon for development by the Idaho Power Company. Application for a license to the Pacific Northwest Power Company (PNPC) to develop, additionally, the remaining lower 58 miles of the Hell's Canyon reach by either of two alternative proposals, two low dams (one each at the Mountain Sheep and Pleasant Valley sites) or a single high dam (at Mountain Sheep), was made in a series of actions over a decade. A license for development of the Mountain Sheep high-dam facility was eventually issued by the FPC in 1964.

The license issued to PNPC was challenged by the secretary of the interior, and the case went to court. In *Udall* v. *Federal Power Commission* (387 U.S. 428, 1967), the Supreme Court, noting that there was no evidence in the record of the hearings on certain issues of consequence, remanded the matter to the FPC for rehearing. Among the important considerations in the Supreme Court's opinion was its concern that the FPC had not adequately considered the issue whether or not any development of the canyon would be in the public interest. Citing Section 10(a) of the Federal Power Act regarding the charge to select projects "best adapted to a comprehensive plan of improving or developing a waterway ... and for other beneficial public uses, including recreational purposes," the Supreme Court said the following:

> The objective of protecting 'recreational purposes' means more than that the reservoir created by the dam will be the best one possible or practical from a recreational viewpoint. There are already eight lower dams on this Columbia River system and a ninth one authorized; and if the Secretary is right in fearing that this additional dam would destroy the waterway as a spawning ground for anadromous fish [salmon and steelhead] or seriously impair that function, the project is put in an entirely different light. The importance of salmon and steelhead in our outdoor life as well as in commerce is so great that there certainly

comes a time when their destruction might necessitate a halt in so-called 'improvement' or 'development' of waterways. The destruction of anadromous fish in our western waters is so notorious that we cannot believe that Congress through the present Act authorized their ultimate demise. (*Udall* v. *FPC*, 1967, pp. 437–8)

And later in the opinion:

The issues of whether deferral of construction would be more in the public interest than immediate construction and whether preservation of the reaches of the river affected would be more desirable and in the public interest than the proposed development are largely unexplored in this record. (*Udall* v. *FPC*, 1967, p. 449)

The question of giving consideration to preservation as well as development under the Federal Power Act was thus introduced explicitly in the Supreme Court's 1967 decision. Accordingly, in September of 1968 the FPC resumed hearings, in part to determine the benefit net of environmental costs of the production of hydroelectric power at the Hell's Canyon site.[17] The analysis and results to be discussed next were developed originally for use in these hearings.[18]

There were, and are, numerous difficulties associated with measuring the benefits from the alternative uses of the resources of Hell's Canyon. In the case of the "improvement," where a multiple-purpose storage reservoir was planned for use in the production of power, reduction of flood damage, and provision of recreation on the river system, there has evolved a

---

[17] During the year prior to the reopening of the hearings, the Washington Public Power Supply System (WPPSS), which had competed with PNPC for license to develop this reach of the river, agreed with the latter to become a joint applicant for the projects. Thus the rehearings dealt with the joint application.

[18] The record of the hearings, which stretched through 1970, was published by the Federal Power Commission (1970).

body of procedures that can be used to provide reasonably good estimates of benefits and costs.[19] Even here, however, the peculiarities of the regional power system of which the Hell's Canyon development was intended to be a part involved the need to find a way to introduce the effects of technical change.

The benefits from a hydroelectric development are conventionally taken to be the savings in costs as compared with the most economical alternative energy source. In a mixed hydro-thermal system, the assumed thermal alternative to hydro for meeting capacity requirements will produce off-peak energy more economically than existing older and less efficient plants. Accordingly, advances in the efficiency of thermal generation of electricity can be credited to the thermal alternative if its off-peak energy displaces energy otherwise produced at higher-cost plants. In an exclusive hydro system without existing thermal facilities, such as the Columbia River system, but with thermal planned as the source for future growth, the introduction of the effects of technological change is more complicated. Initially, with no higher-cost thermal energy to displace, there is no saving in energy costs. But as additional thermal sources enter the system, displacing part of the original thermal load, the cost of the alternative to the hydro is reduced.

Another difficulty arises when, as in this case, the regional power system includes a mix of private, nonfederal public, and federal facilities. In particular, the difficulty is due to the presence of a number of subsidies in the accounting (as against real) costs of public facilities. For example, a subsidy to the construction and operation of federal transmission facilities biases the accounting cost evaluation of alternative energy developments in favor of those more remote from load centers – such as hydroelectric projects. As another example (important in this case), capital costs to a public institution like the Washington Public Power Supply System (WPPSS) are

---

[19] References to the water-resources literature, developed mostly in the 1950s and 1960s, are found in footnote 33 of Chapter 2.

reduced by the tax exemption on interest income from its debt instruments. Yet it is clear that investment outlays, however made, ought to bear a uniform imputed interest rate. Although this is perhaps an elementary point to economists, we emphasize it here because the hearings data were not originally in this form and had to be thoroughly reworked.

Still greater difficulties beset the evaluation of the in situ resources of Hell's Canyon. Responding to an invitation by the FPC to comment on the proposed development (which would flood portions of natural forests), Secretary Freeman of the U.S. Department of Agriculture characterized the recreation and aesthetic resources of the canyon region as follows:

> The Snake River, in its present free-flowing state, is an awesome stream consisting of a series of swift white-water rapids flowing into deep pools in one of the deepest canyons in the United States. The immediate shoreline is principally lined with great boulders interspersed by occasional sand bars in back eddies. There is no doubt that this stretch of the Snake River represents one of the last of this country's great rivers that has been little changed by man and still challenges his best efforts to tame. It represents a scene of ruggedness probably not equaled anywhere in the United States today. (FPC, 1970, p. 5)

And further:

> This canyon of the Snake River is the locality in the United States having the greatest elevation difference between the canyon bottom and the tops of the immediately adjacent canyon rim crags in the Seven Devils Area. There is no way that the some 76 miles which encompass the swift water portions of this canyon can be mitigated or replaced. While there is archeological significance and recreational use significance in the canyon area for recreation associated with the free-flowing river, the outstanding natural resource is the canyon itself with the free-flowing river in it. This

cannot be replaced nor is it duplicated elsewhere in the country. (FPC, 1970, p. 11)

*Research strategy*

It is quite clear that the values Secretary Freeman had in mind are not readily determined. Although recreation values can, with sufficient research resources, be estimated (following an ingenious suggestion in a 1947 letter from Hotelling), it is probably too much to expect the same for such variables as the option value of preserving genetic information or materials for research in the natural sciences.[20] Thus the researchers could not simply apply a formula like equation (5.1), which calls for knowledge of these values, in assessing the efficiency of the Hell's Canyon proposals. The analytical approach will need to be tailored to fit the available information and still play a role in the decision process. How can this be accomplished?

Suppose it could be shown that, even neglecting environmental values, the most profitable development project would yield negative benefits once anticipated technical change and the hidden subsidies mentioned earlier were properly reflected in the calculations. The project could then be judged inefficient without any accounting for the environmental values. As it turns out, one of the two development proposals to emerge from preliminary studies, the two-dam proposal, did indeed fall in this category. The other exhibited positive net benefits. It then became necessary to try to evaluate the in situ uses. But the strategy was, once again, to avoid trying to measure the

---

[20] Hotelling's method, which was sketched in a 1947 letter to the director of the U.S. National Park Service, involves estimating demand for a recreation site from data on travel costs (the "prices") and visit rates (the "quantities") from zones of origin to the site. The method was further developed and applied in a pioneering study by Clawson (1959). A detailed and comprehensive discussion of this method, with applications, can be found in a volume on the economics of outdoor recreation by Clawson and Knetsch (1966). See also the comparative analysis of different methods of evaluating recreation benefits by Knetsch and Davis (1966). A more recent analytical review, with extensions of the theory, was provided by Hanemann (1978).

unmeasurable. For the one-dam project the present value of just the recreation benefits from preserving the environment was found to exceed the present value of the dam. Accordingly, the project could be judged inefficient without a complete accounting for all of the values at stake. Next, some of the numbers behind these conclusions will be presented and discussed.

### Findings

For the Mountain Sheep/Pleasant Valley low-dam project, net benefits are negative in all periods, as shown in Table 5.1.[21] Interestingly, the annual loss falls a bit through time, from a little over $6 million to a little over $5 million. From our earlier discussion of the effects of technical change in the thermal alternative, we might have expected just the reverse. Although this effect is present (indeed, at an assumed rate of 4% per year, based on historical evidence, it accounts for about one-third of the project's estimated $57 million losses), it is countered by an assumed increase in peaking capacity. That is, although the value of the hydro capacity falls per unit with the advance in thermal technology, the total value increases with the increase in the amount of capacity justified for a peak-load operation.

These numbers are dominated by power benefits. What of the flood control and recreation mentioned earlier? Flood-control benefits are positive but very small, on the order of $87,000 annually. Recreation benefits are not included, for a reason of some general interest. The usual practice in benefit–cost analysis of a multipurpose water-resource development project is to compare the benefits with the separable costs for each purpose. If the benefits exceed the costs, the purpose is included as a part of the efficient project design; if they do not, it is dropped. For both of the Hell's Canyon projects, it appears that net recreation benefits will be negative. Accordingly,

---

[21] This table and other results specifically concerning Hell's Canyon presented in this section are taken from Chapters 5 and 6 of the book by Krutilla and Fisher (1975).

Table 5.1. *Costs and benefits, Hell's Canyon hydroelectric projects*

| | Mountain Sheep/ Pleasant Valley | Mountain Sheep |
|---|---|---|
| *1976–80* | | |
| 1. Investment | $305,445[a] | 271,418[a] |
| 2. Annual costs | 48,656 | 43,351 |
| 3. Gross annual benefits | 42,412 | 44,394 |
| 4. Net benefits (3 − 2) | − 6,157 | 1,044 |
| *1981–90* | | |
| 5. Investment | 334,009 | 271,418 |
| 6. Annual costs | 55,707 | 43,351 |
| 7. Gross annual benefits | 50,105 | 44,723 |
| 8. Net annual benefits (7 − 8) | − 5,603 | 1,372 |
| *1991–2025* | | |
| 9. Investment | 388,126 | 271,418 |
| 10. Annual costs | 67,840 | 43,351 |
| 11. Gross annual benefits | 62,604 | 43,635 |
| 12. Net annual benefits (13 − 12) | − 5,236 | 287 |
| 13. Present value 1976–2025 | − 56,833 | 9,861 |

[a]Thousands of dollars, discount rate 10%.
*Source:* Krutilla and Fisher (1975, Chapter 5).

neither benefits nor separable costs are reflected in the figures in Table 5.1.

It may seem odd that recreation benefits should not be substantial for a reservoir with developed access. Indeed, such benefits are often claimed as a justification for water-resource development projects, as they have been for Hell's Canyon. The difficulty is that at current levels of development, a number of close substitutes for an artificial flat-water facility typically exist in an area where another is contemplated. This is certainly true for the Columbia River system, of which the Hell's Canyon reach of the Snake is a part. Considerable excess capacity in reservoir recreation existed as of the date of the FPC hearings (1968–70). Analytically, this translates into a highly elastic demand for the proposed new facility. Under these conditions, the expected consumer surplus from the facility would be very modest.[22]

For the Mountain Sheep high-dam project, net benefits are positive in all periods, as indicated in Table 5.1. The net present value, approximately $10 million, is not especially impressive, although it nearly doubles at an 8% discount rate. In any event, the project appears to be efficient if it is assumed to entail no sacrifice of environmental values. Thus the remainder of the study turns on the question of environmental values.

It was recognized at the outset that estimates of option value (to individual users, to the potentially much larger number benefiting from scientific research involving the natural materials, and so on) would not be obtainable, but the value of the more tangible existing recreational use might be roughly determined. If this exceeded the value attributed to the project, the project could be judged inefficient. As indicated earlier, that was, in fact, what happened. But a closer look at the analysis and results may be of some interest.

The value of existing recreational use of the canyon was estimated in a two-step procedure. First, the levels of use, measured in visitor-days, were estimated with the aid of a survey for some part of the sport fishing and hunting there. Then, values were imputed to each activity-day based on prices paid for similar pursuits elsewhere. The figures obtained are presented in Table 5.2.

Assuming, for the moment, that the 1976 recreational value of approximately $900,000 is representative of later years, and comparing it with the 1976 net benefit from the area of the proposed Mountain Sheep high-dam facility of over $1 million,

---

[22] For a more rigorous discussion of this and related econometric issues in estimating the demand for a recreation site in the presence of substitutes, see the work of Burt and Brewer (1971) and Cicchetti, Fisher, and Smith (1976).

Table 5.2. *Recreation activity, Hell's Canyon*

| Quantified losses (from project) | Visitor-days 1969 | Visitor-days 1976 |
|---|---|---|
| *Stream-based recreation* | | |
| Total of boat counter survey | 28,132 | 51,000 |
| Upstream of Salmon–Snake confluence | 14,439 | 26,000 |
| Nonboat access | | |
| Imnaha–Dug bar | 14,517 | 26,000 |
| Pittsburgh Landing | 14,464 | 26,000 |
| Hell's Canyon downstream | | |
| Boat anglers | 1,000 | 1,800 |
| Bank anglers | 2,333 | 4,000 |
| Total stream use above Salmon River | 46,753 | 84,000 at $5/day = $420,000 |
| | | |
| *Hunting, canyon area* | | |
| Big game | 7,050 | 7,000 at $25/day = $175,000 |
| Upland birds | 1,110 | 1,000 at $10/day = $ 10,000 |
| Diminished value of hunting experience | 18,000 | 29,000 at $10/day = $290,000 |
| Total quantified losses | $895,000 ± 25% | |

*Unevaluated losses*
Unmitigated anadromous fish losses outside impact area
Unmitigated resident fish losses: stream fishing downstream from Mountain Sheep high-dam area
Option value of rare geomorphological-biological-ecological phenomena
Others

*Source:* Krutilla and Fisher (1975, Chapter 6).

which is also approximately the levelized value, the project remains marginally efficient. Moreover, if technical changes in the thermal-powered electricity industry are not taken into account in computing project benefits (i.e., if the analysis is performed in a simpler and more conventional fashion), the benefits will be in the neighborhood of $3 million annually. Clearly, any conclusions we draw from the fragmentary empirical analyses must be powerfully affected by our theoretical framework.

Let us pursue this point further. The near-equality in annual benefits ($900,000 versus $1 million) results from the asymmetric effect of technical change on the values of the alternative uses of the natural environment. One use, the development project, is reduced in value as its gross benefit (the cost of the thermal alternative) falls over time. But what of the recreational value? Should we assume, as we have, that this is unchanging over time? There is considerable evidence to the contrary. The use of the area in question had been increasing at a rate of 20% to 30% per year in the decade or so preceding the original analysis. More generally, U.S. Forest Service estimates of growth in the use of undeveloped areas in the Pacific Northwest have indicated rates between 10% and 15% over a still longer period. It is probable that the value of a given amount of use has also been increasing because of the high education and income elasticities of demand for wilderness recreation that we noted earlier.

On the basis of these trends, some allowance for an increase in annual recreation benefits was made in the original studies. A rather conservative 7.5%–12.5% annual increase in use was assumed for the initial years, falling over time to the rate of growth of the population. Further, an absolute limit on use was set by a capacity constraint determined by the characteristics of the area and the activities it could support. The annual increase in willingness to pay for a given level of use was taken to be 4%–6%, based on an assumed annual productivity increase of 2%–4% and general inflation of 2%, the latter

Table 5.3. *Initial year's preservation benefit needed to equal present value of project*

| Annual rate of increase in willingness to pay | Annual rate of increase in use, up to capacity | | |
|---|---|---|---|
| | 7.5% | 10% | 12.5% |
| $i = 8\%$, $PV_d = \$18,540,000$ | | | |
| 0.04 | $138,276 | $109,149 | $106,613 |
| 0.05 | 85,568 | 70,363 | 70,731 |
| 0.06 | 48,143 | 39,674 | 41,292 |
| $i = 9\%$, $PV_d = \$13,809,000$ | | | |
| 0.04 | $147,422 | $115,008 | $109,691 |
| 0.05 | 101,447 | 80,122 | 78,336 |
| 0.06 | 64,300 | 51,700 | 52,210 |
| $i = 10\%$, $PV_d = \$9,861,000$ | | | |
| 0.04 | $142,335 | $110,240 | $103,030 |
| 0.05 | 103,626 | 80,888 | 77,232 |
| 0.06 | 71,369 | 56,397 | 55,194 |

*Source:* Krutilla and Fisher (1975, Chapter 6).

factored in because it is also present in the nominal discount rates used. The net result of these adjustments is that annual benefits from recreation grow (but at a declining rate) over the life of the project.

This produces a dramatic change in the project evaluation, as reflected in the figures in Table 5.3. Previously, the $900,000 in initial-year recreation benefits appeared to be well under the amount required (some $3 million, if technical change in the thermal alternative is not allowed) to balance project benefits. Even after the introduction of technical change, recreation benefits remain marginally below the $1 million in project benefits. But with more realistic assumptions about growth in recreation benefits (as represented, for example, by the entries in Table 5.3 corresponding to the previously assumed 5% growth rate), the initial year's benefits would need to be only in the range of $70,000 to $100,000 (a full order of magnitude less than estimated) for the present value of preserving the canyon to exceed the present value of the proposed project. Further, the possibility of lowering the discount rate will not help the project as it did when the growing environmental costs were disregarded. Thus an 8% discount rate results in a present value of nearly $19 million for the project, but it also lowers the required initial year's recreation benefit across the board.[23]

### Discussion

These findings can be evaluated in two ways. First, we might take a critical look at some of the procedures and assumptions. Do they seem justified? How would changes in the procedures and assumptions affect the findings? Second, we might consider whether or not, and how, the appearance of new information (in particular, about energy prices) would alter the findings. Such reexamination has yielded the following conclusions. First, the central finding that a development project in Hell's Canyon could not pass a benefit–cost test, once environmental losses are considered, is not driven by strong assumptions about the value of the site in its alternative uses. Further, the ranking of the alternatives is robust to reasonable changes in the variables that determine these values, such as rates of technical change in electric-power generation and rates of increase in recreational activities in wilderness areas like Hell's Canyon. More surprisingly,

---

[23] An interesting potential for "reswitching" arises here. Rather, it does not arise in this particular case but does arise in the general case of high initial (direct) development costs followed by a period of net benefits, and finally by high environmental opportunity costs. In such a case the project can look bad at both very low and very high discount rates, but not at rates in some intermediate range. This point is made by Porter (1978) in a clear and helpful discussion of the theoretical issues treated in this chapter. Viscusi and Zeckhauser (1976) showed that uncertainty about benefits increases the likelihood of reswitching.

perhaps, recent developments in energy markets also do not appear to upset the ranking. One thing that might, however, is a more complete accounting for the environmental costs of the alternative energy sources. These conclusions will be explored in more detail later.

Questions can be raised about the recreational values imputed to the undeveloped site. Ideally these should have been estimated with the Hotelling technique (see footnote 20). To repeat, this consists in estimating demand for a site from data on travel costs (the "price") and visit rates (the "quantity") and then integrating to obtain a measure of consumer surplus. Because of time limits and limits on other research resources, this was not done. Instead, values were assumed on the basis of evidence on prices paid for hunting and fishing rights where these were vested in private parties. How reasonable were the assumed values?

At the time of the original study, prices paid for a day of fishing ranged from around $9 on the better artificial ponds in the United Kingdom to $150 for "prime beats" on the finest chalk streams there. Norwegian Atlantic salmon fishing, similar to steelhead fishing in the Pacific Northwest, commanded a price of up to $500. The imputed value of $5 per day in Table 5.2 accordingly seems very conservative. The prices people were willing to pay for hunting activities ranged from about $25 for a day on unremarkable Texas rangeland to $5,000 for the red stag in central Europe. This is not to suggest that the average American hunter would participate in so aristocratic an activity, but it seems safe to assume that he would pay more than is now customary, were access rationed by price. Again, the imputed price of $10 to $25 per day of hunting is conservative.

Assumptions about the behavior of these values over time are also fairly conservative, as already indicated. Sensitivity analysis of changes in the assumptions reveals very modest effects on computed values. A more-than-proportional effect (i.e., a percentage change in value greater than the change in the driving variable) is found for only one of the relevant variables, the rate of growth in willingness to pay for a recreation day. Changes in value are approximately proportional to changes in one other variable, the rate of technical progress in electric power generation. Were the decision on whether to go ahead with the project a close one, clearly it could be affected by plausible changes in these variables. But, as indicated in Table 5.3, the decision is not close in this case.

Now, what about recent developments in energy markets, in particular the spectacular rise in fuel prices? This obviously makes the project more attractive – assuming that the prices of project inputs have not experienced a similar rise. But does it make enough of a difference to upset the ranking? Probably not. Although most of the popular concern seems to be with oil prices, uranium prices have also gone up by a factor of five or six in the years following 1973, from $6 per pound of $U_3O_8$ to $30 or $40 (where they are expected to remain, in real terms, for some time).[24] This is relevant because the thermal alternative in the study was nuclear power. But fuel costs are only a small fraction of nuclear power costs, about 10% after the price rise.[25] Nuclear power costs have gone up a good deal in the last few years, but this has largely been the result of increases in capital costs, a factor that could affect dam construction costs in much the same way.

But all of this may be irrelevant, because it appears that coal, not nuclear, represents the least-cost thermal alternative. Indeed, this was probably true at the time of the original analysis. A peculiarity in the FPC evaluation procedure

[24] For uranium and other mineral prices, see the annual commodity data summaries of the U.S. Bureau of Mines.
[25] A balanced and concise source of information about this and other aspects of nuclear power is *Nuclear Power Issues and Choices* (Ford, 1977), the report of a study by the Mitre Corporation for the Ford Foundation. The report of the CONAES study of the National Academy of Sciences (1979b), though broader in scope, is also relevant.

Table 5.4. *Bituminous coal, average value ($) per ton*[a]

| | 1968 | 1969 | 1970 | 1971 | 1972 | 1973 | 1974 | 1975 | 1976 |
|---|---|---|---|---|---|---|---|---|---|
| Alabama | 7.04 | 7.47 | 8.09 | 8.15 | 9.63 | 12.43 | 21.79 | 26.53 | 28.37 |
| Alaska | 6.00 | 6.54 | 7.39 | 8.18 | n.a. | n.a. | n.a. | n.a. | n.a. |
| Arizona | — | — | 2.63 | n.a. | n.a. | n.a. | n.a. | n.a. | n.a. |
| Arkansas | 7.47 | 7.90 | 8.30 | 10.30 | 10.93 | 12.97 | 21.28 | 32.76 | 36.15 |
| Colorado | 4.82 | 5.27 | 5.85 | 6.34 | 6.45 | 7.02 | 9.38 | 16.53 | 15.30 |
| Illinois | 4.01 | 4.32 | 4.92 | 5.46 | 6.14 | 6.77 | 10.00 | 14.64 | 15.90 |
| Indiana | 3.88 | 4.13 | 4.60 | 5.18 | 5.58 | 6.05 | 8.36 | 11.15 | 12.34 |
| Iowa | 3.75 | 3.76 | 4.11 | 4.66 | 4.86 | 5.46 | 7.79 | 11.08 | 13.56 |
| Kansas | 5.15 | 5.42 | 5.59 | 5.72 | 6.39 | 6.83 | 7.61 | 19.78 | 19.45 |
| Kentucky | 3.91 | 4.14 | 5.68 | 6.49 | 6.81 | 7.36 | 17.06 | 17.40 | 19.79 |
| Maryland | 3.67 | 3.85 | 5.01 | 6.25 | 5.46 | 7.20 | 20.81 | 19.38 | 21.90 |
| Missouri | 4.20 | 4.33 | 4.39 | 4.87 | 5.20 | 5.35 | 6.36 | 8.52 | 9.37 |
| Montana | 2.34 | 2.13 | 1.85 | 1.82 | 2.03 | 2.82 | 3.90 | 5.06 | 4.90 |

| | | | | | | | | | |
|---|---|---|---|---|---|---|---|---|---|
| New Mexico | 3.94 | 3.66 | 2.89 | 3.26 | 3.61 | 3.55 | n.a. | n.a. | n.a. |
| North Dakota (lignite) | 1.78 | 1.85 | 1.95 | 1.91 | 2.02 | 2.04 | 2.19 | 3.17 | 3.74 |
| Ohio | 3.96 | 4.10 | 4.74 | 5.24 | 5.96 | 7.37 | 12.32 | 16.40 | 16.61 |
| Oklahoma | 5.88 | 5.80 | 6.27 | 6.72 | 7.28 | 7.69 | 10.51 | 16.69 | 15.98 |
| Pennsylvania | 5.37 | 5.87 | 7.27 | 8.52 | 9.14 | 10.73 | 20.35 | 25.09 | 25.33 |
| Tennessee | 3.64 | 3.80 | 4.90 | 6.40 | 7.23 | 7.95 | 18.02 | 17.10 | 16.31 |
| Utah | 5.77 | 6.31 | 7.28 | 7.37 | 8.93 | 9.51 | 12.24 | 19.84 | 22.93 |
| Virginia | 4.84 | 5.42 | 7.03 | 8.32 | 10.11 | 11.59 | 24.94 | 30.46 | 24.12 |
| Washington | 4.63 | 8.21 | 12.81 | 6.72 | 6.61 | 7.05 | n.a. | n.a. | n.a. |
| West Virginia | 5.32 | 5.73 | 7.93 | 9.54 | 10.31 | 11.39 | 21.65 | 29.35 | 30.12 |
| Wyoming | 3.16 | 3.36 | 3.38 | 3.39 | 3.74 | 8.09 | 5.02 | 6.74 | 7.00 |
| United States | 4.67 | 4.99 | 6.26 | 7.07 | 7.66 | 8.42 | 15.75 | 19.23 | 19.43 |

—Dash indicates that no coal was mined; n.a. indicates data not available.

[a]F.O.B. mines, by states.

*Source:* National Coal Association (1978).

(incorporating the taxes that utilities pay as a part of the cost of the energy from a given source) biased the evaluation against coal.

An alternative to the Hell's Canyon project or to a nuclear power plant would have been generation of electricity by use of the thick seams of low-cost coal of eastern Montana that could be strip-mined. However, such an operation would have been charged with a percentage of taxes on investment reflected in the taxes paid by the Montana Power Company. Because of the favorable treatment the Montana Power Company receives from the state public utilities commission in figuring its rate base, it earns very large profits, as determined by the Internal Revenue Service, and thus pays in federal income taxes about 85% more per dollar of investment than the weighted average of all utilities. Accordingly, what the peculiarities of the FPC evaluation produced was a result that reckoned half of the excessive profits of the company as a cost of producing thermal electric power from Montana energy sources.

Assuming that strip-mined eastern Montana coal represented the least-cost thermal alternative in 1968, does this remain true a decade later? The answer is almost certainly yes. Although most sources currently place the cost of nuclear-generated electricity a few percentage points below that from coal, this is an average figure. In coal regions the ranking tends to be reversed, and this is especially true when the coal is as cheap as it is in eastern Montana. A history of coal prices over the period 1968–76, for the United States as a whole and producing states separately, is given in Table 5.4. It should be noted that the Montana coal is actually sub-bituminous and thus has a lower Btu content than the bituminous coal mined in some other states. Correcting for this difference would add $2 or $3 to the Montana price. One additional piece of information is that the (unadjusted) price was $5.73 in 1977, and it was expected to be only slightly higher in 1978. From the figures in Table 5.4 it is clear that coal has generally shared to some extent in the energy commodity price rise of 1973–5. But the Montana price has increased very little in real terms. This may be explained by the impressive economy of mining thick seams by technically advanced, specialized methods. Even taking into account the cost of rehabilitating the areas disturbed by surface mining, it is fairly clear that the real cost of extraction (and, for that matter, the price) has not kept pace with the increases in prices for energy commodities generally.

Although this suggests that coal would have been, and is, the least-cost thermal alternative to the proposed hydroelectric project in Hell's Canyon, it is not clear that it is the least-cost alternative. An intriguing possibility is raised by the studies of the potential for energy conservation discussed in the last chapter. The central finding is that various forms of energy conservation are now increasingly the least-cost means of meeting new energy demands.[26] As another example of what might be done here (in addition to what was reported in the last chapter), it has been calculated that replacing existing refrigerators as they wear out over the next 20 years (approximately the life span of the appliance) with the most energy-efficient models now on the market will save 1,000 MW of electrical generating capacity in California alone. Perhaps the most interesting aspect of this finding is that the cost would be minimal, because there appears to be little correlation between energy efficiency and purchase price. Further, some proposed redesign features could save an additional 1,500 MW, at an estimated cost of $750 million. A rough rule of thumb in energy cost calculations is that a 1,000-MW plant can be constructed for $1 billion; thus the conservation would clearly be cheaper. Some further details are given in Figure 5.2.

[26] See the work of Rosenfeld (1977) and Rosenfeld et al. (1978) for studies of many different conservation options and the aggregate energy savings that are both technically feasible and economically efficient. The example of energy-conserving refrigerators in the following text is taken from Rosenfeld et al., based on an earlier study by Arthur D. Little (1977).

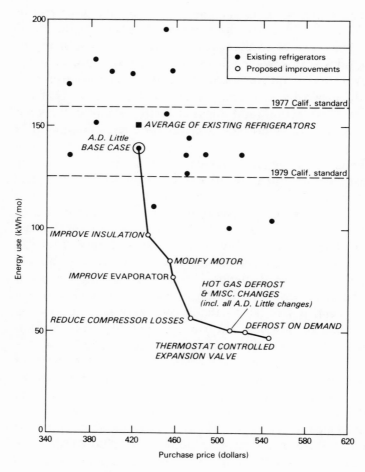

Figure 5.2. Energy use versus purchase price for a number of existing and proposed refrigerators. The filled circles in the upper half of the figure represent 16.0–17.5-cubic-foot top-freezer frost-free refrigerators sold in California in 1976. The open circles in the lower half represent proposed redesigned refrigerators. (From Rosenfeld et al., 1978, p. 9.)

That is the good news. The bad news is that a more complete accounting for the environmental effects of the thermal electric alternatives, coal and nuclear, could conceivably make either or both appear less economic than a new Hell's Canyon dam.[27] This is by no means certain. In the first place, costs of controlling some impacts (most air pollution from coal, land reclamation after strip-mining, thermal pollution from nuclear) are already included in the generating costs for these technologies. And design or other changes to further reduce impacts may not be excessively costly, although this would clearly be true only up to a point.[28] In the second place, not all of the potential impacts of a large new dam have been considered either. Apart from the loss in option value discussed earlier, there is the risk of dam failure, which is roughly similar in probability of occurrence (very low) and consequences (potentially catastrophic) to a nuclear accident.[29] And, like the strip-mining of coal, the quarrying of dam construction materials can disfigure the landscape. But it is at least conceivable that a complete accounting for all impacts of all of the alternatives could affect the rankings.

Having noted this, though, if it is in fact true, as we have just argued, that conservation, not coal (or nuclear), is the least-cost alternative to a Hell's Canyon project, then accounting for all of the environmental impacts of the two alternatives would only strengthen the finding that the project is ineffi-

---

[27] In addition to the references in footnote 25, see the volume by Ramsay (1978) addressed specifically to the comparative environmental effects of coal and nuclear power. For a review of comparative environmental effects of many different energy technologies, see the work of Budnitz and Holdren (1976); for a review with special reference to renewable sources, see the work of Holdren, Morris, and Mintzer (1980).

[28] Recent cost figures on stringent new controls for coal plants can be found in the report of the hearings conducted before the California Energy Commission on a proposal by the Pacific Gas and Electric Company to build a plant in northern California (California Energy Commission, 1979). This would be the cleanest coal-burning plant yet built.

[29] See the work of Holdren, Morris, and Mintzer (1980).

cient. As some preliminary studies of building energy conservation have suggested, there are impacts on the environment, but these are less disruptive than those associated with the alternatives to conservation, including the construction and operation of large dams.[30]

## 5.5. Concluding remarks

In his exposition of the theory of exhaustible resources, Solow (1974*a,* p. 10) observed that the theory "is trying to tell us that, if exhaustible resources really matter, then the balance between present and future is more delicate than we are accustomed to think." Solow's point clearly applies with special force when we come to consider the exhaustible in situ resources of natural environments.

The combination of technical change (which in effect expands the supply of conventional inputs, but not the in situ resources) and a shift in preference in favor of environmental amenities is likely to lead to a rise in the value of the in situ resources. Because their loss to one or another form of development is, as we have argued, likely to be difficult or impossible to restore in important cases, the balance between present and future must be weighed carefully indeed. Modifications to the usual benefit–cost criteria, which suggest proceeding very cautiously where an irreversible step is contemplated, can guide decisions about the fate of natural environments in the absence of information about all of the costs and benefits of their development.

These considerations, of course, apply to all long-lived environmental disruptions, including some types of pollution. But numerous other considerations have arisen with respect to

[30] For a fairly comprehensive accounting of the possible environmental impacts of energy conservation, see the work of Anderson (1980). Perhaps the most serious threat, at least in the building sector, is to indoor air quality, resulting from the tighter building shells. However, this can be mitigated, at a cost, by means of heat exchangers.

pollution in particular. It is interesting that in contrast to the dynamic approach emphasized thus far, a static analysis is adequate to handle many of the problems presented by pollution and its control, although in some cases dynamic considerations will be relevant. The next chapter will take up a number of aspects of pollution: what causes it, how to control it, and how to measure the benefits and costs of control.

# 6

## Environmental pollution

### 6.1. Introduction

Pollution, in its many forms, is widely regarded as our major environmental problem. Pigou (1932) was perhaps the first academic economist to take it seriously, but recorded expressions of concern go back much further. The use of coal was prohibited in London in 1273, and at least one person was put to death for this offense some time around 1300.[1] Why did it take economists so long to recognize and analyze the problem? Apart from the concern of Pigou, little was done until the 1960s, although elements of the theory of externalities and public goods that would later be useful were developed largely in the 1950s.[2]

One plausible explanation for this lack of interest is that the problem has only recently become competitive, in its severity, with others we face. True, there have been local and temporary episodes, as the unfortunate Londoner would attest, but it is only recently that we have come to fear that "environmental

---

[1] For a history of air-pollution control in Britain, see the work of Gilpin (1963).

[2] See the introduction to Chapter 5, and especially footnote 2 there. For a review of this literature, with many additional references, see the work of Mishan (1971a).

reservoirs" may be filling up over large areas and in ways that may be difficult to reverse.[3]

This view of the world has, in fact, been advanced in some conceptual contributions from economists. Boulding's "spaceship earth" (1966) suggested that pollution, or at least material residuals from production and consumption activities, must always and increasingly be with us, because the earth is, like a spaceship, a closed system with respect to materials. A related concept developed by Ayres and Kneese (1969) is that of materials balance. According to the physical law of conservation of mass, residuals will be roughly equal, in mass, to the total amount of fuels, foods, and raw materials entering the economy. If the economy is growing, then so is pollution. It follows, too, that pollution will be pervasive, associated with most economic activities, not just the few that the theorists of the 1950s and before struggled to find.[4]

[3] One example of this phenomenon is the increasing concentration of $CO_2$ from fossil-fuel combustion in the global atmosphere. The fear is that this may lead to a warming and melting of the polar ice caps, with attendant adverse effects, including the flooding of coastal areas. For further discussion, see the work of Ehrlich, Ehrlich, and Holdren (1977) and Williams (1978). A useful review of the $CO_2$ and related global environmental problems for economists was provided by Kneese (1971). Nordhaus (1976a) made some calculations of an implied shadow price for $CO_2$ emissions.

[4] The connection between growth and pollution is, of course, not as simple as stated in the text, even in the absence of policies to control pollution. For one thing, some material is accumulated as inventory, or is immediately recycled, and hence is not released to the environment. For another, the damage done by residuals depends on their physical properties, when and where they are released, and so on. Clearly, only harmful materials should be classified as pollution. Still, in the absence of controls, at least, it is likely that the relationship between activity levels and pollution will be positive.

The materials-balance model was developed by Ayres and Kneese, as noted in the text. They credited the idea to an unpublished dissertation by F. A. Smith (1968). A more detailed exposition can be found in the work of Kneese, Ayres, and d'Arge (1970). Modifications that deal with inventory accumulation and physical relationships in the environment were proposed by Noll and Trijonis (1971) and Victor (1972).

Of course, to say that pollution is a major social problem is not to advance the discussion of how to deal with it very far. But I think it is fair to say that, having recognized the problem, economists have also developed a body of theory and measurement techniques that can be important components of a solution. Specifically, we can answer questions such as these: (1) What is the optimal amount of pollution or, if one prefers, of pollution control? (2) What policy instruments can be most helpful in achieving it? We also know a good deal about how to evaluate the damages from pollution and the costs of control, a precondition for determining optimal levels in practice.

In this chapter we shall look at these questions in some detail. In the next section a model will be developed to determine the conditions that characterize a socially efficient, or Pareto-optimal, allocation of resources in the presence of pollution externalities. There we shall also see how the allocation can be supported, not by the market, but by a marketlike policy instrument, a tax on pollution. A potentially important qualification, arising from the connection between externality and a kind of nonconvexity, will be considered. In Section 6.3, advantages and disadvantages of a tax as compared with other commonly suggested methods of controlling pollution (private bargaining, direct controls, a subsidy, and a permit system) will be explored. In Section 6.4 we shall consider methods for estimating pollution damage and control costs. A sampling of empirical results will also be presented.

### 6.2. Pollution externalities and economic efficiency

The setting of the problem is as follows. The production of commodities by firms generates an externality (call it smoke) that, in the aggregate, adversely affects each consumer. It is convenient to think of the smoke generated by each firm as a factor of production for the firm, in the sense that it can be substituted for other (costly) inputs, like labor and capital. For example, a given output can be produced by a process that involves the generation of 10 tons of smoke or, alternatively, by one that, through the employment of a device that catches the smoke, generates just 5 tons. In either case the smoke generated by the activities of all producers constitutes the externality, which then enters the utility functions of all consumers.

The externality is a pure public good – or bad. What one person "consumes" does not affect the amount available for consumption by others.[5] Although pollution is clearly a public-good externality in this sense, equally clearly it varies geographically; some areas are more polluted than others. We might say that the same aggregate emissions enter all utility functions, but the disutility suffered by any consumer also depends in part on his consumption of land, or, in other words, on where he lives.[6]

Now let us state the problem formally. It is to maximize the utility of any one individual, subject to the restrictions that no one else is made worse off and that the indicated outputs are feasible. The control variables are the consumption of each commodity by each individual and the production and input (including smoke) use by each firm. It is clearly not realistic to imagine a planner directly controlling the behavior of such a system down to the level of the consumption, by each consumer, of each commodity. We simply set up the problem in this form in order to (eventually) determine the value of a much less ambitious, and more realistic, control: a tax on pollution that makes a decentralized competitive equilibrium Pareto-optimal.

The problem, then, is as follows:

$$\text{maximize } u^1(x_{11}, \ldots, x_{n1}, s) \tag{6.1}$$

---

[5] In addition to the classic article by Samuelson (1954), see also the work of Head (1962) for a discussion of the attributes of public goods.

[6] Problems for pollution-control policy raised by spatial variations in pollution concentrations will be considered in Section 6.3.

subject to

$$u^j(x_{1j}, \ldots, x_{nj}, s) \geq u^{j*} \qquad (j = 2, \ldots, m) \qquad (6.2)$$

$$f^k(y_{1k}, \ldots, y_{nk}, s_k) = 0 \qquad (k = 1, \ldots, h) \qquad (6.3)$$

and

$$\sum_{j=1}^{m} x_{ij} - \sum_{k=1}^{h} y_{ik} \leq r_i \qquad (i = 1, \ldots, n) \qquad (6.4)$$

where $u^j(\ )$ is individual $j$'s utility function, $x_{ij}$ is the amount of good or resource $i$ consumed by individual $j$, $y_{ik}$ is the amount of good or resource $i$ produced ($y_{ik} > 0$) or used ($y_{ik} < 0$) by firm $k$, $r_i$ is the amount of resource $i$ available, $s_k$ is the smoke emitted by firm $k$, $s = \Sigma_k s_k$ is the smoke externality, and $f^k(\cdot)$ is firm $k$'s production function.

This is clearly a general-equilibrium system, particularly if it is recognized that one of the goods $x_{ij}$ entering individual $j$'s utility function can be leisure or labor. Although the analysis of externalities and optimal taxes often has proceeded in a partial-equilibrium framework, the general-equilibrium approach allows us to take account of important interdependencies. For example, we noted earlier that the impact of an externality will depend on the location decisions of individuals. These decisions and others that may influence the impact (such as whether or not trees are planted or air conditioning is installed, and so on) are in principle part of the general equilibrium we are modeling. As we shall demonstrate later, the potential for adjustments like these, which would not be picked up in the ordinary partial analysis, may be important for policy. Note, however, that the model, as given in equations (6.1) through (6.4), does not explicitly reflect the interdependence implied by materials-balance considerations.[7]

[7] The model developed and used here is based on one in the Baumol and Oates (1975*a*) volume on the theory of environmental policy. Other general-equilibrium models include those of Ayres and Kneese (1969), Kneese, Ayres, and d'Arge (1970), Meyer (1969), Tietenberg (1973, 1974*a*), Page (1973*a*), and Mäler (1974).

Also, the model is not dynamic. An obvious alternative would be to extend the optimal-depletion models of Chapters 2 and 3 to reflect pollution, or its costs. But, as we have noted, this is already implicit. Making it explicit would not add much to our knowledge of the sources, effects, and control of pollution. In my judgment, the problems are essentially those of static misallocation. This is not to deny that pollution can accumulate (or be assimilated) over time or that other dynamic processes might be relevant (e.g., building a stock of control equipment). Dynamic analyses have, in fact, been developed that go beyond simply extending the models of optimal depletion.[8] Where specially relevant, as, for example, to a choice among policy instruments, results will be indicated. But I continue to feel (other students of the matter may, of course, feel differently) that the basic concepts (how externalities arise, what are their optimal levels, how a decentralized

Kneese and his collaborators did take account of materials balance, but not substitution in production, including substitution of other factors for pollution. Mäler's analysis is a good deal more abstract than the others, employing the methods of algebraic topology now standard in the general-equilibrium literature. More recently, models combining general-equilibrium features and dynamic features have been developed (Gruver, 1976; Comolli, 1977; Forster, 1977). Dynamic models will be discussed later, as well as in the next footnote.

[8] The accumulation of waste over time is introduced in a highly aggregated materials-balance model by d'Arge (1972) and d'Arge and Kogiku (1973) that includes resource extraction. Several other dynamic models of waste accumulation have also been developed, although these have not always included extraction and full materials balance. See the work of Keeler, Spence, and Zeckhauser (1972), Plourde (1972), V. L. Smith (1972), Mäler (1974), and Rausser and Lapan (1979). Mäler's analysis did account explicitly for materials balance. These dynamic models are, in essence, optimal-growth models extended to consider the residuals or pollution generated by consumption. As in the case of optimal-growth models with an extractive-resource constraint, the key question is whether or not a steady state exists. And again, substitution possibilities, here for pollution, are clearly decisive. In other words, the question is whether or not (and at what rate) pollution per unit of output (and also pollution accumulations) can be reduced. Other questions relating to the dynamics of investment in pollution control were treated by Gruver (1976), Forster (1977), Comolli (1977), and Zilberman and Just (1980).

economy can be controlled to bring these about) can be elucidated without introducing the more complicated dynamics.

Now let us consider, briefly, the point of each equation in the model. The thing to note about the objective, consumer 1's utility function, is that it contains an argument, $s$, representing the externality. This same argument appears in the utility function of each consumer, as indicated in equation (6.2), the first constraint. This constraint says that the utility of each consumer other than the one whose utility is being maximized must be at least equal to some prespecified level ($u^{j^*}$ for consumer $j$). The second constraint, equation (6.3), is the set of production functions. The thing to note here is that $s_k$, the smoke emitted by firm $k$, appears in the firm's production function, where it is treated in effect as a factor of production. Finally, the third constraint, equation (6.4), is a general-equilibrium condition. It says that no more of a commodity can be consumed, or a resource used, in the aggregate, than is available to the economy.

The objective and constraints can be combined in the Lagrangian expression

$$L = u^1(\cdot) + \sum_{j=2}^{m} \lambda_j [-u^{j^*} + u^j(\cdot)] - \sum_{k=1}^{h} \mu_k f^k(\cdot)$$

$$+ \sum_{i=1}^{n} \omega_i \left( r_i - \sum_{j=1}^{m} x_{ij} + \sum_{k=1}^{h} y_{ik} \right) \qquad (6.5)$$

Differentiating with respect to the $x_{ij}$, $y_{ik}$, and $s_k$, and assuming no corner solutions, we obtain the first-order conditions for a maximum:

$$\lambda_j u_i^j - \omega_i = 0 \qquad \text{(all } i, j) \qquad (6.6)$$

$$-\mu_k f_i^k + \omega_i = 0 \qquad \text{(all } i, k) \qquad (6.7)$$

$$u_s^1 + \sum_{j=2}^{m} \lambda_j u_s^j - \mu_k f_{s_k}^k = 0 \qquad \text{(all } k). \qquad (6.8)$$

The interesting result here is equation (6.8), which tells us that each firm should emit or employ smoke only to the point that the marginal benefit from doing so, the value of the marginal product of smoke, $\mu_k f^k_{s_k}$, is just equal to the marginal cost, literally the value of the weighted sum of marginal disutilities, $u^1_s + \Sigma^m_{j=2} \lambda_j u^j_s$. However, because neither the disutilities nor the weights are observable, the result as stated is not very useful. A little further analysis can yield one that is.

Let $x_{\bar{i}}$ be a good consumed by everyone. From equation (6.6), $\lambda_j = \omega_{\bar{i}}/u^j_{\bar{i}}$. The value of the marginal damage from pollution then becomes $\omega_{\bar{i}}\Sigma_j u^j_s/u^j_{\bar{i}}$. And, as is well known, along an indifference curve between two goods (here pollution and $x_{\bar{i}}$) the ratio of marginal utilities $u^j_s/u^j_{\bar{i}} = -dx_{\bar{i}j}/ds$, the marginal rate of substitution between the two. This leaves us with the value of damage equal to $\omega_{\bar{i}}\Sigma_j(-dx_{\bar{i}j}/ds)$, the value of the $x_{\bar{i}}$ needed to offset an increment of pollution. If we further let $x_{\bar{i}}$ be the numeraire in this system, then the value of damage is just the amount of $x_{\bar{i}}$ needed, $\Sigma_j(-dx_{\bar{i}j}/ds)$.[9] In any case, the value is, at least in principle, observable.

Now let us obtain the conditions that characterize a competitive equilibrium. By making the polluting firms subject to a tax, we then readily derive the optimal tax (i.e., the tax required to make the competitive allocation Pareto-optimal). Almost as a by-product of this analysis we shall derive another result that sheds some light on an old controversy in the literature concerning the compensation of victims. Some have argued for compensation, which presumably could be paid out of the proceeds of the tax. Others have disagreed, on the grounds that it makes more sense to tax the "victim," because

---

[9] Notice that this is just Samuelson's condition (1954) for the optimal supply of a public good: The marginal cost is equated to the sum of marginal rates of substitution between the good and a numeraire private good. In this case, of course, the good is a "bad" (pollution), and so it is the marginal benefit from its use that is equated to the sum of (positive) marginal rates of substitution.

by his action (e.g., moving next to a smoky factory) he increases the damage done by the smoke and therefore the tax paid by the factory owner and, ultimately, the losses to owners of factors of production and to consumers of the factory's output. What we shall show is that the optimal compensation is either zero or a lump sum that does not vary with the victim's actions and hence the damage he suffers.

Formally, the consumer's problem is to maximize his utility subject to a slightly unusual budget constraint. Expenditures are $\Sigma_{i=1}^{n'} p_i x_{ij}$, where $p_i$ is the price of $x_i$, and $n' < n$. Income is $\Sigma_{i=n'}^{n} p_i x_{ij}$, where $x_{n'j}$ to $x_{nj}$ are services sold by the consumer (there may be just one, labor). To this we add a term, $t^j$, as compensation for smoke damage suffered. The budget constraint then takes the form $\Sigma_{i=1}^{n'} p_i x_{ij} \leq \Sigma_{i=n'}^{n} p_i x_{ij} + t^j$, or, letting services sold be represented by negative values of $x_{ij}$,

$$\sum_{i=1}^{n} p_i x_{ij} \leq t^j \tag{6.9}$$

The Lagrangian expression for this problem is

$$L_j = u^j(\cdot) + \alpha_j(t^j - \sum_i p_i x_{ij}) \tag{6.10}$$

Differentiating with respect to the $x_{ij}$, and again ignoring corner solutions, we obtain

$$u_i^j + \alpha_j (t_i^j - p_i) = 0 \tag{6.11}$$

For the firm, the problem is to maximize profits subject to a production constraint. The only novel feature in this analysis is that the firm's profit function includes a term, $t_k s_k$, representing tax payments, at a per unit rate $t_k$, for the smoke it emits.

The Lagrangian expression then is

$$L_k = \sum_{i=1}^{n} p_i y_{ik} - t_k s_k - \beta_k f^k(\cdot) \tag{6.12}$$

Differentiating with respect to the $y_{ik}$ and $s_k$, and once again ignoring corner solutions, we obtain

$$p_i - \beta_k f_i^k = 0 \qquad (6.13)$$

and

$$-t_k - \beta_k f_{s_k}^k = 0 \qquad (6.14)$$

Comparing these conditions, and equation (6.11), to the corresponding ones for a Pareto optimum, equations (6.6) through (6.8), it is clear that for them to coincide, the following must hold

$$p_i = \omega_i, \qquad \lambda_j = 1/\alpha_j, \qquad \mu_k = \beta_k \qquad (6.15a)$$

and

$$t_i^j = 0, \qquad t_k = -u_s^1 - \sum_{j=2}^{m} \lambda_j u_s^j \qquad (6.15b)$$

The interesting results are in equation (6.15b). Looking at the smoke tax, $t_k$, we see that it is uniform (i.e., is the same for all firms) and is just equal to the value of the marginal damage from smoke at the Pareto-optimal smoke level. From our earlier discussion of an observable expression for this value, the tax can also be written as

$$t_k = \sum_j dx_{ij}/ds \qquad (6.15c)$$

Notice that the tax is not on output. It is sometimes suggested that the output of a good whose marginal social cost diverges from its marginal private cost (as would be true where smoke or other pollution is involved) ought to be reduced by means of a tax. Clearly this is not correct. It is the smoke that is optimally taxed and correspondingly reduced, and if possibilities for substitution (away from smoke) in production are good, the effect on output may be negligible.[10]

---

[10] The distinction between a tax on pollution (as an input to production) and a tax on output was made by Plott (1966), who showed that if pollution is an inferior input it will be increased by a tax on output.

The other result of interest here is that $t_i^j = 0$. This tells us that compensation must not vary with changes in the victim's consumption levels. Specifically, if he moves next to a smoky factory, thereby suffering an increase in smoke damage, he should neither be compensated for this increase nor taxed to prevent it. In other words, the compensation is not really compensation, in the sense of a compensating variation in income. A lump-sum payment can, of course, be made, but this will not (indeed, must not) affect the allocation of resources.

Our first result, that a pollution tax ought to be set equal to the marginal damage from pollution, is generally well understood (apart from the confusion about whether or not the tax applies to the polluting product). Although most derivations are in a partial-equilibrium setting, whereas ours (along with a few others cited in footnote 7) is part of a general equilibrium, the intuition behind the result is clear. This is probably less true for the no-compensation rule. Those who sympathize with pollution victims may be disturbed, and those (sterner individuals) who argue that the optimal compensation is, in fact, negative (i.e., the victims ought to be taxed) may also feel let down.

Let us try to indicate why the result makes economic sense.[11] Consider an external economy that, like pollution, is also a public good in the sense that what one individual consumes does not reduce the amount available for others. Examples (assuming no congestion) might be a bridge crossing, or a scenic view, or, if one is fortunate enough to live in the San Francisco Bay area, the Golden Gate Bridge, which is both. If the external economy is not a gift of nature, but must be produced, the same reasoning that established the optimality of a tax on a diseconomy suggests a subsidy to the producers.[12]

---

[11] The discussion here is drawn from Baumol and Oates (1975a). See also the work of Page (1973a) and Mäler (1974).

[12] Our framework does not explicitly allow for public production, but as pointed out by Kneese and his collaborators, the optimal provision of a public-good externality may require this, along with fiscal incentives for individuals. In the case of pollution control,

What about a charge to the consumers, perhaps to cover the subsidy? Again assuming no congestion, the optimal charge is clearly zero. The reason is that any positive charge will lead to a reduction in consumption, when its marginal social cost is zero.

The case of the external diseconomy is exactly analogous. The producers should indeed be taxed, but the consumers should not be compensated, or at least not in proportion to their consumption. By inhaling smoke, consumer $j$ does not provide a benefit to consumer $j'$, unless, of course, $j'$ is a malevolent individual and derives satisfaction from $j$'s misfortune. But ignoring the possibility of a consumption externality of this type, no compensation is required. Moreover, just as a charge on consumption of the public good would lead to too little being consumed, compensation for damages from the public bad would tend to lead to too much being "consumed." If the potential victim were fully compensated for the damage he suffers by living next to the smoky factory, he would have no incentive to adjust his consumption behavior to reduce the damage, as, for example, by moving or by not locating there in the first place. Note, finally, that negative compensation (a tax) is equally unjustified. The victim absorbs the full social cost of his decision to live near the factory and needs no additional incentive to look elsewhere.

One important qualification to this discussion is that the public-good or public-bad externality be excludable, in the sense that an individual can be excluded from consumption. Some public goods (national defense comes to mind) are nonexcludable, and this has sometimes been taken as a defining characteristic, along with nonrivalry in consumption (what one consumes does not reduce the amount available for others). We have specified only that pollution exhibits nonrivalry. If it were completely nonexcludable as well, compensa-

public investment in treatment facilities can complement a tax on polluters. The optimal mix of these control elements was studied by Bohm (1972*a*).

tion could be justified. Suppose an individual has no real option of living away from a polluted area, and there are no other actions he can take to substantially reduce or eliminate the impact of the pollution. Then compensation, which may be desirable for reasons of equity, will not impair allocative efficiency. The same reasoning, of course, applies to the external economy. If it were completely nonexcludable, a charge would not lead to less being consumed; only the distribution of income would be affected.

### A qualification: externality and nonconvexity

In the introduction to this chapter we noted a different qualification to the optimal tax solution, related to the presence of a nonconvexity. The basic difficulty is that externalities can be associated with nonconvexities in affected preference of production sets, and these nonconvexities can lead to multiple tax equilibria. This sounds rather formidable, but I think the point can be made fairly simply with the aid of diagrams and examples.[13]

Consider the case of an individual faced with increasing marginal damage from pollution. As our general-equilibrium analysis suggests, he need not accept this indefinitely. He may, instead, take action to protect himself (e.g., installing some sort of filtering system, or ceasing to use the contaminated medium where this is possible, as in the case of a polluted swimming place, or moving away).[14] As a result, the marginal damage falls, perhaps to zero. The situation is represented in

---

[13] The view of nonconvexity developed here is based on that of Starrett and Zeckhauser (1974). A more rigorous abstract analysis was presented by Starrett (1972). Other treatments of the connection between externality and nonconvexity include those of Portes (1970), Kolm (1971), Baumol and Bradford (1972), Baumol and Oates (1975a), Kohn and Aucamp (1976), and Gould (1977).

[14] These and other alternatives were emphasized, under the general heading of "averting behavior," by Zeckhauser and Fisher (1976). Averting behavior is simply an aspect of the general-equilibrium adjustment of an economy to a disturbance, such as an increase in pollution.

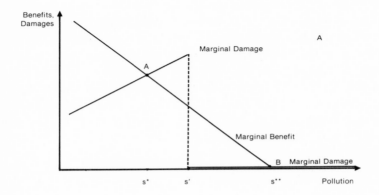

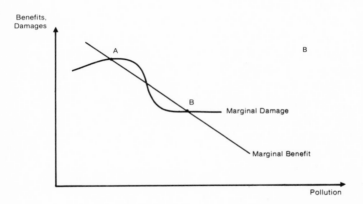

Figure 6.1. Externality, nonconvexity, and multiple equilibria. A: One individual. B: Many individuals.

Figure 6.1A, where a well-behaved marginal product, or benefit, of pollution curve is also shown.

The nonconvexity is introduced by the defensive action taken at the point where pollution reaches the concentration denoted by *s'* in the diagram. At this point the marginal-damage curve drops sharply, to zero. As a result, two equilibria exist: at point *A*, and again at point *B*, where the marginal-benefit curve reaches zero and again intersects the marginal-damage curve, this time at a much higher concentration. Note that it is not necessary that marginal damage drop to zero; it need only fall far enough to intersect the marginal-benefit curve a second time. Further, the drop need not be sharp. Suppose many individuals are affected, as in our model and, more important, as in the typical pollution case. Doubtless they will not all react to the increasing damage at precisely the same point, but as increasing numbers do so over some range of concentrations, the sum of marginal damages will begin to fall. Such a situation, with the potential for a second equilibrium, is represented in Figure 6.1B. Note that, especially in this case, multiple equilibria cannot be ruled out.

Why does any of this matter? The reason is easily seen when we consider the imposition of a tax, set as in equation (6.15) equal to marginal damage at the optimal point. Suppose the *ex ante* pollution concentration is at a point where marginal damage is still rising. On the somewhat simpler Figure 6.1A, this will mean at some $s < s'$. Then a tax $t^*$, set as indicated, will clearly lead to the $A$ equilibrium, where $s = s^*$. If the *ex ante* $s > s^*$, the tax is greater than the marginal benefit, and pollution is accordingly reduced. If the *ex ante* $s < s^*$, the tax is less than the marginal benefit, and pollution is increased. The equilibrium is at $s = s^*$.

Now suppose the *ex ante* concentration is at $s > s'$. Here marginal damage has fallen to zero, and a tax that reflects this must lead to the $B$ equilibrium, where $s = s^{**}$. For *ex ante* $s$ between $s'$ and $s^{**}$ the optimal tax is just zero, and thus it remains below the marginal benefit until $s = s^{**}$.

The problem this poses is that a pollution tax, or indeed any policy instrument based (appropriately) on marginal-efficiency conditions, may produce an outcome that depends on pollution levels and related adjustments in force at the time it is imposed. Because damages are generally not internalized (although this is changing), adjustments will be made that result in low observed marginal damages. In other words, by consulting marginal conditions in the neighborhood of the *ex* ante point, which is probably all we can do, we are likely to end up at the high-pollution $B$ equilibrium rather than at the low-pollution $A$ equilibrium. This may be globally optimal, but the point is that we do not know. A benefit–cost analysis of the move from $A$ to $B$, or vice versa, will be required to determine whether or not the likely local maximum at $B$ is also a global maximum. The question is whether or not (in Figure 6.1A) the area under the marginal-benefit curve from $s^*$ to $s^{**}$ exceeds the area under the marginal-damage curve from $s^*$ to $s^{**}$, or, as in this case, where marginal damage falls to zero at $s'$, from $s^*$ to $s'$. An empirical analysis of the move back from $B$ to $A$ could be difficult, as one would have to determine what adjustments had already been made or would be made if pollution loads were cut back.

### 6.3. Pollution-control policies: a comparative analysis

We have just seen that a tax on pollution can lead to an optimal degree of control, although the potential for adjustments by victims can make attainment of a global optimum difficult. In fact, the other methods we shall discuss (direct control, subsidy, pollution rights market) face the same difficulty, and so this is not necessarily an argument against a tax. There are, indeed, numerous advantages of a tax, as compared with those methods. In this section we shall be mainly concerned with the comparative strengths and weaknesses of the several alternatives. First, however, we shall consider a rather novel challenge to all. It was raised by Coase (1960) specifically against a tax, as the traditional remedy advocated by Pigou, but it would seem to apply to all of the other forms of collective action as well.

#### *The Coase theorem: a challenge to pollution policy*

Coase's "theorem" can be stated simply: With a clear definition of property rights, resources will be put to their highest-value (Pareto-optimal) use without any need for government intervention.[15] What has this to do with pollution? Consider the case of a factory dumping wastes in a stream also used as a source of irrigation water by a farm. Suppose the farmer has no protected right to the water, and there is no law against dumping. The farmer presumably will be willing to pay the factory for each gallon of wastewater not discharged, as long as the payment is not greater than the marginal damage. The factory, for its part, will require a payment not less than the marginal benefit of dumping. Thus the equilibrium payment results in an amount of dumping that equates the marginal benefit to the marginal damage.

Now suppose the farmer enjoys a right to clean water from the stream. The factory will be willing to pay to discharge each gallon of wastewater as long as the payment does not exceed the saving. And the farmer will require a payment at least equal to the damage done by the discharge. Again, equilibrium comes where the marginal benefit from dumping equals the marginal damage.

This is shown in a slightly different way in Figure 6.2, an illustration of the theorem derived from the work of Turvey (1963). If the farmer is not entitled to clean water, he will be willing to pay, in total, an amount up to $c + d$ to secure a reduction in discharge to $s^*$, whereas the factory will cut back to this level for a payment of anything over $d$. If the farmer does have rights, the factory will be willing to pay up to $a + b$ for the privilege of discharging $s^*$, and the farmer will accept the damage for a payment of anything over $b$.

We have established the following: that the allocation of resources will be the same regardless of the assignment of

---

[15] Coase's original article is much richer in detail than this suggests, and there is a bit more to the theorem. Indeed, Coase may have been the first to emphasize the potential for the kind of averting behavior or adjustment to externality we discussed in the preceding section. For a clear presentation of Coase's analysis, as well as extensions and criticisms, see the work of Randall (1972) and Page (1973*a*).

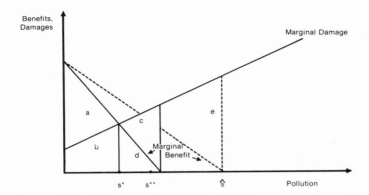

Figure 6.2. Coase theorem.

property rights; that the allocation will maximize the value of production; that no intervention by government is required to achieve this result. In short, we have established the Coase theorem. However, there are several objections that can be raised to the assumptions needed to obtain this result, and in my view, these rob the theorem of any practical applicability to pollution problems. There is even a question whether or not it is correct on its own terms.

In our example, the only affected party was the farmer, but stream pollution ordinarily will affect many parties: other producers, like the farmer, and, perhaps more important, consumers. Recreational opportunities will be diminished, there may be public health impacts, and so on. Thousands or even millions of people could be affected. Coase explicitly assumed no transaction costs, which was realistic in the two-party setting of his examples (a rancher whose wandering cattle trample a farmer's crops, a confectioner whose machinery disturbs a doctor in an adjacent office, and so on). But in the typical many-party pollution case, it is clear that transaction costs will be prohibitive. All of the affected parties will have to be assembled and asked what they will be willing to pay or will require in compensation depending on the assignment of property rights. Suppose the damage, in the aggregate, exceeds the benefit from a projected increase in pollution. If the damaged parties do not have the right to clean water, the costs of getting together and negotiating a payment can be so high that it might not be done. The stream water will not go to its highest-value use, nor will this use be independent of the assignment of property rights.

I believe that this argument is generally well known. Not so well known, perhaps, is the interesting counterargument posed by Demsetz (1964): Where transaction costs block a private-bargaining solution to an environmental problem, as in the example just given, the status quo must be optimal in the sense that the benefits from moving are less than the costs, including the transaction costs. The difficulty with this argument is that it does not address the question of the desirability of an alternative-solution mechanism, such as a tax on (or other government regulation of) the environmental impact. We might counter the counterargument by saying that when transaction costs block the formation of a market, the relevant comparison is between doing nothing, letting the environmental damage take its course, on the one hand, and imposing some collective control, on the other. It is by no means obvious that the former will always be preferred.

Even if the barrier of transaction costs could somehow be overcome, there is another barrier to a bargaining solution. When many parties are involved, there will be an incentive for each to engage in strategic misrepresentation of preferences. Suppose, again, that damages exceed benefits and that the victims have no rights. Each will have an incentive to under-state its willingness to contribute to a bribe to the polluter, on the assumption that this will not appreciably affect the total. But if enough parties behave in this fashion, the total will indeed fall below the amount required to compensate the polluter, and once again stream water will be allocated ineffi-ciently. In other words, when the externality is a public good, as pollution normally is, the conditions required for the theorem to hold are not met.[16]

Questions have also been raised as to the validity of the theorem in a two-party setting. Let us return to our original example of factory and farm. Even here, there seems to be scope for strategic behavior that will upset the Coasian equilibrium. The factory can claim that its marginal-benefit curve, in Figure 6.2, is really farther to the right (e.g., through point $\hat{s}$). Then the bribe it can extract from the farmer is increased by an amount equal to $e$ in Figure 6.2, and a new equilibrium, at $s^{**}$, is established. If the potential gains from this sort of behavior are large enough, one can imagine that real resources will be used (wastefully, from a social point of view) for the purpose of establishing a credible threat. The factory might, for example, at least begin to build an effluent outfall larger than needed in order to frighten the farmer into offering a larger bribe.[17]

Another difficulty for the theorem is the presence of income effects, which can drive a wedge between the amount an individual is willing to pay for clean water, for example, and the amount he will require in compensation for the loss of this good. In our example, and in Coase's example, the two parties are producers, so that this difficulty is not likely to arise. The

---

[16] This argument (that publicness and the large numbers associated with it make the Coase theorem inapplicable) was developed originally by Wellisz (1964) and by Kneese (1964), with special reference to water pollution. Schulze and d'Arge (1974) provided a detailed analysis of the ramifications of transaction costs. For more on the effect of transaction costs on the bargaining behavior of large and small groups, not confined to externality situations, see the work of Olson (1964). Buchanan and Stubblebine (1962) showed that a pollution tax can lead to too little pollution, because the victims will bribe the polluters to reduce pollution beyond the optimal point induced by the tax. The significance of this result is clearly weakened, in my judgment, by the prohibitive transaction costs in the typical large-numbers pollution case.

[17] The insight into the potential for strategic behavior even in a two-party setting is due to Wellisz (1964). Mumey (1971) discussed the possibility that resources will be channeled into threatening actions or processes.

loss to the farmer is measured unambiguously by the loss of output or the cost of obtaining clean water, whichever is less. But when the damaged party is a consumer (and this, we have argued, is the more typical case), willingness to pay may differ from required compensation because the former is constrained by the consumer's income. The result is that the assignment of property rights will affect resource use.[18]

In summary, it appears that the Coase theorem fails as a challenge to pollution-control policy involving some form of public intervention. It does offer an insight into the virtues of the market in dealing with certain kinds of externalities, but generally not those associated with pollution or other environmental disruption.

### The cost-effectiveness of a tax

Another kind of challenge to a pollution tax comes not from a school of academic economists, as in the case of the Coase theorem, but from noneconomists. The contention is that the information required to implement a tax (the marginal damage, at the optimal point, to all pollution receivers) is not available and is not likely to be. One implication is that neither a tax nor the economic theory on which it rests is particularly relevant to practical attempts to deal with pollution. Many economists accept, at least provisionally, the claim that we do not know enough about damage functions to design a tax to achieve full Pareto optimality.[19] But these same economists have shown how a tax can be used to achieve the more modest, but still important, objective of cost-effective control.[20]

---

[18] Income effects were analyzed by Dolbear (1967) and Mishan (1967). For an amusing critique of the Coase theorem and extensions as applied to pollution, see Mishan's "Pangloss on Pollution" (1971*b*).

[19] Methods of estimating damages will be discussed in detail in the next section.

[20] Versions of this result have been obtained and discussed by many people. See, for example, the work of Kneese (1964), Ruff (1970),

Suppose we view the problem as one of choosing, through the political process, a standard of environmental quality (much as we choose amounts of other public goods, such as national defense) and then seeking a method to achieve it at least cost. In what follows we shall show that a tax will do this and that direct controls on emissions, a method favored by many noneconomists, probably will not. However, there are circumstances in which controls may be superior to a tax or can usefully supplement a tax. Our approach in proving the cost-minimization theorem is similar to the one adopted in the preceding section. We shall first derive necessary conditions for achieving a preselected level of pollution at minimum cost and then show that the same conditions are satisfied by the decentralized decisions of polluting firms subject to an appropriate tax.

Formally, the planner's problem is to minimize the sum of expenditures on two kinds of inputs (those used to produce conventional goods and services and those used to control pollution), subject to restrictions on production, on pollution, and on the relationship between production and pollution. Previously, we considered pollution as just another factor of production. This, of course, implied some expenditure on control, because less pollution meant more of other costly inputs. Here, however, the expenditure is made explicit in order to obtain an expression for the indicated pollution tax in terms of the cost of control. This has some advantages in interpretation and in comparing the costs of a tax with those of other methods, such as direct controls, but it sacrifices some

Baumol and Oates (1971, 1975*a*), Baumol (1972), and Mishan (1974). The clear nontechnical discussion by Ruff can be particularly recommended to noneconomists. A detailed empirical study of the comparative costs of taxes or effluent charges as opposed to uniform controls (discussed in the following text) to achieve a desired level of water quality in the Delaware estuary was discussed by Kneese (1977). The conclusion of the study was that the desired quality could be achieved for about half the cost with taxes.

detail in modeling the role of pollution within the firm, as we shall see.[21]

In symbols, the problem is as follows:

$$\text{minimize} \sum_i \sum_k p_i r_{ik} + \sum_k p_v v_k \qquad (6.16)$$

subject to

$$f^k(r_{1k}, \ldots, r_{nk}) = y_k^* \qquad (k = 1, \ldots, h) \qquad (6.17)$$

$$g^k(y_k^*, v_k) = s_k \qquad (k = 1, \ldots, h) \qquad (6.18)$$

and

$$\sum_k s_k \leq s^* \qquad (6.19)$$

where $r_{ik}$ is the amount of input $i$ and $v_k$ is the amount of control input $v$ employed by firm $k$, $p_v$ is the price of $v$, $y_k^*$ is the output of firm $k$, $g^k(\cdot)$ is a function that relates smoke emissions to levels of output and control for each firm, $s^*$ is the environmental-quality standard, and the other symbols are as previously defined.

There are at least two features of this model that deserve further explanation. As indicated in equation (6.18), smoke emissions are determined by two things: the level of output, $y^*$, and the input, $v$, devoted to abatement or control. This formulation is not as rigid as it may seem, because the control input can be understood rather broadly as a method or technique for reducing emissions in combination with physical factors such as labor and capital. Just one such input is specified for simplicity without loss of generality.

A vector of outputs, the $y_k^*$, is specified, because otherwise the problem would be trivial. By having the firms produce nothing or very little, the planner obviously can minimize costs and satisfy the smoke constraint. What we are interested in are

---

[21] For an approach that treats pollution as an input, but is similar in other respects to ours, see the work of Baumol and Oates (1975a).

the conditions for minimizing costs associated with any given output, just as in the ordinary theory of the firm. The output actually selected presumably will depend on demand and on the planner's objective or the firm's objective. We assume only that it is desired to produce the chosen output at least cost, and we seek the conditions that will assure this. As before, we do not suppose that a planner can really determine input use at the firm level. We simply pose the problem in order to show how a much less ambitious approach, the setting of a (uniform) tax, can achieve the same results.

Proceeding with the solution, the Lagrangian expression can be written, first substituting $g^k(\cdot)$ directly for $s_k$, as

$$L = \sum_i \sum_k p_i r_{ik} + \sum_k p_v v_k$$
$$+ \sum_k \lambda_k [y_k^* - f^k(\cdot)] + \lambda \left[ \sum_k g^k(\cdot) - s^* \right] \quad (6.20)$$

Differentiating with respect to the $r_{ik}$ and $v_k$, and assuming no corner solutions, we obtain the necessary conditions for a minimum:

$$p_i - \lambda_k f_i^k = 0 \qquad \text{(all } i,k) \qquad\qquad (6.21)$$

$$p_v + \lambda g_v^k = 0 \qquad \text{(all } k) \qquad\qquad (6.22)$$

Now suppose the decisions on input levels will be made by the individual firms. The problem facing each is to minimize the sum of expenditures on inputs and a pollution tax, subject to the same restrictions on production and on the relationship between production and pollution. Note that our results will apply to imperfectly competitive firms as well, because we may assume that they are interested in keeping costs down, however much they choose to produce.[22]

---

[22] We must also assume that the firms are price takers in factor markets, importantly including the market for pollution. That is, the tax rate is not influenced by firm activities. This issue was further discussed by Bohm (1970) and Baumol and Oates (1975a). A potential difficulty with the factor price assumption is that after

Thus the firm's problem is as follows:

$$\text{minimize} \sum_i p_i r_{ik} + p_v v_k + t_k s_k \qquad (6.23)$$

subject to equations (6.17) and (6.18). The Lagrangian expression, again subsituting $g^k(\cdot)$ for $s_k$, is

$$L^k = \sum_i p_i r_{ik} + p_v v_k + t_k g^k(\cdot)$$

$$+ \alpha_k [ y_k^* - f^k(\cdot)] \qquad (6.24)$$

where $t_k$ is the pollution tax. Differentiating with respect to the $r_{ik}$ and $v_k$, we obtain

$$p_i - \alpha_k f^k_i = 0 \qquad \text{(all } i) \qquad (6.25)$$

and

$$p_v + t_k g^k_v = 0 \qquad (6.26)$$

Comparing these conditions to equations (6.21) and (6.22), it is clear that they are the same, provided the tax $t_k$ is set equal to $\lambda$, the shadow price of the pollution constraint, for all $k$.[23] It is clear that $\lambda$ depends on the standard, $s^*$. For full efficiency, $s^*$ would be set where the marginal damage from pollution just equals the marginal benefit, but this would bring us back to the preceding section's approach, which we have suggested is impaired by lack of information about damages.

Still, we have shown a great deal. Let us take stock. We have shown that a uniform tax on polluters ($t_k = \lambda$, all $k$) will achieve a preselected standard for environmental quality at minimum cost, provided the tax is set appropriately. It is important that the result emerges from the decentralized

imposition of a tax, the prices either may be changed or may no longer reflect real factor scarcities (assuming they did so in the original problem of social-cost minimization). My guess is that this difficulty is likely to be of little empirical importance.

[23] It must also be true that $\alpha_k = \lambda_k$. Because the equations and parameters are the same in both cases (provided $t_k = \lambda$), the solution values of the parameters, including $\alpha_k$, must be the same. Away from equilibrium, $\alpha_k$ is, in general, not equal to $\lambda_k$.

decisions of the polluting firms. The central authority need know nothing about the control options facing each firm in setting the tax, and it need do nothing beyond setting the tax. On the other hand, to set the tax appropriately, the authority must solve for $\lambda$, the change in the minimum expenditure on production and control associated with a small change in the pollution constraint. This is a kind of aggregate marginal cost of control, and in practice it might be estimated from knowledge of the costs of an "average" polluter.[24] Even when this is not feasible, however, a uniform tax has the desirable property of minimizing the cost of achieving some quality standard, and doing so in a decentralized fashion.

To see this, consider the expression for the tax implicit in equation (6.26). Rewriting to make the tax explicit, we have

$$t = -p_v/g_v^k \qquad (6.27)$$

The RHS is the price of the control input divided by its marginal product, or the marginal cost of control. Now, suppose the tax required to achieve a given quality standard, call it $q^*$, where $q^*$ represents units of pollution abated and is inversely related to $s^*$, is not known. Instead, a tax is set that will result in a different quality, $q^{**}$. The marginal cost of control will still be equated across sources of pollution, because each will push control to the point that the marginal cost equals the common tax. This is shown for two sources with different control costs in Figure 6.3. A tax $t^*$ will achieve the desired quality level $q^*$ at the least cost, but a tax $t^{**}$ will achieve $q^{**}$ at the least cost.

The advantage of a tax over direct controls on emissions is easily demonstrated in this format as well. Suppose the two sources in Figure 6.3 are producing the same amount of

---

[24] For more on this suggestion, see the work of Kneese and Bower (1968). The reader seeking a discussion of some of the theoretical efficiency issues treated in this chapter, especially taxes versus direct controls, in a detailed and realistic setting might wish to consult the Kneese-Bower volume on the economics, technology, and institutions of water-quality management.

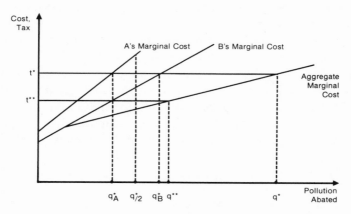

Figure 6.3. Minimum-cost tax.

pollution, before the tax or other control. Now it is desired to achieve a reduction to $q^*$. One obvious way to do this is to impose a uniform control on each source: a reduction of $q^*/2$. The difficulty is that in general this will result in violation of the cost-minimizing equimarginal outcome assured by the tax. As long as marginal costs differ, the cost of achieving $q^*$ can be reduced by shifting a unit of abatement from the high-cost source to the low-cost source. Of course, a uniform reduction (which can also be stated in percentage terms for sources of different sizes) may have some appeal on grounds of equity, but it certainly will not be cost-effective.

Alternatively, the control can be tailored to the individual source to achieve the standard at least cost, as under the tax. In Figure 6.3 this will involve setting a standard of $q_A^*$ for source $A$ and $q_B^*$ for $B$. The difficulty here is that the central authority will need to know the control cost function for each individual source. When there are just two sources, the difficulty may not be serious, although even in this case the incentive to misrepresent is clear. And when there are a great many sources, it is not realistic to imagine that the central authority can be informed about the types and costs of options available to each for controlling pollution.

Another advantage that has been claimed for a tax, as opposed to direct controls, is that the tax provides a continuing incentive to the polluter to cut back on emissions. No matter how low they already are, cutting back further will reduce tax payments. This may be especially important in a dynamic setting, where polluters are encouraged to seek new low-cost ways of cutting back.[25]

A disadvantage of a tax is that extensive monitoring of emissions is required. Thus far, we have tended to ignore the administrative costs of the policy alternatives. Yet it is clear (as noneconomists, especially, have argued in their attacks on the feasibility of a tax) that the real resource costs of monitoring can be substantial.

A first response to this criticism is that it appears to apply to direct controls as well as to other alternatives such as a subsidy or a permit system. Certainly this is true for controls on emissions, whether uniform or individually tailored. However, monitoring costs may be considerably lower for another form of control: a requirement that the polluter use a particular type of control technology. This is a popular approach in the management of both air quality and water quality in the United States.

My impression is that there is no reason to believe that mandated technology will be cost-effective, any more than other controls. Horror stories of almost perverse inefficiency in

---

[25] Kneese and Schultze (1975), in a nontechnical discussion of the history of air- and water-pollution policies in the United States and desirable changes in these policies, argued that the incentive for technical change in pollution control may be the most important criterion for judging a policy. Discussions of tax effects on control technology have been provided by V. L. Smith (1972), Orr (1976), and, most rigorously and comprehensively, Magat (1978). For a comparison of technical change under a subsidy for pollution control, as opposed to a tax, see the work of Wenders (unpublished). The conclusion is that a tax provides superior incentives.

specific instances are common knowledge among students of environmental economics.[26] And as the history of mandated emission-control devices on automobiles suggests, continuing inspection may be required to ensure that the devices are functioning properly (indeed, that they are in place and functioning at all). Prospects are perhaps better in other areas, but it is difficult to imagine a technology that does not require some monitoring. A fair conclusion might be that the question of which approach to pollution control accomplishes a desired degree of control at the least cost, including monitoring cost, is an empirical one. It is conceivable that there are cases in which a mandated technology will represent the least-cost alternative.

There are a couple of other situations in which direct controls may be an improvement over a tax. One occurs when the desired emission level is zero, as, for example, with a highly toxic substance. In this situation, a simple ban on use may be indicated.[27] A second situation occurs when rapid or temporary variation in emission levels is desired, as a consequence, for example, of changing weather patterns. Taxes, subsidies, and the number of pollution permits sold can all be varied to meet changing emission targets, but this may be impractical over short periods. Changing prices can be costly, and this is presumably one reason that peak or time-of-day prices are not more widely employed. An in-place tax system, on air pollu-

[26] For example, recycling, considered by many to be the ideal control technology, is not among the mandated technologies that qualify for water-pollution-control subsidies (Kneese and Schultze, 1975), with the result that the choice of technology is biased away from recycling. Similarly, low-sulfur western U.S. coal is discriminated against by the proposed New Source Performance Standards (NSPS) for coal-burning plants that mandate scrubbers. The advantage of the low-sulfur coal is that it does not need scrubbers to meet almost any reasonable ambient air-quality standard; yet this natural advantage is impaired by the mandate.

[27] For a detailed discussion of the alternatives for dealing with toxic substances, see the work of Portney (1978), which appears in an RFF volume containing articles on several aspects of U.S. environmental policy.

tion, for instance, could be usefully supplemented by direct controls on emissions in unusual circumstances, such as an atmospheric inversion that inhibits the dispersal of pollution.[28]

### Tax versus subsidy

With the exceptions of the cases just discussed, a tax appears generally superior to direct controls. But a tax is not the only fiscal instrument that can be used to reduce pollution. Some economists have suggested that a subsidy, or payment to reduce pollution, will work just as well. In its strongest form, the suggestion is that resource allocation, including the emission of pollutants, does not depend on the assignment of environmental property rights. Whether the polluter is paid for the emissions he abates or is taxed for those he does not, the outcomes will be the same. Only the distribution of income is affected.

This may sound familiar, and indeed it has been called a Coasian position, although Coase considered mainly two-party situations and advocated direct negotiation between the parties, as opposed to government intervention in the form of either a tax or a subsidy. Still, if we accept the proposition that some form of intervention is necessary in the typical large-numbers pollution case, the question whether or not tax and subsidy are equivalent, in their allocative effects (and, if not, which is superior), seems legitimate. We shall show that they are not equivalent and that the tax is superior, although there is a superficially plausible case for equivalence. The reasoning here is somewhat similar to that in our earlier analysis of the Coase theorem and its application to pollution control.

Before proceeding, we should take note of another kind of subsidy that is a central feature of U.S. environmental policy: payment of part or all of the cost of pollution control. The payment can be direct, as in the case of federal grants to municipalities for construction of wastewater-treatment facili-

---

[28] This suggestion is due to Baumol and Oates (1975*b*).

ties, or indirect, as in the case of tax credits to firms for investment in certain types of control equipment. From the point of view of economic efficiency, this subsidy has serious drawbacks. These will be considered following discussion of the first, or Coasian, subsidy.

The Coasian subsidy takes the following form. Starting from a benchmark level, the polluter is paid for each unit reduction in emissions. If the benchmark is $s*$, actual emissions are $s$, and payment is at rate $t$, then the subsidy is $t(s* - s)$. It is easy to see that this is just equivalent to a lump-sum transfer to the polluter, $ts*$, coupled to a tax, $-ts$. Because behavior presumably is not affected by a lump-sum transfer, it appears that the allocative effects of a tax and subsidy must be the same. Income distribution is, of course, affected by the disposition of the lump sum $ts*$.

There are, however, two distinct difficulties with this result. One, discussed in connection with the Coase theorem, is that because the size of the lump-sum payment depends on the benchmark emission level, the polluter has a clear incentive to misrepresent and even misallocate resources to establish a favorable benchmark. The fundamental difficulty is that the benchmark is set arbitrarily. One plausible way to do this (perhaps the only practical way) is on the basis of previous emission levels. But this creates an incentive for emissions above even what the firm would find profitable in the absence of any control, for an interim period during which the benchmark is established. Moreover, setting the benchmark on the basis of observed emissions penalizes the clean firm, the one that has already installed control equipment or uses a less polluting process. It may be that an appropriate method can be devised to determine a benchmark for each polluter, but clearly this is not a trivial problem.[29]

---

[29] It was recognized in a number of early contributions to the tax-versus-subsidy literature, or, as it is also known, the bribes-versus-charges literature. See, for example, the work of Kamien, Schwartz, and Dolbear (1966), Freeman (1967), and Mills (1968).

A second reason for questioning the symmetry between tax and subsidy arises when the lump sum is considered more carefully. The difficulty is that in the longer run the lump sum can have an effect on the polluting firm's decisions. Because it has an effect on profits, it can influence the firm's decision whether or not to stay in business, or to enter a polluting business in the first place. Thus, even though a subsidy leads to a reduction in pollution by each polluter, just as a tax does, it will tend to increase the number of polluters and correspondingly the total amount of pollution. Over the longer run, when entry and exit are permitted, the allocative effects of a subsidy will not be the same as those of a tax.[30]

There is a qualification to this proposition, but it is not likely to be important in practice. Suppose that the lump-sum payment is not made contingent on whether or not the firm that receives it remains in the "pollution business." That is, the firm will continue to receive the payment even if it goes into another line of activity or shuts down completely. Because this component of profit does not depend on any decision by the firm, the subsidy will not hold the firm in the pollution business.

The reason that this is not likely to be important in practice is that the payment will have to go indefinitely not only to the firm that leaves the pollution business or shuts down but also to the potential polluter. The objective is to keep firms from staying in or entering a polluting activity merely to qualify for the subsidy, and this requires indefinite payments to all in a position to do either.

Let us now look at the second kind of subsidy. Current U.S. environmental policy features direct or indirect payment by the government of a portion of the polluter's control costs. For example, the federal government now pays 75% of the

---

[30] The differing implications of tax and subsidy for firm profits were noted by Bramhall and Mills (1966). For an analysis of long-run effects on resource allocation among industries, see the work of Porter (1974) and Baumol and Oates (1975a).

construction costs for plants to treat municipal waste (water), up from about 50% in previous years. The difficulties with this arrangement are, first, that construction and operation of a plant still constitute a losing proposition for the municipality and, second, that the choice of control technology is biased.[31]

Unless 100% of the cost is paid, construction still entails a loss in revenue. If those who will benefit from the plant are largely in "downstream" jurisdictions, the incentive to build "upstream" is weakened. Further, the incentive to operate the plant efficiently (indeed, to operate it at all) is similarly weakened, because operating costs are borne entirely by the municipality.

The second objection to the subsidy as currently constituted is that it biases the choice of control technology. If capital costs are heavily subsidized and operating costs are not, one will expect overly capital-intensive methods of waste treatment to be popular. The results can be somewhat perverse. Current policy provides a subsidy in the form of tax advantages to industrial polluters for the installation of certain types of control equipment. Recovery and recycling of residuals do not qualify under this heading. Yet, in at least some cases, recycling represents the least-cost method of waste treatment.

### *Uniformity, spatial variation, and the administrative costs of a tax*

One of the advantages of a tax is that it is uniform. Discrimination among polluters is not required to assure either the efficient outcome or the cost-effective outcome. When comparing a tax to direct controls, for example, we found that the same tax imposed on all polluters would lead to a given

---

[31] For a detailed critique of current subsidy policy along these lines, see the work of Kneese and Bower (1968) and Kneese and Schultze (1975). Various issues involving more efficient and more equitable operation of the subsidy program were discussed by Renshaw (1974). He also suggested an argument for a subsidy, namely, that a tax could be regressive in its impact on income distribution.

reduction in the total amount of pollution at the least cost. In other words, the environmental authority need not tailor the tax to each polluter's individual circumstances. With direct controls, on the other hand, quotas will have to be determined based on individual control cost functions. The low administrative cost of a tax, in this respect, is one of its attractive features.

But there is a problem with the uniform-tax solution that casts doubt on the claim of low administrative cost. Consider two sources of pollution, one in an area where the capacity of the environment to disperse or assimilate emissions is high, the other in an area where it is low. Should emissions from each really be taxed at the same rate? Intuitively, it seems that the answer should be no; the tax ought to be higher where emissions contribute more to pollution, in order to discourage polluters from locating there. This is easily shown in the framework of our model of a cost-minimizing tax.

The only assumption in the model that needs to be changed is that emissions from individual sources were added together to produce "pollution." Instead, we shall assume that pollution is a function (not necessarily linear) of individual emissions. That is, whereas we previously defined pollution as aggregate emissions $\Sigma_k s_k$, let us now define it as a function $\phi(s_1, \ldots, s_h)$ of individual emissions. We require only that emissions by each firm contribute positively to pollution, that $\partial \phi / \partial s_k > 0$ for all $k$.

Constraint (6.19) now becomes

$$\phi(s_1, \ldots, s_h) \leq s^* \tag{6.19'}$$

and the necessary condition (6.22) becomes

$$p_v + \lambda \phi_{g^k} g_v^k = 0 \tag{6.22'}$$

The other necessary conditions are not affected, so that the tax on firm $k$, $t_k$, must be set equal to $\lambda \phi_{g^k}$, which obviously is not the same, in general, as the tax on firm $k'$, $t_{k'} = \lambda \phi_{g^{k'}}$. The tax on emissions by each source, in other words, is no longer uniform; instead, it is weighted by the contribution of emissions by that source to pollution.[32]

Does this significantly weaken the case for a tax? Clearly, if there are numerous sources in a region, and something like our $\phi_{g^k}$ term must be assessed for each, the tax loses some of its appeal. A practical solution to the dilemma might be to make a fairly broad cut at discriminating among sources. In the simplest case, for example, just two classes of sources might be defined (those characterized by high assimilative capacity of the receiving medium and those characterized by a low capacity) and a uniform tax set within each. A study of taxes versus direct controls on water pollution in the Delaware estuary (to be discussed in detail in the next section) represents a considerably more ambitious approach, in that it distinguishes between a uniform tax and one that varies by zone, for some 30 different zones. The additional flexibility introduced by this variation does have an impact on control costs, although the major impact is still produced by the move from uniform direct controls (equal percentage reductions) to a uniform tax. In other words, fairly substantial spatial differentiation appears to be computationally feasible and will yield a savings in control costs, but even without this, a tax is superior to direct controls.

Still another instrument, the sale of pollution permits or rights, is sometimes advocated as being superior to a tax on several grounds, including the ability to deal with spatial

---

[32] A result like this was obtained in the more richly detailed analyses of Tietenberg (1973, 1974*a*, 1974*b*) and Hamlen (1978). An important contribution of these analyses, especially Hamlen's, was the modeling of spatial diffusion of emissions. Atkinson and Lewis (1976) considered some issues that arose in the setting of standards and taxes in a theoretical and empirical model of air pollution in the St. Louis area. See the work of Rose-Ackerman (1973) for discussion of a variety of difficulties with a uniform tax. The spatial dimension may have been introduced into formal externalities models by Førsund (1972).

variation. In the remainder of this section we shall consider the relative merits of tax schemes and pollution-rights schemes.

*Tax versus pollution rights: price versus quantity rationing*

In principle, a tax and a rights auction ought to lead to the same result. The tax is set to cut emissions to some desired level, whereas the auction sells rights to produce the same emissions. In either case, polluters have an incentive to pursue controls to the point that the cost reaches the price they would pay for polluting. But a number of economists have suggested that the rights auction might have some advantages in practice.[33]

One advantage, as just indicated, is a superior ability to deal with spatial variation. The idea is that fewer permits will be auctioned in "bad" areas. Alternatively, of course, the tax could be set higher in such areas, but Baumol and Oates (1979) have argued that this sort of discrimination would be politically difficult. Perhaps they were right, but it is not clear to me why, if polluters are going to complain about paying a higher tax price than their competitors in other areas, they will not complain about being offered fewer rights. Note that both the number of permits and the tax could also be manipulated to shift the time distribution of emissions. We said earlier that this would not be practical for short periods, such as those associated with atmospheric inversions. But for longer periods, such as a season, it might well be.

Another alleged advantage of an auction is its superior ability to achieve the desired degree of control. We saw earlier that to achieve this, the environmental authority must know something of the aggregate control cost function. When this

[33] The rights auction was perhaps first and most prominently associated with the work of Dales (1968*a*, 1968*b*). For further discussion of the advantages (and some disadvantages), see the work of Ferrar and Whinston (1972), Tietenberg (1974*c*), and Baumol and Oates (1979).

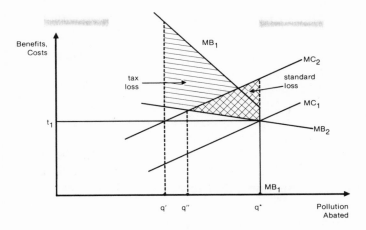

Figure 6.4. Tax and standard compared.

knowledge is lacking, there is a risk that the target will not be achieved, in particular that too much pollution will result. The situation is represented in Figure 6.4. Suppose the target is $q^*$. If the environmental authority believes that marginal control costs are approximately $MC_1$, the appropriate tax is $t_1$. But if marginal control costs are really more like $MC_2$, then only $q' < q^*$ will be achieved. Baumol and Oates suggested that this is one reason that taxes, although persistently recommended by economists, are viewed with skepticism by policy makers. Of course, a tax is not set in concrete. If it does not achieve the desired objective, it can be moved. But there may be a good deal less flexibility *ex post*. The initial tax presumably will lead to investments in control, and once these are in place, the costs of adjustment in response to a change in the tax could be substantial.[34]

Thus the skepticism of policy makers (and some economists)

[34] For a formal analysis of adjustment costs in pollution control, see the work of Harford (1976).

may be well-founded. On the other hand, setting a standard and sticking by it carries a risk of its own. The costs of compliance can reach unacceptable levels. This possibility is also illustrated in Figure 6.4. Suppose, again, that the target is $q^*$, set because the environmental authority believes that marginal control costs are in the neighborhood of $MC_1$. If they are really nearer $MC_2$, achieving the target will entail substantially higher costs, which may imply unacceptable sacrifices of other social objectives.[35]

It appears, then, that both tax and standard carry the risk of large anticipated losses in environmental amenities or other goods and services. The source of the difficulty, along with the control cost uncertainty, is that neither tax nor standard is set with regard to the relationship between costs and benefits. It follows that some knowledge of benefits may be helpful. The question is, What kind of (imperfect) knowledge can in fact be helpful?

Suppose we have reason to believe that marginal damages from the pollution in question rise sharply at some point or, in other words, that marginal benefits from control fall sharply. Then the marginal-benefit curve will look very much like $MB_1$ in Figure 6.4, which becomes inelastic at around $q^*$. In this case the environmental authority ought to auction off rights just sufficient to attain $q^*$, rather than take a chance on a tax that could lead to an inefficiently low level of environmental quality, if control costs have been underestimated. In Figure 6.4, tax $t_1$, based on a cost estimate (underestimate) of $MC_1$, results in large losses, as measured by the area between curves $MB_1$ and $MC_2$ from $q'$ to $q^*$.

Now suppose that the marginal-benefit function is believed to be quite elastic, like $MB_2$ in the figure. Again estimating control costs as $MC_1$, the environmental authority sets a standard $q^*$. If costs are really $MC_2$, losses are once again

[35] This was also recognized by Baumol and Oates (1979) in their discussion of the advantages of a rights auction over a tax.

incurred, measured by the area between curves $MC_2$ and $MB_2$ from $q''$ to $q^*$. This time, however, the losses result not from too much pollution but from too little, in the sense that more is being spent on control than it is worth.

To sum up, when the marginal-control cost curve is uncertain, knowledge of the shape of the marginal-benefit curve can be helpful in choosing between a pollution tax and a standard-and-auction approach to avoid the risk of large losses. An inelastic benefit curve will favor a standard, which it resembles, whereas an elastic curve will favor a tax, which it resembles.[36]

We do not know if it is realistic to expect that an environmental body will have at its disposal even the limited knowledge of benefits called for in this approach. But in view of the potential for loss if it does not, research to determine if (and where) benefit curves exhibit sharp drops (or damage curves exhibit sharp rises) similarly has a potential for a large payoff. Lacking such knowledge, the choice between tax and standard might simply be based on avoiding what appears to the decision maker to be the larger risk. When there is concern that environmental quality reach at least a certain minimal level, for example, the standard-and-auction approach seems indicated. When the concern is more for the possibly excessive costs of reaching a standard, on the other hand, a tax is appropriate.

Thus far, a case has not been made, in my judgment, for the general superiority of a pollution-rights auction as opposed to a tax. Either might be varied for cost-effectiveness, time and political constraints permitting. And uncertainty about control costs can cut in favor of either, depending, as we have just seen, on the nature of benefits. But two considerations from

---

[36] For a more formal derivation of this and other results on the effects of uncertainty on the choice of control instruments, see the work of Adar and Griffin (1976). Formal analyses of control under uncertainty were also provided by Fishelson (1976) and Yohe (1976).

outside the realm of static efficiency analysis do seem to pose special difficulties for a tax.[37]

In a growing economy, tax rates will need to be adjusted frequently to maintain a desired quality of the environment. With a rights market, the price of a right to pollute will rise automatically (i.e., without government intervention). As the demand for rights increases, this should be reflected in a higher price, just as for other scarce resources. A tax can be adjusted to reflect this, but the point is that the rights market will do so automatically.

A closely related argument concerns the effect of inflation on environmental quality under the two regimes. Again, without frequent adjustment of rates, quality will be inadvertently eroded under a tax. However, a permit system will maintain quality while the price of the permit or right simply shares in the general inflationary rise. Thus in a dynamic setting, where growth and inflation may be significant, a rights auction is likely to do a better job of protecting the environment than a tax. Still, we should not overlook entirely the advantage of a tax in holding the line on costs.

### 6.4 Pollution damages and control costs

In order to make effective use of any of the instruments for pollution control that we have just described, we must know something of the damage done by pollution, as well as the costs of control. This section is mainly concerned with methods for assessing damages or, as we should put it where a change for the better is under consideration, the benefits of control. Some attention is also given to the more straightforward problem of assessing the costs of control. Rather than simply presenting a bewildering variety of results from the hundreds of diverse empirical studies, we shall stress some of

---

[37] These considerations were raised by several of the authors who discussed the merits of the rights auction. See footnote 33 for references.

| Economic Activity | Emissions | Ambient Conditions | Damages | Costs |
|---|---|---|---|---|
| level and composition of activity in a region | tons of $SO_2$, raw sewage, etc., emitted at given time and place | ppm of $SO_2$ or of dissolved oxygen, etc., at given time and place | thousands of cases of lung cancer, or of dead fish, etc. | value of reduction in mortality rate, or of fish, etc. |

Figure 6.5. Steps in going from activity to costs.

the more important and interesting theoretical issues that arise in the formulation and interpretation of these studies. A sampling of results will also be presented. The discussion will be specially relevant to air pollution, because the theory and practice of damage estimation have been mainly directed to this. It should be obvious, as we go along, where the discussion applies also to other types of pollution or related disamenities such as noise.

### Damage estimation

To understand how damages are estimated, it is helpful to place them in a large framework. This is done in Figure 6.5. Starting on the left in the figure, the pattern of economic activity in a region leads to a pattern of residuals discharge: so many tons of particulates emitted to the atmosphere, so many gallons of raw or treated sewage dumped into streams, and so on.[38] These waste residuals move through the receiving

---

[38] The connection between the level and composition of economic activity and the pattern of residuals is provided by augmented input-output models. Along with conventional materials flows, these show residuals flows and include a pollution-abatement "sector." The original suggestion for a model of this sort was probably due to Cumberland (1966). An operational version that also took account of materials balance was presented by Cumberland and Korbach (1973). During this period, a somewhat different model that featured a pollution-abatement sector but did

medium, possibly undergoing some physical or chemical transformation in the process, and appear at concentrations varying with the time and distance from the source of the discharge.[39] Ambient concentrations, in turn, produce physical damages: crop loss, increased human mortality, and so on.[40]

Our problem is to evaluate the damages. Obviously, one way to do this is first to determine the physical magnitudes and then impute a value to each. An alternative and somewhat neater way, if it can be done, is to infer values directly from pollutant concentrations. This avoids the risk, in the first method, of failing to capture all of the separate effects. For example, some of the disutility of pollution is clearly aesthetic, but it is difficult to measure aesthetic damage. What are the appropriate units? Alternatively, aesthetic damage may be reflected in property values in polluted and unpolluted areas.

not account for materials balance was developed by Leontief (1970). More complete models that sought to account for materials flows back and forth from the natural environment to the economy were suggested by Isard (1969) and Victor (1972). Victor developed such a model and also provided a detailed review of the literature. More recently, dating from about 1974, an expanded and improved version of the early models, the Strategic Environmental Assessment System (SEAS) model, has been developed and used by the U.S. Environmental Protection Agency. For a detailed (and sometimes critical) discussion of the properties of SEAS and related models, see the work of Holdren, Harte, and Tonnessen (1980).

[39] These processes are described with the aid of physical-diffusion models. For some discussion and use of diffusion models by economists, see the work of Atkinson and Lewis (1974) and Hamlen (1978).

[40] There have been hundreds of studies of the impact of pollutant concentrations, for the most part, naturally enough, by noneconomists. Two useful reviews for economists are those by Freeman (1979*a*) and Hamilton (1979). Much of the discussion in the following text is drawn from these two sources and from a third (Scotchmer, 1979) described in the next footnote. For comprehensive surveys of studies linking air pollution and human health, see the work of Lave and Seskin (1977) and Freeman (1979*b*). A review of evidence linking environmental factors to cancer and suggestions for policies to deal with this problem were provided by Kneese and Schulze (1976).

Other things being equal, we would expect a house in a polluted area to sell for less than one in an unpolluted area, and the difference is just the value of damage, including aesthetic damage.

Actually assessing values is more complicated than this suggests, and ordinarily it will require a combination of methods. The state of the art is currently such that some effects (aesthetic losses, and perhaps materials and some vegetation damage) can be better evaluated by means of a sophisticated version of the comparison of property values just described. Risks to human health, on the other hand, may not be captured in this fashion, at least in part because they are not accurately perceived. A separate evaluation of health damage will be required.

In summary, there are two methods of evaluating damages. The first, a two-step method, determines the physical effects of pollution and then imputes a value to each. The second estimates a relationship directly between ambient concentrations and a measure of value, ordinarily residential property value. We shall consider both.[41]

---

[41] Both methods were discussed by Freeman (1979a). A useful feature of his discussion was treatment of the welfare foundations of damage, or benefit, estimation. Empirical results were also reviewed. A detailed review of both of the steps in the first method was provided by Hamilton (1979). Hamilton's work was part of a study by the Public Interest Economics Foundation for the California Air Resources Board concerning methods of estimating and evaluating pollution damages. Another part of the study provided a review and analysis of the second method (Scotchmer, 1979). See also the collection of studies on the valuation of social cost edited by Pearce (1978); for a discussion of issues in the benefit–cost analysis of water-quality programs, see the studies in Peskin and Seskin (1975). Recently, a group of environmental economists centered at the University of Wyoming, working under contract to the U.S. Environmental Protection Agency (EPA), has mounted a major study of methods of evaluating damages and has come up with new and interesting empirical results as well. In addition to separate papers by members of the group, which will be referenced where appropriate, see the reports to the EPA by Crocker et al. (1979) and Brookshire et al. (1979).

*Measurement of damages, imputation of values:*
*impacts on vegetation and materials*

In principle, valuation of impacts on commercial plant and animal species seems straightforward. The observed loss in units of biomass is simply multiplied by the price per unit to obtain a measure of value. Something like this has been done in many studies of local impacts of particular pollutants, and the results may be reasonably accurate. However, there are pitfalls even here, as revealed by economic and econometric theory.

In the first place, how is the loss observed? Two methods are available: statistical field study, in which actual crop yields, for example, are statistically related to a variety of influences, including differences in pollutant concentrations; controlled dose–response experiments, in which the effect of a substance on a laboratory specimen is studied. An obvious difficulty with the statistical approach is the presence of other factors that influence yield. If one or more of these are also related to pollution, the estimated relationship between pollution and yield will exhibit either bias (if the other influences are left out of the regression equation) or multicollinearity. It is also difficult to disentangle the effects of different types of pollution, some of which tend to appear in concert and may act synergistically.

Another pitfall in interpreting the statistical results is revealed by our theoretical analysis of the general-equilibrium adjustments to pollution. For example, rather than suffer heavy crop damage, a farmer might plant a crop strain that is less valuable but more pollution-resistant, and in so doing limit his damage. The real loss from pollution in this case is the reduction in new-crop yield plus the difference in value between the old crop and the new crop, but only the former will tend to be captured in the statistical analysis.[42]

[42] This problem was discussed further by Hamilton (1979), with

Fortunately, in the case of environmental impacts that do not involve humans, such potentially incomplete or biased results can be supplemented by laboratory experiment. Thus damage to the original crop can be studied in a controlled environment. But note that this will tend to produce an overestimate of the loss from pollution, because possibilities for defensive adjustments are ignored.

Whether biomass and materials losses are estimated from statistical field studies or from dose–response experiments or, perhaps best of all, from a mixture of both, the problem of imputing values remains. Although market price is the obvious measure, at least a couple of rather subtle pitfalls must be avoided. One is the effect of a pollution-induced quantity change on price. If the quantity change is substantial and the demand is inelastic, market price can be affected. Further, in a general-equilibrium system, other prices will in turn be affected – for commodities related in consumption, and for factors of production. This is a potentially troublesome issue, because the price changes imply in each case changes in consumers' or producers' surpluses. Clearly the researcher must hope that price effects can be safely ignored, and some evidence suggests they can.[43]

A different problem is presented by effects of pollution other than simple reductions in yield. There is substantial evidence that the quality of crops is also changed, generally for

references to studies of actual crop shifts in response to pollution. In principle, a way to overcome the problem is to take the property-value capitalization approach. As will be discussed later, virtually all such studies have concerned residential property values. I am aware of one study of the effect of pollution on the price of agricultural land (Crocker, 1971). One special disadvantage of this approach in the agricultural setting is the possible correlation between air pollution (which presumably depresses values) and encroaching urban development (which presumably raises values).

[43] It has been estimated that crop damage from air pollution in California, although alarming in some absolute sense, represents less than 1% of the total value of California crops and less than 0.25% of the total value of U.S. crops (Millecan, 1976).

the worse, and that vegetation is made more susceptible to damage by insects and disease. The compounding effect probably cannot be ignored. One study estimated the annual value of damage to vegetation from air pollution in the United States at $134 million, but another suggested that taking the indirect damages into account would put the figure at over $1 billion.[44]

Thus it appears that even the relatively straightforward task of valuing the nonhuman impacts of pollution must be approached with a great deal of care. In saying this, we certainly do not wish to give the impression that the results obtained to date are not significant. On the contrary, the hundreds of statistical and experimental studies have clearly documented large and costly impacts on vegetation, on (commercial) marine life, on materials, and so on. But challenging theoretical issues must be faced in refining and interpreting the results. My impression is that actual damages probably are substantially greater than even the studies suggest, for two reasons. First, they have tended to be based on postadjustment high-pollution equilibria, where some of the damage is invisible. Second, many of the effects of pollution, including synergistic effects such as lowering the resistance of vegetation to pest attack, are not yet well understood.

### Evaluating impacts on human health

Lack of knowledge is a problem especially for a class of effects we have not yet discussed – effects on human health. Measurement and evaluation here run into all of the difficulties already noted, and then some. For example, one reason it is difficult to estimate the effects of pollution on human health is that controlled experiments cannot be carried out in the same way they can on plants or mice. The researcher must rely almost exclusively on statistical analyses of public health data.

[44] Studies describing effects on various quality characteristics were discussed by Hamilton (1979). The estimate of $134 million was by the Stanford Research Institute (1973), and that of over $1 billion was by Heck and Brandt (1977).

There has been a great deal of work in this area, probably the best-known (to economists, at least) being the careful and comprehensive statistical analyses of the relationship between air pollution and human health by Lave and Seskin (1977). The results are not free of controversy, but I think it is fair to say that Lave and Seskin and others have demonstrated that there is a relationship between either or both of the main stationary-source pollutants, sulfates and particulates, and human health.[45]

But the most difficult aspect of evaluating the damage done by pollution may well be imputing a value to effects on human health. For impacts on commercial plant and animal species, and on materials, market prices can serve as measures of value, subject to the qualifications noted. When it comes to evaluating changes in human mortality rates, however, the researcher is confronted with the lack of a measure of value, a willingness to pay analogous to the price for a bushel of wheat or a pound of shrimp. Several indirect methods for valuing lives have been suggested, but none, in my judgment, is entirely satisfactory.

At the outset it ought to be clear that we are talking about statistical life, as opposed to the life of a given individual. Obviously, I would be willing to pay (if I had it) an infinite amount to prevent my certain loss of life tomorrow. And there is considerable evidence that society is similarly willing to go to enormous expense to save or prolong the life of a given individual. But this is not germane to the evaluation of pollution damages. What is to be evaluated in this case is not the certain loss of life of a given individual but rather a

---

[45] The first in a series of publications by Lave and Seskin was a 1970 *Science* article. Their 1977 book provided a much more comprehensive analysis and discussion of results. For a critical review of statistical studies of the relationship between air pollution and human health, see the work of Freeman (1979*b*). Recent studies have appeared to cast doubt on the Lave and Seskin results, although none has claimed that there is no association between pollution and health. The Wyoming group, for example, found a weak relationship between pollution and mortality, but a much stronger one between pollution and morbidity.

relatively modest increase in the probability of loss of life for each individual member of a larger population at risk: in short, statistical life. It is clear that individuals and governments routinely make choices that involve trading off money, time, or other goods for small changes in the probability of loss of life. The methods we shall discuss seek in one way or another to infer, from these trade-offs, the value of statistical life.

A commonly suggested source of information about this value is the expenditure on public programs to save lives. From data on expenditures and lives saved it is possible to calculate the expenditure per life saved, which might be assumed to be the value attached by society to a statistical life. There are problems, however. Most important, the procedure is circular. The relevant value, instead of being determined by analytical methods and then given to the political process to use as it chooses in assessing and deciding on programs, is itself extracted from the political process. Thus one is simply looking at the outcomes of past program decisions and feeding them back into current assessment. Not surprisingly, because the decisions generally have not reflected any sort of optimization, a very wide range of values (expenditures per life saved) has been observed, spanning three orders of magnitude (Table 6.1).[46] On the other hand, when public agencies adopt an explicit benefit–cost framework for making these decisions, the values are just those calculated by other methods. In this case the political process provides no independent information.[47]

Perhaps the most common approach, and the one taken by Lave and Seskin in valuing their estimated health effects, is the human-capital approach. The idea is that the death of an

---

[46] For example, Bailey (1978) inferred values ranging from $1.9 million to $625 million for a statistical life on the basis of standards promulgated by the U.S. Occupational Safety and Health Administration.

[47] For example, the U.S. Federal Highway Administration and the National Highway Traffic Safety Administration both use a figure of about $250,000 (Hapgood, 1979) derived from explicit risk–benefit analyses.

Table 6.1. *Estimates from assorted sources of the value of saving a statistical life and averting associated illness and disability*

| Source of evidence | Estimated value (1,000s of $) | Reference |
|---|---|---|
| *Human capital* | | |
| Discounted future earnings plus total medical costs | 89 | Cooper and Rice (1976) |
| *Surveys* | | |
| Willingness to pay for emergency coronary care | 28–43 | Acton (1973) |
| Willingness to pay for flight on airline with better safety record | 5,000 | Jones-Lee (1976) |
| *Political process* | | |
| Office of Science and Technology | 140 | OST (1972) |
| National Academy of Sciences | 200 | NAS (1974*b*) |
| Federal Highway Administration | 250 | Hapgood (1979) |
| National Highway Traffic Safety Administration | 287 | Hapgood (1979) |
| U.S. Air Force | 270–4,500 | Usher (1973) |
| Occupational Safety and Health Administration | 1,900–625,000 | Bailey (1978) |
| Consumer Product Safety Commission | 240–1,920 | Bailey (1978) |
| *Labor Market* | | |
| Extra wages of workers in risky occupations | 136–260 | Thaler and Rosen (1976) |
| Extra wages of workers in risky industries | 1,500–5,000 | R. S. Smith (1974, 1976) |
| Extra wages of underground miners | 68–318 | Usher (1973) |
| Hazard pay for pilots | 161 | Usher (1973) |
| Hazard pay for pilots | 1,800–2,700 | Viscusi 1976) |
| *Other evidence* | | |
| Seat belts and time preference | 160–551 | Blomquist (1977) |

*Source:* Hamilton (1979).

individual causes losses to society in the form of both medical costs and forgone future contributions to the national product, the latter measured by the individual's wage or salary. One difficulty with this approach is its failure to capture any disutility of illness or death apart from that associated with losing income. The failure is particularly serious when the affected individual is not in the labor force.

A more basic difficulty is that forgone earnings do not provide information about what an individual would be willing to pay to obtain a given reduction in the probability of loss of life, which is, after all, what we are interested in. For example, suppose I am offered a safer widget, one that will reduce the probability of my suffering a fatal accident during its use from 0.01 to 0.0001 (in other words, by a factor of 100). The human-capital approach implies that I would be willing to pay 1% of the present value of my future earnings for this opportunity. Yet I might be willing to pay a good deal more than this.[48] The human-capital approach is conservative, likely to underestimate the value of statistical life. It may be useful, as a lower bound, when no better information is available.

If willingness to pay is the measure of value, why can't we simply ask people what they would be willing to pay for a product or program carrying a specified reduction in probability of loss of life? There have been three or four such surveys that I am aware of, and their results have varied widely (Table 6.1). There are, in addition, the usual reasons for concern about the accuracy of responses to hypothetical questions and distortions due to strategic behavior by the respondents.

The final approach we shall consider also focuses, correctly, on willingness to pay, but on the basis of observed behavior, generally in the labor market. People routinely make choices about jobs carrying different degrees of risk. This approach seeks to infer the value attached to an increment of risk of loss

---

[48] This conjecture was proved by Conley (1976), who showed that willingness to pay would necessarily exceed the present value of earnings.

of life from the resulting pattern of wage differences. The method used is statistical regression analysis of wages on a variety of influences, such as age, education, region, and, of course, degree of risk. The estimated risk coefficient then gives a measure of the extra compensation required for the individual to bear extra risk, or his willingness to pay for reduced risk.[49]

In principle, this is an appropriate method for valuing impacts on health, because it seeks the right value (willingness to pay for a reduction in risk) and does so on the basis of observed behavior. In practice, there are a number of difficulties. To begin with, much of the modern theory of the labor market calls into question the assumptions of perfect mobility and perfect competition required for observed wage differences to faithfully reflect attitudes toward risk. If mobility, for example, is restricted, wages will not be bid up to attract or hold workers to a risky job.

Second, the attitudes reflected may be the wrong attitudes for purposes of evaluating the effects of pollution on health. People who take risky jobs do require compensation for bearing the extra risk, but probably less than people affected by pollution would require for bearing the same risk from the pollution. The risk in a risky job often is quite exciting, whereas there is nothing exciting about sickening and dying from air pollution. Again, observed wage differences will underestimate willingness to pay for a reduction in risk from pollution.

Finally, the method assumes that workers correctly perceive risks. For example, in regard to the risk of development of cancer from prolonged exposure to certain industrial materials whose dangers are only now coming to light, it is not likely that

[49] Probably the best-known work here is that of Thaler and Rosen (1976), who provided a theoretical and empirical analysis of interoccupational wage differences, especially as related to risk differences. However, there have been many other studies as well. For references, see the work of Hamilton (1979) and Table 6.1.

the risk has been accurately perceived by the workers. For this reason, too, wage differentials will underestimate the value of statistical life. Misperception of risk can, of course, cut in either direction; workers may be unduly concerned about the risk of exposure to a substance from which, in fact, they are effectively shielded or a substance that turns out to be relatively harmless.

In raising these questions about the labor-market approach, I do not wish to deny its potential usefulness. Again, I believe that, in principle, it is appropriate. But it must be used with care and with an eye on the qualifications suggested by labor-market theory. For example, wage–risk differences within occupations probably will be superior to differences between occupations, because they are less likely to be impaired by restrictions on mobility.[50]

### A brief look at empirical results

Some estimates of the value of statistical life from one or another kind of labor-market evidence are presented in Table 6.1, along with the human-capital estimates and government-expenditure estimates. Note also an estimate based, correctly, on observed willingness to pay for reduced risk in a different situation. In Table 6.2, a few estimates of the values of pollution damages are presented.

A number of tentative conclusions can be drawn from the results reported in these tables. With respect to the value of statistical life (Table 6.1), the human-capital value does indeed generally fall below the value estimated from labor-market behavior and other observed behavior. One will therefore certainly not be guilty of overvaluing life in employing the human-capital figure. Further, because even the labor-market figures tend to be biased downward, they probably are preferable, as furnishing a tighter bound on the true value. A

---

[50] A study by Usher (1973) looked at intraoccupational differences for miners. His estimates were in the same range as those of Thaler and Rosen (Table 6.1).

Table 6.2. *Selected estimates of U.S. air- and water-pollution damages*

| Type of damage | Value (annual) | Source |
|---|---|---|
| Stationary-source air pollution | $10.8 billion ($4.3 billion health, $1.1 billion materials, $5.4 billion aesthetics and soiling) | Waddell (1974), for Environmental Protection Agency |
| Automotive air pollution | $5 billion | National Academy of Sciences (1974b) |
| Air pollution: health benefits of 58% abatement of particulates, 88% abatement of sulfates, consistent with 1979 compliance with 1970 Clean Air Act amendments | $16.1 billion (1973 dollars) | Lave and Seskin (1977) |
| Air-pollution damage to vegetation | $2.9 billion | Heintz, Hershaft, and Horak (1976), for Environmental Protection Agency |

| | | |
|---|---|---|
| Water pollution (U.S.): benefits of Clean Water Act amendments of 1972 | $5.5 billion by 1985 | National Commission on Water Quality (1976) |
| Water pollution | $10.1 billion (60% due to loss of recreation opportunities, 17% due to production losses) | Heintz, Hershaft, and Horak (1976), for Environmental Protection Agency |
| Air pollution: benefits from reduction in pollution since 1970 (to 1978), approximately 20% improvement in air quality | $21.4 billion | Freeman (1979b), for Council on Environmental Quality |
| Water pollution: benefits to be realized by 1985, when "best available technology" for controlling discharges is assumed to be in place; point sources only | $12.3 billion | Freeman (1979b) |

commonly suggested central tendency for the labor-market
value is in the neighborhood of $300,000 in 1979 dollars.

The results in Table 6.2 are sketchy. The health damages
appear to be a good deal larger than those to vegetation or
structures. This is true even though they are underestimates,
based on the human-capital valuation. Note also that adjustments for inflation will raise all of the figures somewhat.

An interesting question, in view of the motivation for this
whole discussion, is whether or not the calculated values tell us
anything about pollution-control policies. Specifically, we
might ask if suggested ambient standards for particular pollutants are justified on efficiency grounds. To answer this, we
must know something of the costs of attaining the standards.
In one case, at least, that of air pollution from sulfates and
particulates, there may be sufficient information about both
costs and benefits. Lave and Seskin used EPA estimates of the
costs and came up with a total in the neighborhood of $9.5
billion in 1973 dollars. This is compared with their estimate of
$16.1 billion in benefits, again in 1973 dollars, from the same
standards. Thus the standards are justified in a rough way,
especially if we bear in mind that only health benefits have
been included, and probably conservatively. Further calculations will be required to determine "optimal" standards, those
that will result in marginal benefits just equal to marginal
costs.

*Direct estimation of values: pollution and
property values*

An alternative to the two-step piecemeal approach to
estimating values is to estimate them directly as a function of
differences in ambient concentrations. As noted earlier, this is
normally done by relating differences in land or property
values to differences in air-pollution levels. Well over a dozen
studies of this type have been carried out over the last decade.[51]

[51] The pioneering work here, to my knowledge, is due to Ridker
(1967) and Ridker and Henning (1967). For references to the

The results are difficult to characterize with precision, because different measures of the key variables (pollution and property values) were used, and the data were drawn from different times and places.[52] But it is probably fair to say that at least the existence of a relationship between air pollution and residential property values has been demonstrated.[53]

One of the potentially attractive features of this approach is that, in principle, it captures all of the separate effects of pollution (experienced around the place of residence), effects on aesthetics, on health, on materials, and so on. However, as noted earlier, it seems doubtful that health effects are reflected in residential property values, because they probably have not been accurately perceived.

Another difficulty that this approach shares with all of the examples of statistical estimation we have discussed is the presence of other variables that may bias the estimate. Clearly, land values are affected by a variety of factors aside from pollution. And we cannot look to experimental data to disentangle all the effects of pollution, as we can, for example, when attempting to infer its effect on crop yields.

But there is a positive side to the story that deserves further

many studies undertaken since, and brief descriptions, see the work of Freeman (1979a). For an application to noise consistent with the theory described in the following text, see the work of Nelson (1978), and for a review of studies of the relationship between noise and property values and an application to airport siting in the London area, see the work of Walters (1975). An estimate of the relationship between lakeshore property values and lake water quality was made by David (1968). Freeman (1979a) suggested an adaptation to water quality for the theory originally developed to evaluate differences in air quality.

[52] A concise guided tour of data, methods, and results for each study was provided by Freeman (1979a).

[53] Two of the early theoretical analyses of the relationship between pollution and property values, by Strotz (1968) and Lind (1973), focused on land as a productive input, rather than a residential site. Other theoretical analyses, including those of Freeman (1974, 1979a), Polinsky and Shavell (1975, 1976), Polinsky and Rubinfeld (1977), and Harrison and Rubinfeld (1978a, 1978b), considered residential property values, as did most of the empirical studies.

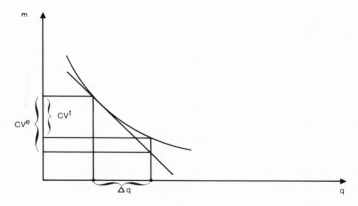

Figure 6.6. Compensating-variation measure of the value of an environmental improvement.

discussion, because it is both important and special to the property-value method. It is my impression that researchers originally believed that in order to estimate the benefits from a reduction in pollution, the change in property values that would result from the reduction would have to be predicted. Clearly, this raises the question of how to account for general-equilibrium adjustments to property values everywhere in the system. Even assuming that no prices are affected outside the area experiencing the reduction, as could be the case if the area is sufficiently small, the supply of low-pollution sites will be increased and the price of such sites presumably decreased. And if outside prices are affected, demand for the improved sites will also shift, influencing price in an undetermined direction.

Fortunately, it can be shown that prediction of a new set of property values (even for the directly affected sites) is not required to estimate benefits.[54] There is sufficient information in the existing property-value–pollution relationship to infer a

---

[54] The discussion that follows is based on the theoretical analyses of Scotchmer (1979) and Freeman (1979a).

correct compensating-variation measure of the benefits of an improvement. We shall show this by proceeding indirectly, via the relationship between income and a reduction in pollution, or an improvement in environmental quality.

Figure 6.6 shows a consumer's indifference curve for a numeraire, income net of land rent (where rent is the amount paid per period for the site, a flow measure related to the site's capital value by an appropriate discount factor), and environmental quality. The numeraire represents an aggregate private good. For a marginal change in quality, $dq$, the compensating variation is the change in net income, $dm$ in Figure 6.6, that will keep the consumer on the same indifference curve. For a sufficiently small change, this is approximated by the slope of the tangent to the curve at the appropriate point.

There is a qualification, easily demonstrated in the figure. Suppose we are considering a nonmarginal change, say $\Delta q$. The true compensating variation, read from the indifference curve, is $CV^t$. But if the compensating variation is computed from a point estimate of the income–quality relationship, such as the slope of the tangent line, an overestimate, $CV^e$ in the figure, will result. Thus, for a nonmarginal improvement, a technique such as the one we are about to discuss, based on a point estimate, will yield an upper bound to the value of the improvement.[55] Conversely, the value of a nonmarginal deterioration in quality, the amount of the numeraire that will be required in compensation, will be underestimated.

Now let us redefine the indifference curve in Figure 6.6 in terms of land rent $R$, instead of the numeraire $m = Y - R$ (where $Y$ is income). The new curve is a mirror image of the old one, as indicated in Figure 6.7. Next, we draw in an opportunity locus for the individual that describes the relationship between land rent and environmental quality, keeping constant the other site characteristics that might influence rent. This relationship between the price of a site and its

---

[55] For an estimate of the magnitude of the bias, see the work of Harrison and Rubinfeld (1978$b$).

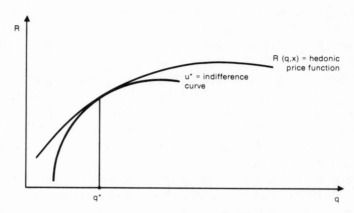

Figure 6.7 Hedonic price-function equilibrium.

characteristics is often called a hedonic price function. Although we will normally expect the partial relationship between rent and quality to be positive, as indicated in Figure 6.7, a noncorner solution requires only that the indifference curves be more sharply curved than the rent–quality locus.

Where is the equilibrium? Clearly, at the point of tangency, where quality is $q^*$. Any other point on the opportunity locus yields inferior utility. And points on indifference curves to the right of the one shown, though preferable, are unattainable.

The value of a change in quality (around $q^*$) is then given by the slope of the tangent line at $q^*$, which is just the value of the derivative of the opportunity locus, or hedonic price function, at $q^*$. The value of a change that affects several sites (as any conceivable change in the public good, environmental quality, will) is the sum of the individual-site values.

An important qualification, or perhaps we should call it an assumption needed for the procedure to yield sensible results, is that the area experiencing the change be "open" (i.e., that there be no restrictions on mobility). Suppose that pollution is decreased in an area. This represents a consumer surplus benefit to residents, but the benefit will not be capitalized into property values unless there is some mechanism to transfer the surplus from residents to property owners. Competition from potential in-migrants for the improved sites will normally do this. However, when there are barriers to entry (and note that even significant costs of migration will fall into this category), some part of the surplus may not be captured in property values. In this case the estimated pollution–property-value relationship will be biased downward. Note that we are not talking here about whether or not property values will actually adjust in an area in which an environmental program is being contemplated. We have already shown that this is irrelevant to an assessment of benefits, although it is related to the question of how the benefits are distributed. Rather, the point is that the (prior) statistical estimate of the pollution–property-value relationship must ideally reflect a full adjustment of property values.

There is another potential source of (downward) bias of considerable theoretical interest. Thus far we (along with most researchers who have studied the relationship between pollution and property values) have ignored the role of wage differences. This is not unreasonable. Within a single urban labor market, the type of area that has been studied, differences in pollution levels cannot be reflected in differences in wage compensation. Subject to the qualifications noted, only rent provides a site-specific measure of value related to pollution. On the other hand, it seems plausible that individuals might be attracted to a polluted area in a different labor market by higher wages there.[56]

The question is whether the compensation required to hold an individual at a polluted site comes in the form of lower rents or higher wages or both. There have been a few empirical studies of the relationship between wages and environmental

---

[56] The persistence of wage differences seems inconsistent with the theorem of factor price equalization. But as Freeman (1979a) and Scotchmer (1979) showed, the conditions for the theorem to hold probably are not met in this situation.

quality across urban areas, but they have not really addressed this question, any more than have the more numerous studies of the relationship between property values and quality within urban areas. Recent theoretical analyses have suggested that differences in both rents and wages will contribute to the required compensation, over a broad range of conditions.[57]

Clearly, the econometric problems involved in an attempt to disentangle and identify both components of value would be formidable. This is probably one reason that no such study exists, to my knowledge.[58] Yet, to the extent that wage differences are relevant, the value of a change in quality will be underestimated by an approach that takes into account only differences in intraurban rents or property values. Still a further source of downward bias, even if wage differences are appropriately counted, is the existence of cost or other barriers to labor mobility, exactly as in the property-value estimation.

We have exposed a number of pitfalls (sources of bias that have nothing to do with econometric or data problems) in using comparative property values to infer environmental values.[59] But let me reaffirm the usefulness of this approach. It

---

[57] See the work of Freeman (1979*a*) and Scotchmer (1979). For estimates of the relationship between urban amenities or disamenities and wage rates, see the work of Hoch (1972), Nordhaus and Tobin (1973), Tolley (1974), Meyer and Leone (1977), and Cropper (1979).

[58] For a discussion of how a study might be set up, the kinds of data needed, and the econometric considerations, see the work of Scotchmer (1979).

[59] A potential source of bias of an indeterminate nature that involves both theory (under what conditions surplus will be capitalized in property values) and econometric procedure is housing-market segmentation. That is, if an urban housing market is really a set of separate markets, with barriers to mobility between them, separate hedonic price functions will have to be estimated. This issue was first raised by Straszheim (1974) and was discussed by Freeman (1979*a*). A study by Harrison and Rubinfeld (1978*a*) suggested substantial variation in estimated benefits from an air-quality improvement in the Boston area, depending on how the market is stratified. On the other hand, Nelson (1978) found no significant difference between urban and suburban hedonic price functions in the Washington, D.C., area.

is rooted in economic theory. It depends on observed behavior. And each of the difficulties we have identified can be characterized as leading unambiguously to an underestimate or overestimate of the environmental value at stake. Where a deterioration in quality is concerned, an estimated relationship between quality and property values can be interpreted unambiguously as a lower bound, subject to the identification of still other, conflicting, sources of bias. Where an improvement is concerned, if it is nonmarginal, the direction of bias is theoretically indeterminate, although all but one of the identified sources will lead to an underestimate of the value. In an actual case, the researcher might well have sufficient feel for the data to at least determine the direction of bias.[60]

If one is nevertheless unsatisfied with this and all of the other approaches considered thus far, there remains the possibility of simply asking people what an improvement in quality would be worth to them. The difficulties with surveys here are the same as noted in connection with surveys designed to elicit information about the value of life. First, people may not know how to respond to a hypothetical question. Second, they will ordinarily have an incentive to behave strategically, to not reveal the "truth," even if they know what it is. Still, given the difficulties with the alternative approaches, the use of surveys ought not to be rejected out of hand. A number of bidding games designed to elicit honest responses to questions about the worth of environmental improvements have been developed and applied, with results that appear reasonable and consistent (with each other and with those of alternative schemes).[61]

---

[60] One other pitfall here that is not really behavioral (rather, it has to do with the form in which the data are likely to come, as suggested by Niskanen and Hanke, 1977) is the existence of income and (especially) property taxes. See also the work of Freeman (1979*a*) for a detailed discussion and some estimates of the size and direction of bias in studies that ignore tax effects.

[61] Both Freeman (1979*a*) and Scotchmer (1979) provided discussions, with references, of survey approaches to public-good valuation generally. An illuminating discussion of the new "demand-revealing" processes can be found in a companion volume in the

Before moving on to discuss the estimation of control costs, I should acknowledge that the discussion of benefits has neglected the question of how they are distributed. Because environmental policy decisions will surely be affected by this, it is clear that empirical studies ought to try to develop information about the distribution, as well as the magnitude, of expected benefits and costs. Several studies have done this, especially for air-pollution controls.[62]

## *Estimation of control costs*

Control costs are those entailed by changing in some respect the pattern of economic activity that gives rise to pollution. For example, a polluting firm might invest in waste-treatment facilities, relocate, or change its product mix – or pursue some combination of these and other measures. Whatever it does, the consequences will show up on the firm's balance sheet, in dollars and cents. As such, they are much easier to grasp, and certainly to evaluate, than the benefits of control. This is probably one reason that some environmental

Cambridge University Press series by Mueller (1979). Studies specifically directed to valuing pollution abatement are those of Randall, Ives, and Eastman (1974), Brookshire, Ives, and Schulze (1976), and Rowe, d'Arge, and Brookshire (1980).

[62] An early empirical study of some aspects of the distribution of air- and water-pollution damages in the United States was that of Freeman (1972). More recent studies include the following: Zupan (1973), for air quality in the New York area; Harrison (1975), for costs of air-pollution control; Dorfman and Snow (1975), for costs of pollution control generally; Dorfman (1976), for benefits and costs of environmental programs; Spofford, Russell, and Kelly (1976), for benefits and costs of controlling air and water pollution in the Delaware estuary; Freeman (1977), for costs of controlling automotive air pollution; Gianessi, Peskin, and Wolff (1977), for air-pollution policy in the United States; Peskin (1978), for the U.S. Clean Air Act amendments of 1970; Harrison and Rubinfeld (1978a), for benefits from automobile emission controls in the Boston area.

Distributional considerations were introduced into models of representative or legislative environmental decision making by Haefele (1973) and Dorfman and Jacoby (1973). For a review and further analysis, see the work of Portney, Sonstelie, and Kneese (1974) and Kneese and Bower (1979).

economists prefer to focus on the control costs associated with the alternatives (taxes, subsidies, etc.) for achieving a reduction in pollution specified without regard to benefits.

In order to determine these costs, it helps to have a theory or model of the way a polluter will respond to, say, a tax. We outlined such a theory in earlier sections of this chapter, but for the purpose of drawing some qualitative conclusion (about the optimal tax, about the cost of reduction under a tax as opposed to other policy instruments, and so on). Here we are interested more in the detailed modeling of adjustments.

Such modeling has been done, especially for water pollution. One approach is extension of the neoclassical (smooth-isoquant) model of the firm to include decisions about how, and how much, to reduce pollution in response to a charge or other control. Within this framework, pollution has been considered both as an input to production, along the lines of our optimal tax model in Section 6.2, and as a by-product amenable to treatment, somewhat along the lines of our cost-effective tax model in Section 6.3.[63] Another approach is a still more detailed engineering-economic analysis of discrete process options, at the plant level, for responding to a control. In the more recent applications, a formal optimizing procedure, linear programming, often has been used to select the options and their levels.[64]

[63] For an example of the former, see the work of Sims (1979); for the latter, see the work of Etheridge (1973).

[64] Early RFF studies of industrial water use, such as the one by Löf and Kneese (1968) for the beet sugar industry, exemplified the first relatively informal phase of this line of research. Later RFF studies expanded the scope of the analysis to take account of all residuals, not just waterborne ones. In this category are studies of petroleum refining (Russell, 1971, 1973), steel production (Russell and Vaughan, 1974, 1976), pulp and paper (Bower, Löf, and Hearon, 1971), and steel-scrap recycling (Sawyer, 1974).

The linear-programming approach of the Russell studies was further developed in independent work by Thompson and associates (Thompson and Young, 1973; Calloway, Schwartz, and Thompson, 1974; Singleton, Calloway, and Thompson, 1975; Calloway and Thompson, 1976). The Calloway and Thompson study (1976) is noteworthy in that it considered several related

Whatever the underlying model, the key question is, How can the costs be estimated in an actual case? Here the engineering-economic process model has an advantage, in that it is already in a computational format. The effect on a cost or profit function of a tax or other constraint on pollution is readily determined in a linear program. However, for such an abstract representation of a production process to yield usable results, a great deal of very detailed technical information is required. The difficulty in acquiring this information may be compounded by the fact that some of it will be proprietary.

An alternative way of proceeding in these circumstances (indicated, in any case, to give empirical content to the neoclassical model) is by means of statistical regression analysis of industry data. The idea is to estimate changes in inputs, outputs, and costs of production in response to the specified control.[65] Much of the interesting detail of the process model is lost, of course, but it may not have been available to begin with, and the econometric model may do reasonably well in tracing the movements of broad aggregates. Indeed, econometric models have been used to predict the effects of environ-

industries in a region (the Texas gulf coast): petroleum refining, electric power production, and chemicals. Finally, an explicitly regional approach, focusing on all residuals in a geographic area, was taken in the RFF studies of the Delaware estuary by Russell and Spofford (1972), Spofford, Russell, and Kelly (1976), and Russell and Spofford (1977).

Much of this work was reviewed in a recent volume by Kneese and Bower (1979). For a further review of studies of industrial water-pollution control in the RFF tradition, see the work of Hanke and Gutmanis (1975). The linear-programming approach was applied to air pollution in a series of papers by Kohn (1971a, 1971b, 1972, 1975). In seeking to minimize the cost of achieving ambient air-quality standards in St. Louis, Kohn assumed that the annual mean concentration of a pollutant was a constant times annual emissions. Using a more sophisticated diffusion model, Atkinson and Lewis (1974) found that abatement costs could be reduced substantially below Kohn's figures by allowing emissions to vary by time and place.

[65] For such studies of a tax on the sulfur content of fuels in the electric power industry, see the work of Griffin (1974a, 1974b) and Chapman (1974). For an application to an effluent charge in the Canadian brewing industry, see the work of Sims (1979).

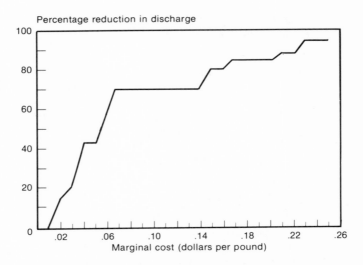

Figure 6.8 Marginal costs of BOD discharge reductions in petroleum refining. (From Russell, 1973, p. 143.)

mental policies on the broadest aggregates: GNP, the price level, unemployment, and so on.[66]

Several results stand out from the many and varied studies. First, there is in most cases considerable scope for reducing pollution, and by a variety of methods in addition to end-of-pipe treatment of wastes.[67] Second, however, beyond some point the marginal cost of control rises steeply. Fortunately, this generally occurs at high levels of control. For example, as shown in Figure 6.8, the marginal cost of BOD discharge reduction in petroleum refining begins to rise steeply only after a 70% reduction has already been achieved.

A third finding is that a given reduction in aggregate discharges (or improvement in environmental quality) in a

---

[66] See the report from Data Resources, Inc. (DRI) (1979), and for a review and discussion of some earlier studies, see the work of Haveman and Smith (1978).

[67] See the work of Kneese and Bower (1979). The range of choices in water-pollution control was emphasized in an early RFF study by Davis (1968).

Table 6.3 *Costs of water-pollution abatement under taxes and direct controls, Delaware estuary*[a]

| Dissolved oxygen (ppm) | Program | | |
| --- | --- | --- | --- |
| | Uniform treatment controls | Uniform tax | Zone tax |
| 2 | 5.0 | 2.4 | 2.4 |
| 3–4 | 20.0 | 12.0 | 8.6 |

[a]Costs in millions of dollars per year.
*Source:* Kneese (1977).

region can be brought about more cheaply by a tax on the discharges than by uniform direct controls on them. This is shown in Table 6.3 for water pollution in the Delaware estuary. For example, to achieve a 3–4-ppm level of dissolved oxygen in the water, the cost will be $20 million annually, under uniform treatment controls (each source reducing discharges by the same percentage). A uniform tax on discharges will accomplish the same result, but at a cost of just $12 million. Finally, a tax that is varied by zone, over 30 zones along the river, will produce the cleanup at a cost of $8.6 million. All of this is quite consistent with our theoretical discussion of the cost-effectiveness of a tax.

A final interesting empirical result is that the macroeconomic effects of current U.S. environmental policies (and also those of at least a couple of other countries for which studies have been done) are likely to be relatively modest. That is, the studies do not lend support to either of two extreme positions that have been advanced in the political debate about environmental policies: (a) that current policies will lead to sizable reductions in output, or rises in prices, as opponents claim, (b) that they will greatly stimulate employment, as proponents claim. A study done for the Environmental Protection Agency and the Council on Environmental Quality suggested that over the period 1970–86, federal environmental legislation of the 1970s has had, or will have, the following effects.[68] First, inflation will be stimulated, but only slightly. Prices will be less than 4% higher at the end of the period than they would have been without the legislation. Second, the level of economic activity, as measured by real GNP, will first be stimulated by the extra investment in pollution-control and related industries, but ultimately (by 1981) will fall below the "without" case, as a consequence of the reduced productivity and higher inflation. The gain, in the early 1970s, was about 0.9%, and the shortfall, by 1986, is projected also at 0.9%. Again, both impacts will be modest. Finally, unemployment rates will be consistently lower over the period, reflecting the jobs created in the early years in manufacturing and installing control equipment and in later years in operating and maintaining it. Once again, the impact will be modest – a reduction in unemployment rates of around 0.2 percentage point.

## 6.5 Concluding remarks

Although pollution is not the only environmental problem, it is clearly the one people tend to focus on when they worry about the environment. There are good reasons for this, as indicated by the magnitude of the damage estimates (many billions of dollars annually) presented in this chapter. These numbers may not be sufficient to upset the relatively optimistic conclusion, discussed in a preceding chapter, to the effect that the real cost of extractive output is declining, but neither, it seems to me, can one reject this possibility out of hand.

Empirical studies by economists in collaboration with others have established not only ballpark damage estimates but also costs of control in many situations. Theoretical analyses have

---

[68] The study was carried out by the large economic consulting firm Data Resources, Inc. (DRI), in 1979, using its own macroeconometric model of the U.S. economy.

provided a framework for environmental policy decisions based on the damage and cost estimates. In fact, given the partial and fragmentary nature of the damage estimates, the major contribution of the theoretical work (and I would argue that it is indeed a major contribution, in terms of both the power of the concepts and the potential for real resource savings) has been to elucidate the likely cost differences among contending policy instruments for achieving a given environmental quality standard.

It seems fair to say that fiscal instruments have been shown to be superior to direct controls. That is, they will tend to produce the same outcome (e.g., a desired reduction in aggregate emissions of a particular pollutant) at a lower cost. This essentially theoretical finding has received some support from numerical simulations. Further, among fiscal instruments, either a tax on emissions or a marketable permit to emit is likely to work better than a subsidy to reduce emissions or to defray part of the cost of doing so.

An interesting question, and one we leave for the next chapter, is why, in the light of these findings, U.S. environmental policy continues to rely primarily on a mix of direct controls and cost subsidies.

# 7

## Some concluding thoughts: the role of economics in the study of resource and environmental problems

We began this volume by noting, as evidence of widespread interest in the subject, several items dealing with natural resources and the environment in an average edition of a local (San Francisco) daily newspaper. The items dealt with technical and policy options for controlling pollution, energy conservation, and prospects for oil production and gold mining in California. In each case the story was developed with little or no reference to the findings and insights of economic analysis. This is not surprising. It may not be an exaggeration to say that the "conventional wisdom," as we have heard it expressed by those concerned with issues of resource depletion and environmental protection, holds that economics can contribute little to their resolution (or, worse, that the problems we face are due to the depredations of an economic system explained, justified, and occasionally guided by economists). To the extent that economics is seen as relevant, it follows that what is needed is a radical shift, away from the system characterized by advanced industrial technology, growth, and a largely market-determined allocation of resources, such as is found in the United States and other developed Western countries. According to this view, the discipline of economics is itself in need of a radical restructuring.[1]

[1] For perhaps the most prominent among many expressions of this

233

This volume can be viewed as an exercise in developing the implications of a somewhat different view: first, that economic analysis is relevant to resource and environmental issues; second, that a radical reorientation of economics, or of "the system," is neither necessary nor sufficient to resolve them.

I should say that in making the case for economics against its detractors, I do not wish to associate myself with the view of some others, usually economists, to the effect that there is nothing new or special about, for example, exhaustible resources, that everything worth knowing about (the economics of) these resources is already contained in the standard concepts and models, and/or that everything is best left to the market to decide, in any case. The detractors have a point. The natural environment does impose constraints that ought to be reflected in our models and in the advice we give policy makers. This volume can also be viewed as a series of explorations in the application and extension of economic method to deal with resource and environmental issues. But if it is agreed that there is anything of value in the earlier chapters (e.g., any insight into the ways in which exhaustible and renewable resources are depleted under different market and institutional arrangements, any useful suggestion for environmental policy), then perhaps this second purpose needs no further explication here.

Much the same can be said with respect to the contention by noneconomists that economics is not relevant to the environmental choices we face. Even the most committed environmentalist presumably will be interested to learn that both economic theory and some empirical evidence suggest that a given degree of pollution control can be attained more cheaply (often, much more cheaply) by means of a decentralized fiscal mechanism such as a tax on emissions than by the usual mix of direct controls. Such a finding can be crucial to the fate of

view, see the work of Commoner (1976) and the limits-to-growth arguments of Meadows et al. (1972).

environmental programs in the current atmosphere of concern over government spending and regulation.

This leaves us with the attack on technology, growth, the market, economics, or some combination of all four as the source of our resource and environmental problems. Much has been written on this subject (much too much, one might say), and I promise to be brief. But I should like, in concluding what has been a long labor, to offer a few reflections, in a sense in defense of that labor. Clearly these cannot serve to answer all of the points that have been raised. For one thing, I do not disagree with all of the points. Resources do have some special characteristics, and market failures do exist. But let me try to indicate why I think the main lines of the attack are misleading, at best.

First, about technology and growth. It is certainly true that an expanding economy can lead to serious and even catastrophic environmental disruption and resource depletion. But these grave events could and presumably would occur, if somewhat later, even with no further increase in personal incomes. The point is that the increase in incomes is beside the point. We (as analysts and as a society) shall have to deal directly with the problems posed by pollution and depletion. As a consequence, conventional measures of economic welfare, such as personal incomes or GNP, will, of course, be affected. But the point is (to put it positively now) to aim our policies where they will have the greatest effect, directly at the evils we have identified.

Is continued growth physically impossible? If we define growth solely in physical terms, the answer will have to be yes, although only beyond a point that is almost certainly several decades, at least, in the future (i.e., only beyond almost any reasonable planning horizon). But I think most economists would argue that the definition is too narrow. Clean air, for example, is a "good," although it is only imperfectly, if at all, reflected in physical measures of the size of the economy, or even in GNP. There is no reason we cannot take some of the fruits of our expanded productive capacity in the form of cleaner air. More generally, consumption of goods and services that are environmentally benign can continue to grow even as consumption of the more destructive items stabilizes or declines. Stopping some ill-defined aggregate, "growth" of the "economic system," is neither necessary nor sufficient to protect the environment. This is fortunate, because it is not at all clear how this would by done in the near or medium term, without substantial harm to the prospects of poor people for a better life here in the United States and especially in developing countries around the world.

The same arguments also apply to technology. There is little doubt that many of our environmental problems can be traced to the technology that has powered growth. But there is similarly little doubt that an environmental policy that changes the incentives faced by those who will use, or misuse, our environmental resources will affect their choice of technology. Both economic theory and a considerable body of empirical evidence suggest that as it becomes expensive to dump harmful substances in the air or in the water, methods of production will be devised and employed that will greatly decrease the dumping of harmful substances.

Well, then, what about "the system"? Is the unregulated market economy the source of our difficulties? I believe there are elements of truth in the view that it is. We have seen that efficiency in the presence of environmental externalities generally requires some form of collective action or government intervention. We have also described potential market failures in the allocation of exhaustible resources over long periods of time. But is radical change (presumably to a socialist system, with or without benefit of revolution) the solution? My answer, once again, is that this is neither necessary nor sufficient.

Various policy instruments to control environmental externalities have been proposed, none requiring radical change. This is true whether we are speaking of some form of direct control, a subsidy tied to a particular control technology, or an indirect fiscal measure such as a tax on emissions. If the difficulty is that exhaustible resources are being used too rapidly, another kind of tax, a severance tax, will keep them in the ground. Some of these measures are already in force, in the United States and elsewhere, and the others clearly could be. One who believes that the environment is not adequately protected or that resources are not adequately conserved under the current mix of market and government controls may, of course, advocate a different mix, or one that sets more ambitious targets. But it is difficult to see where socialism, in the sense of government ownership of the means of production, is necessary.

Nor is it sufficient. Theory suggests that socialist managers of productive (and polluting) enterprises, whether they are driven to meet output targets or, as under proposed reforms, to generate profits, will take no more account of the environment or the claims of future generations than do their market-economy or capitalist counterparts. Of course, claims of the environment, or of the future, may be addressed at other, higher levels. But then the question is how they are to influence the behavior of individual polluters or resource users, and we are back to debating the merits of direct controls versus financial penalties, and so on. A different mix may well work better in the institutional setting of a socialist system; this is certainly a legitimate question. But even a casual acquaintance with the serious air- and water-quality problems that plague the Soviet Union and other socialist countries confirms the presumption that neither revolution nor socialism is a sufficient condition for a pristine environment.[2]

We come, finally, to the discipline of economics itself. Does it, as alleged, foster a distorted view of the world, one that justifies, even encourages, destruction of the environment and exhaustion of resources? I think that possibly a couple of

---

[2] For a great wealth of detail on Soviet environmental problems, see the work of Goldman (1972).

different kinds of confusion underlie this charge. One is confusion between economics and the preferences of some economists. Thus, it is not economics that sets up something like "maximization of the GNP" as a goal, as the critics seem to think. Certainly many individual economists (in capitalist, socialist, and developing countries alike) favor policies to enhance growth of per capita GNP, a quite different proposition. Some may even favor maximization of GNP without the "per capita." But in any case, economics as a body of theorems about resource allocation, or quantitative estimates of costs and benefits, demand and supply responses, and so on, does not set up anything like a goal of maximizing, or even increasing, GNP. Further, it is my impression that even the individual economists who favor growth in GNP or per capita GNP are sensitive to other aspects of welfare, such as how the GNP is distributed and how (uncontrolled) growth affects the environment.

A second kind of confusion is that of analysis with advocacy. As an example, economics is criticized for models that show it is "rational" to exploit a renewable resource to the point of extinction. What the models show is that in some (unusual) circumstances it is rational for a harvester concerned only with maximizing the commercial (present) value of a species to exploit it in this fashion. Now, I would argue that this is perfectly proper. Any benefit from preserving a viable stock not captured by the harvester ought not to be included in a model that purports to explain or predict his behavior. But this is not to say that such benefit (e.g., as arising from the conservation of genetic information) does not exist or should not be taken into account in a social choice about use of the resource.

Further, if the resource is, like an ocean fishery, a common property, there will, as we have seen, be an even greater tendency to overexploitation, with a correspondingly greater risk of extinction. The point I wish to make here is that to explain behavior in a common-property setting is not to endorse it. Saying that economics "justifies" overexploitation is much like saying that the study of ecology "justifies" an imbalance in nature simply because it is capable of explaining the source of the imbalance. As a matter of fact, economists typically recommend stringent controls to protect common-property resources from overexploitation. Yet it cannot be denied that our recommendations, here as elsewhere in the resource and environmental area, tend to be disregarded by those who make policy in this area. Let me conclude by considering briefly why this is so, and what we, as economists, might do about it.

It is customary to conclude a volume such as this with a call for further research. Certainly I believe that this is appropriate, and for the purpose of influencing policy as well as the more traditional one of contributing to knowledge. Our advice on managing common-property resources, for example, will carry more weight when we are able to identify more precisely maximum sustainable yields, steady-state optimal stocks, and so on.

But I believe more is needed. One reason for our lack of influence is that we have paid relatively little attention to problems of implementation. Take the case of pollution control. We have shown that either a marketable permit system or an emissions charge will normally be superior, in the abstract, to the currently employed mix of direct controls and subsidies. But how would the permit system for example, actually work? Who should be allowed to bid? Just existing polluters, within a region? Existing and potential polluters, within and without, if the market is thin? Environmental groups, to allow for a reduction in emissions below the specified level? And should permits be issued for a year at a time, or perhaps for longer periods to encourage investment in control technology?

My feeling is that a substantially larger share of the research into problems of pollution control, and other environmental and resource problems as well, might profitably focus on implementation. Of course, there is a place for more abstract investigations, but the insights yielded may fail to carry over from the pages of academic journals to the policy arena unless there is explicit attention to the mechanisms for accomplishing this.

A short statement of the themes of this concluding chapter might run as follows. Economics is relevant to the solution of resource and environmental problems; radical change is needed in neither the discipline nor "the system"; we shall have to work harder to convey to the general public and to the policy community the arguments underlying these propositions.

# REFERENCES

Acton, J. P. *Evaluating Public Programs to Save Lives.* Santa Monica: Rand Corporation, 1973.

Adams, F. G., and Griffin, J. M. "Energy and Fuel Substitution Elasticities: Results from an International Cross Section Study." Unpublished manuscript, Department of Economics, University of Pennsylvania, October 1974.

Adar, Z., and Griffin, J. M. "Uncertainty and the Choice of Pollution Control Instruments." *Journal of Environmental Economics and Management* 3:178–88, October 1976.

Adelman, M. A. "Economics of Exploration for Petroleum and Other Minerals." *Geoexploration* 8:131–50, 1970.

Adelman, M. A. *The World Petroleum Market.* Baltimore: Johns Hopkins Press, 1972.

Agria, S. R. "Special Tax Treatment of Mineral Industries." In *Taxation of Income from Capital,* edited by A. C. Harberger and M. J. Bailey. Washington: Brookings Institution, 1969.

Allais, M. "Method of Appraising Economic Prospects of Mining Exploration Over Large Territories: Algerian Sahara Case Study." *Management Science* 3:285–347, 1957.

Almon, C. *Matrix Methods in Economics.* Reading, Mass.: Addison-Wesley, 1967.

Anderson, K. B. "Integrated Assessment Issues Raised by the Environmental Effects of Energy Conservation: A Case Study of Space Conditioning in Residential Buildings." Energy and Resources Group working paper no. 80-4, University of California, Berkeley, March 1980.

Anderson, K. P. "Optimal Growth When the Stock of Resources Is Finite and Depletable." *Journal of Economic Theory* 4:256–67, 1972.

Anderson, L. G. "The Relationship Between Firm and Industry in Common Property Fisheries." *Land Economics* 52(2):179–91, 1976.

Anderson, R. C., and Spiegelman, R. D. "Tax Policy and Secondary Material Use." *Journal of Environmental Economics and Management* 4:68–82, 1977.

Anderson, R. J., Jr., and Crocker, T. D. "Air Pollution and Residential Property Values." *Urban Studies* 8:171–80, 1971.

Arrow, K. J. "Optimal Capital Policy with Irreversible Investment." In *Value, Capital and Growth,* edited by J. N. Wolfe. Chicago: Aldine-Atherton, 1968.

Arrow, K. J. "The Organization of Economic Activity: Issues Pertinent to the Choice of Market vs. Nonmarket Allocations." In U.S. Congress, Joint Economic Committee, *The Analysis and Evaluation of Public Expenditures: The PPB System.* Washington: U.S. Government Printing Office, 1969.

Arrow, K. J. "Rawls' Principle of Just Saving." *Swedish Journal of Economics* 75:323–35, 1974.

Arrow, K. J., and Chang, S. "Optimal Pricing, Use and Exploration of Uncertain Natural Resource Stocks." Technical report no. 31, Project on Efficiency of Decision-making in Economic Systems, Harvard University, 1978.

Arrow, K. J., and Fisher, A. C. "Environmental Preservation, Uncertainty, and Irreversibility." *Quarterly Journal of Economics* 88:312–19, 1974.

Arrow, K. J., and Kurz, M. *Public Investment, the Rate of Return, and Optimal Fiscal Policy.* Baltimore: Johns Hopkins Press, 1970.

Arrow, K. J., and Lind, R. C. "Uncertainty and the Evaluation of Public Investment Decisions." *American Economic Review* 60:364–78, 1970.

Atkinson, S. E., and Lewis, D. H. "A Cost Effectiveness Analysis of Alternative Air Quality Control Strategies." *Journal of Environmental Economics and Management* 1:237–50, 1974.

Atkinson, S. E., and Lewis, D. H. "Determination and Implementation of Optimal Air Quality Standards." *Journal of Environmental Economics and Management* 3:363–80, 1976.

Ayres, R. U., and Kneese, A. V. "Production, Consumption, and Externalities." *American Economic Review* 59:282–97, 1969.

Bailey, M. J. "Measuring the Benefits of Life-Saving." Unpublished manuscript, University of Maryland, 1978.

Banks, F. E. "A Note on Some Theoretical Issues of Resource Depletion." *Journal of Economic Theory* 9:238–43, 1974.

Barger, H., and Schurr, S. H. *The Mining Industries, 1899–1939.* New York: National Bureau of Economic Research, 1944.

Barnett, H. J. "Energy Use and Supplies, 1939, 1947, 1965." Bureau of Mines information circular 7582. Washington: U.S. Department of the Interior, October 1950.

Barnett, H. J. "Scarcity and Growth Revisited." In *Scarcity and Growth Reconsidered,* edited by V. K. Smith. Baltimore: Johns Hopkins Press, 1979.

Barnett, H. J., and Morse, C. *Scarcity and Growth: The Economics of Natural Resource Scarcity.* Baltimore: Johns Hopkins Press, 1963.

Barnett, L. B., and Waddell, T. E. *The Cost of Air Pollution Damages.* Publication number AP-85. Research Triangle Park, N.C.: U.S. Environmental Protection Agency, February 1973.

Bator, F. "The Anatomy of Market Failure." *Quarterly Journal of Economics* 72:351–79, 1958.

Baughman, M. L., and Joskow, P. L. "Interfuel Substitution in the Consumption of Energy in the United States." M.I.T. Energy Laboratory working paper, May 1974.

Baumol, W. J. "On the Social Rate of Discount." *American Economic Review* 58:788–802, 1968.

Baumol, W. J. "On Taxation and the Control of Externalities." *American Economic Review* 62:307–22, 1972.

Baumol, W. J., and Bradford, D. F. "Detrimental Externalities and Non-Convexity of the Production Set." *Economica* 39:160–76, 1972.

Baumol, W. J., and Oates, W. E. "The Use of Standards and Prices for Protection of the Environment." *Swedish Journal of Economics* 73:42–54, 1971.

Baumol, W. J., and Oates, W. E. *The Theory of Environmental Policy.* Englewood Cliffs, N.J.: Prentice-Hall, 1975a.

Baumol, W. J., and Oates, W. E. "The Instruments for Environmental Policy." In *Economic Analysis and Environmental Problems,* edited by E. S. Mills. New York: Columbia University Press for the NBER, 1975b.

Baumol, W. J., and Oates, W. E. *Economics, Environmental Policy, and the Quality of Life.* Englewood Cliffs, N.J.: Prentice-Hall, 1979.

Beckerman, W. "Economists, Scientists and Environmental Catastrophe." *Oxford Economic Papers* 24:237–44, 1972.

Beckmann, M. J. "A Note on the Optimal Rates of Resource Exhaustion." *Review of Economic Studies, Symposium on the Economics of Exhaustible Resources* 121–2, 1974.

Beddington, J. R., Watts, C. M. K., and Wright, W. D. C. "Optimal Cropping of Self-Reproducible Natural Resources." *Econometrica* 43:789–802, 1975.

Bell, F. W. "The Pope and the Price of Fish." *American Economic Review* 58:1346–50, 1968.

Bell, F. W. "Technological Externalities and Common Property Resources: An Empirical Study of the U.S. Northern Lobster Fishery." *Journal of Political Economy* 80:148–58, 1972.

Berck, P. "Open Access and Extinction." *Econometrica* 47:877–82, 1979a.

Berck, P. "The Economics of Timber: A Renewable Resource in the Long Run." *Bell Journal of Economics* 10:447–62, 1979b.

Bergman, L. *Energy and Economic Growth in Sweden.* Stockholm: Economic Research Institute, Stockholm School of Economics, 1977.

Berndt, E. R., and Wood, D. "Technology, Prices, and the Derived Demand for Energy." *Review of Economics and Statistics* 57:259–68, 1975.

Beverton, R. J. H., and Holt, S. L. *On the Dynamics of Exploited Fish Populations.* Ministry of Agriculture, Fisheries and Food, Fishery Investigations, Series II, Vol. 19. London: Her Majesty's Stationery Office, 1957.

Bieniewski, C. L., Persse, F. H., and Brauch, E. F. *Availability of Uranium at Various Prices from Resources in the United States.* U.S. Bureau of Mines information circular 8501. Washington: U.S. Government Printing Office, 1971.

Blitzer, C., Meeraus, A., and Stoutjesdijk, A. "A Dynamic Model of OPEC Trade and Production." *Journal of Development Economics* Fall 1975.

Blomquist, G. "Value of Life: Implications of Automobile Seat Use." Ph.D. dissertation, University of Chicago, 1977.

Boerema, L. K., and Obarrio, J. L. "The Case for Regulation of the Shrimp Industry." In *Economic Effects of Fisheries Regulation,* edited by R. Hamlisch, pp. 537–44. FAO Fisheries Reports, no. 5. Rome: Food and Agriculture Organisation, 1962.

Bohm, P. "Pollution, Purification, and the Theory of External Effects." *Swedish Journal of Economics* 72:153–66, 1970.

Bohm, P. "Pollution: Taxation or Purification?" *Kyklos* 25:501–17, 1972*a*.

Bohm, P. "Estimating Demand for Public Goods: An Experiment." *European Economic Review* 3:111–30, 1972*b*.

Boulding, K. E. "The Economics of the Coming Spaceship Earth." In *Environmental Quality in a Growing Economy,* edited by H. Jarrett. Baltimore: Johns Hopkins Press, 1966.

Bower, B. T., Löf, G., and Hearon, W. M. "Residuals Management in the Pulp and Paper Industry." *Natural Resources Journal* 11:605–23, 1971.

Bradley, P. G. *The Economics of Crude Petroleum Production.* Amsterdam: North-Holland Publishing, 1967.

Bradley, P. G. "Some Seasonal Models of the Fishing Industry." In *Economics of Fisheries Management: A Symposium,* edited by A. D. Scott, pp. 33–44. Vancouver: Institute for Animal Resource Ecology, University of British Columbia, 1970.

Bramhall, D. E., and Mills, E. S. "A Note on the Asymmetry between Fees and Payments." *Water Resources Research* 2:615–16, 1966.

Brannon, G. M. *Energy Taxes and Subsidies.* Cambridge, Mass.: Ballinger, 1975.

Brobst, D. A. "The Systems Approach to the Analysis of Resource Scarcity." In *Scarcity and Growth Reconsidered,* edited by V. K. Smith. Baltimore: Johns Hopkins Press, 1979.

Brobst, D. A., and Pratt, W. P., eds. *U.S. Mineral Resources.* USGS professional paper 820. Washington: U.S. Government Printing Office, 1973.

Brooks, D. B. "The Lead-Zinc Anomaly." In *Proceedings, Council of Economics, American Institute of Mining, Metallurgical and Petroleum Engineers,* pp. 144–59. New York: AIME, 1967.

Brookshire, D. S., d'Arge, R. C., Schulze, W., and Thayer, M. A. *Methods Development for Assessing Tradeoffs in Environmental Management. Vol. II, Experiments in Valuing Nonmarket Goods.* Washington: Environmental Protection Agency, 1979.

Brookshire, D. S., Ives, B. C., and Schulze, W. D. "The Valuation of Esthetic Preferences." *Journal of Environmental Economics and Management* 3:325–46, 1976.

Brown, G. M. "An Optimal Program for Managing Common Property Resources with Congestion Externalities." *Journal of Political Economy* 82:163–75, 1974.

Brown, G. M., and Field, B. C. "Implication of Alternative Measures of Natural Resource Scarcity." *Journal of Political Economy* 86:229–43, 1978.

Brown, G. M., and Hammack, J. "A Preliminary Investigation of the Economics of Migratory Waterfowl." In *Natural Environments: Studies in Theoretical and Applied Analysis,* edited by J. V. Krutilla. Baltimore: Johns Hopkins Press, 1972.

Brown, G. M., and Hammack, J. "Dynamic Economic Management of Migratory Waterfowl." *Review of Economics and Statistics* 55:73–90, 1973.

Buchanan, J., and Stubblebine, W. C. "Externality." *Economica* 29:371–84, 1962.

Budnitz, R., and Holdren, J. P. "Social and Environmental Costs of Energy Systems." *Annual Review of Energy* 1:553–80, 1976.

Burness, H. S. "On the Taxation of Nonreplenishable Natural Resources." *Journal of Environmental Economics and Management* 3:289–311, 1976.

Burt, O. R. "Optimal Use of Resources Over Time." *Management Science* 2:80–93, 1964.

Burt, O. R. "Groundwater Management Under Quadratic Criterion Functions." *Water Resources Research* 3:673–82, 1967.

Burt, O. R. "Groundwater Storage Control under Institutional Restrictions." *Water Resources Research* 6:1540–8, 1970.

Burt, O. R., and Brewer, D. "Estimation of Net Social Benefits from Outdoor Recreation." *Econometrica* 39:813–27, 1971.

Burt, O. R., and Cummings, R. G. "Production and Investment in Natural Resource Industries." *American Economic Review* 60:576–90, 1970.

Butlin, J. "Optimal Depletion of a Replenishable Resource: An Evaluation of Recent Contributions to Fisheries Economics." In *The Economics of Natural Resource Depletion,* edited by D. W. Pearce and J. Rose, pp. 140–76. New York: John Wiley & Sons, 1975.

California Energy Commission. *Final Report: Fossil 1 and 2,* July 12, 1979.

Calloway, J. A., Schwartz, A. K., and Thompson, R. G. "Industrial Economic Model of Water Use and Waste Treatment for Ammonia." *Water Resources Research* 10:650–8, 1974.

Calloway, J. A., and Thompson, R. G. "An Integrated Industry Model of Petroleum Refining, Electric Power, and Chemicals Industries for Costing Pollution Control and Estimating Energy Prices." *Engineering and Process Economics* 1:199–216, 1976.

Calvo, G. "Some Notes on Time Inconsistency and Rawls' Maximin Criterion." *Review of Economic Studies* 45:97–102, 1978.

Capen, E. C., Clapp, R. V., and Campbell, W. M. "Competitive Bidding in High-Risk Situations." *Journal of Petroleum Technology* 23:641–53, 1971.

Carlisle, D. "The Economics of a Fund Resource with Particular Reference to Mining." *American Economic Review* 44:595–616, 1954.

Cazalet, E. G. "Generalized Equilibrium Modeling: The Methodology of the SRI/Gulf Energy Model." Decision Focus, Palo Alto, California, 1977.

Chapman, D. "Internalizing an Externality: A Sulfur Emission Tax and the Electric Utility Industry." In *Energy: Demand, Conservation, and Institutional Problems,* edited by M. S. Macrakis. Cambridge, Mass.: M.I.T. Press, 1974.

Cheung, S. N. S. "Contractual Arrangements and Resource Allocation in Marine Fisheries." In *Economics of Fisheries Management: A Symposium,* edited by A. D. Scott, pp. 97–108. Vancouver: Institute for Animal Resource Ecology, University of British Columbia, 1970.

Christy, F. T. "Property Rights in the World Ocean." *Natural Resources Journal* 15:695–712, 1975.

Christy, F. T., and Scott, A. D. *The Common Wealth of Ocean Fisheries.* Baltimore: Johns Hopkins Press, 1965.

Cicchetti, C. J. *Alaskan Oil: Alternative Routes and Markets.* Baltimore: Johns Hopkins Press, 1972.

Cicchetti, C. J., Fisher, A. C., and Smith, V. K. "An Econometric Evaluation of a Generalized Consumer Surplus Measure: The Mineral King Controversy." *Econometrica* 44:1259–76, 1976.

Cicchetti, C. J., and Freeman, A. M., III. "Option Demand and Consumer Surplus: Further Comment." *Quarterly Journal of Economics* 85:528–39, 1971.

Clark, C. W. "Profit Maximization and the Extinction of Animal Species." *Journal of Political Economy* 81:950–60, 1973.

Clark, C. W. *Mathematical Bioeconomics.* New York: John Wiley & Sons, 1976.

Clark, C. W., and Munro, G. R. "The Economics of Fishing and Modern Capital Theory." *Journal of Environmental Economics and Management* 2:92–106, 1975.

Clark, C. W., and Munro, G. R. "Renewable Resources and Extinction: The Consequences of Irreversibility." Mimeographed. Resources paper no. 2, Research Programme on Natural Resource Utilization, University of British Columbia, July 1976.

Clawson, M. "Methods of Measuring Demand for and Value of Outdoor Recreation." Resources for the Future, reprint 10. Washington: RFF, 1959.

Clawson, M., and Knetsch, J. L. *Economics of Outdoor Recreation.* Baltimore: Johns Hopkins Press, 1966.

Coase, R. H. "The Problem of Social Cost." *Journal of Law and Economics* 3:1–44, 1960.

Comitini, S., and Huang, D. S. "A Study of Production and Factor Shares in the Halibut Fishing Industry." *Journal of Political Economy* 75:366–72, 1967.

Common, M., and Pearce, D. W. "Adaptive Mechanisms, Growth and the Environment: The Case of Natural Resources." *Canadian Journal of Economics* 6:289–300, 1973.

Commoner, B. *The Poverty of Power.* New York: Knopf, 1976.

Comolli, P. M. "Pollution Control in a Simplified General Equilibrium Model with Production Externalities." *Journal of Environmental Economics and Management* 4:289–304, 1977.

CONAES. *Energy in Transition, 1985–2010.* Final report of the Committee on Nuclear and Alternative Energy Systems, National Academy of Sciences. San Francisco: Freeman, 1979.

CONAES Demand Panel. *Alternative Energy Demand Futures to 2010.* Washington: National Academy of Sciences, 1979*a.*

CONAES Modeling Resource Group. *Energy Modeling for an Uncertain Future.* Washington: National Academy of Sciences, 1978.

Conley, B. C. "The Value of Human Life in the Demand for Safety." *American Economic Review* 66:45–55, 1976.

Conrad, R. F. "Output Taxes and the Quantity-Quality Trade-Off in the Mining Firm." Unpublished manuscript, Duke University, 1980.

Converse, A. O. "On the Extension of Input-Output Analysis to Account for Environmental Externalities." *American Economic Review* 61:197–8, 1971.

Cooper, B. S., and Rice, D. P. "The Economic Cost of Illness Revisited." *Social Security Bulletin* 39:21–36, 1976.

Cooper, R. N. "Resource Needs Revisited." *Brookings Papers* 1:238–45, 1975.

Courtney, L. H. "Jevons' Coal Question: Thirty Years After." *Journal of the Royal Statistical Society* 15:789–810, 1897.

Cowing, T. G., and Smith, V. K. *A Survey of Econometric Models of the Supply and Cost Structure of Electricity.* Palo Alto: Electric Power Research Institute, 1978.

Cox, D. P., et al. "Copper." In *United States Mineral Resources,* edited by D. A. Brobst and W. P. Pratt, pp. 163–90. U.S. Geological Survey professional paper no. 820. Washington: U.S. Government Printing Office, 1973.

Cox, J. C. "The Determinants of Investment in Petroleum Reserves and Their Implications for Public Policy." *American Economic Review* 66:153–67, 1976.

Cox, J. C., and Wright, A. W. "The Cost-effectiveness of Federal Tax

Subsidies for Petroleum Reserves." In *Studies in Energy Tax Policy,* edited by G. M. Brannon, pp. 177–202. Cambridge, Mass.: Ballinger, 1975.

Crabbé, P. J. "L'exploration des ressources extractives non renouvelables: théorie économique, processus stochastique et vérification." *L'Actualité Economique* 53:559–86, 1977.

Crabbé, P. J. "The Contribution of L. C. Gray to the Economic Theory of Exhaustible Resources." Unpublished manuscript, University of Ottawa, 1980.

Cremer, J., and Weitzman, M. "OPEC and the Monopoly Price of World Oil." *European Economic Review* 8:155–64, 1976.

Crocker, T. D. "Externalities, Property Rights, and Transaction Costs: An Empirical Study." *Journal of Law and Economics* 14:451–64, 1971.

Crocker, T. D., Schulze, W., Ben-David, S., and Kneese, A. V. *Methods Development for Assessing Air Pollution Control Benefits, Vol. I, Experiments in the Economics of Epidemiology.* Washington: Environmental Protection Agency, 1979.

Crommelin, M., and Thompson, A. R., eds. *Mineral Leasing as an Instrument of Public Policy.* Vancouver: University of British Columbia Press, 1977.

Cropper, M. L. "The Valuation of Locational Amenities, An Alternative to the Hedonic Price Approach." In *Methods Development for Assessing Air Pollution Control Benefits, Vol. IV, Studies on Partial Equilibrium Approaches to Valuation of Environmental Amenities.* Washington: Environmental Protection Agency, 1979.

Crutchfield, J. A. "The Marine Fisheries: A Problem of International Cooperation." *American Economic Review* 54:207–18, 1964.

Crutchfield, J. A., and Zellner, A. "Economic Aspects of the Pacific Halibut Fishery." *Fishery Industrial Research* 1, 1962.

Cumberland, J. H. "A Regional Interindustry Model for Analysis of Development Objectives." *The Regional Science Association Papers* 17:65–94, 1966.

Cumberland, J. H., and Korbach, R. J. "A Regional Interindustry Environmental Model." *The Regional Science Association Papers* 30:61–75, 1973.

Cummings, R. G. "Some Extensions of the Economic Theory of Exhaustible Resources." *Western Economic Journal* 7:201–10, 1969.

Cummings, R. G. "Optimum Exploitation of Groundwater Reserves with Saltwater Intrusion." *Water Resources Research* 7:1415–24, 1971.

Cummings, R. G., and Norton, V. "The Economics of Environmental Preservation: Comment." *American Economic Review* 64:1021–4, 1974.

Dales, J. H. "Land, Water, and Ownership." *Canadian Journal of Economics* 1:791–804, 1968a.

Dales, J. H. *Pollution, Property and Prices.* Toronto: University of Toronto Press, 1968b.

d'Arge, R. C. "Economic Growth and the Natural Environment." In

*Environmental Quality Analysis,* edited by A. V. Kneese and B. T. Bower. Baltimore: Johns Hopkins Press, 1972.

d'Arge, R. C., and Kogiku, K. C. "Economic Growth and the Environment." *Review of Economic Studies* 40:61–78, 1973.

Darmstadter, J., Dunkerley, J., and Alterman, J. *How Industrial Societies Use Energy: A Comparative Analysis.* Baltimore: Johns Hopkins Press, 1977.

Darmstadter, J., Teitelbaum, P., and Polach, J. *Energy in the World Economy: A Statistical Review of Trends in Output, Trade, and Consumption Since 1925.* Baltimore: Johns Hopkins Press, 1971.

Dasgupta, P. "On Some Alternative Criteria for Justice Between Generations." *Journal of Public Economics* 3:405–23, 1974.

Dasgupta, P., and Heal, G. "The Optimal Depletion of Exhaustible Resources." *Review of Economic Studies, Symposium on the Economics of Exhaustible Resources* 3–28, 1974.

Dasgupta, P., Heal, G., and Majumdar, M. "Resource Depletion and Research and Development." Technical report no. 18, Institute for Mathematical Studies in the Social Sciences, Stanford University, 1976.

Dasgupta, P., and Stiglitz, J. E. "Uncertainty and the Rate of Extraction under Alternative Institutional Arrangements." Unpublished manuscript, Stanford University, 1975.

Data Resources, Inc. "The Macroeconomic Impact of Federal Pollution Control Programs: 1978 Assessment." Submitted to the Environmental Protection Agency and the Council on Environmental Quality, January 1979.

David, E. L. "Lake Shore Property Values: A Guide to Public Investment in Recreation." *Water Resources Research* 4:697–707, 1968.

Davidson, P. "Public Policy Problems of the Domestic Crude Oil Industry." *American Economic Review* 53:85–108, 1963.

Davidson, P., Adams, F. G., and Seneca, J. "The Social Value of Water Recreational Facilities Resulting from an Improvement in Water Quality: The Delaware Estuary." In *Water Research,* edited by A. V. Kneese and S. C. Smith. Baltimore: Johns Hopkins Press, 1966.

Davis, R. K. "The Value of Big Game Hunting in a Private Forest." In *Transactions of the 29th North American Wildlife and Natural Resources Conference,* pp. 393–403. Washington: Wildlife Management Institute, 1964.

Davis, R. K. *The Range of Choice in Water Management.* Baltimore: Johns Hopkins Press, 1968.

Demsetz, H. "The Exchange and Enforcement of Property Rights." *Journal of Law and Economics* 7:11–26, 1964.

Deshmukh, S. D., and Pliska, S. R. "Optimal Consumption and Exploration of Nonrenewable Resources under Uncertainty." Discussion paper no. 317, Center for Mathematical Studies in Economics and Management Science, Northwestern University, 1978.

Devarajan, S. *Natural Resource Extraction and Exploration Under*

*Uncertainty.* Ph.D. dissertation, University of California, Berkeley, 1980.

Devarajan, S., and Fisher, A. C. "Exploration and Scarcity." IP-290, Working Papers in Economic Theory and Econometrics, University of California, Berkeley, 1980.

Dewhurst, J. F. *America's Needs and Resources,* 2nd rev. ed. New York: Twentieth Century Fund, 1955.

Dolbear, F. T. "On the Theory of Optimum Externality." *American Economic Review* 57:90–103, 1967.

Dorfman, N. S., and Snow, A. "Who Will Pay for Pollution Control?" *National Tax Journal* 28:101–15, 1975.

Dorfman, R. "An Economic Interpretation of Optimal Control Theory." *American Economic Review* 59:817–31, 1969.

Dorfman, R. "Conceptual Model of a Regional Water Quality Authority." In *Models for Managing Regional Water Quality,* edited by R. Dorfman, H. D. Jacoby, and H. A. Thomas, Jr., pp. 42–83. Cambridge, Mass.: Harvard University Press, 1972.

Dorfman, R. "The Technical Basis for Decision Making." In *The Governance of Common Property Resources,* edited by E. T. Haefele. Baltimore: Johns Hopkins Press, 1975.

Dorfman, R. "Incidence of the Benefits and Costs of Environmental Programs." Discussion paper 510, Harvard Institute of Economic Research, October 1976.

Dorfman, R., and Jacoby, H. "An Illustrative Model of River Basin Pollution Control." In *Models for Managing Regional Water Quality,* edited by R. Dorfman, H. Jacoby, and H. A. Thomas, Jr. Cambridge, Mass.: Harvard University Press, 1973.

Dowdle, B., ed. "The Economics of Sustained Yield Forestry: A Symposium." Unpublished. College of Forest Resources, University of Washington, Seattle, 1974.

Eckstein, O. *Water Resource Development: The Economics of Project Evaluation.* Cambridge, Mass.: Harvard University Press, 1958.

Ehrlich, P. R., and Ehrlich, A. H. *The Extinction of Species.* New York: Random House, 1981.

Ehrlich, P. R., Ehrlich, A. H., and Holdren, J. P. *Ecoscience: Population, Resources, Environment.* San Francisco: W. H. Freeman, 1977.

Epple, D. *Petroleum Discoveries and Government Policy.* Cambridge, Mass.: Ballinger, 1976.

Erickson, G. K. "Alaska's Petroleum Leasing Policy." *Alaska Review of Business and Economic Conditions* 7, 1970.

Etheridge, D. "The Inclusion of Wastes in the Theory of the Firm." *Journal of Political Economy* 81:1430–41, 1973.

Evans, M. K. "A Forecasting Model Applied to Pollution Control Costs." *American Economic Review* 63:244–53, 1973.

Federal Power Commission. *In The Matter of: Pacific Northwest Power Company and Washington Public Power Supply System.* Hearings: Lewiston, Idaho; Portland, Oregon; and Washington, D. C., 1970.

Feldstein, M. S. "The Social Time Preference Discount Rate in Cost-Benefit Analysis." *Economic Journal* 74:360–79, 1964.

Ferrar, T. A., and Whinston, A. B. "Taxation and Water Pollution Control." *Natural Resources Journal* 12:307–17, 1972.

Fischman, L. L., and Landsberg, H. H. "Adequacy of Nonfuel Minerals and Forest Resources." In *Population, Resources, and the Environment,* edited by R. G. Ridker. Washington: U.S. Government Printing Office, 1972.

Fishelson, G. "Emission Control Policies Under Uncertainty." *Journal of Environmental Economics and Management* 3:189–97, 1976.

Fisher, A. C. "Environmental Externalities and the Arrow-Lind Public Investment Theorem." *American Economic Review* 63:722–5, 1973.

Fisher, A. C. "On Measures of Natural Resource Scarcity." Research report 77-19, International Institute for Applied Systems Analysis, 1977.

Fisher, A. C., and Krutilla, J. V. "Valuing Long Run Ecological Consequences and Irreversibilities." *Journal of Environmental Economics and Management* 1:96–108, 1974.

Fisher, A. C., and Krutilla, J. V. "Resource Conservation, Environmental Preservation, and the Rate of Discount." *Quarterly Journal of Economics* 89:358–70, 1975.

Fisher, A. C., Krutilla, J. V., and Cicchetti, C. J. "The Economics of Environmental Preservation: A Theoretical and Empirical Analysis." *American Economic Review* 62:605–19, 1972.

Fisher, A. C., and Peterson, F. M. "The Environment in Economics." *Journal of Economic Literature* 14:1–33, 1976.

Fisher, F. M. *Supply and Costs in the U.S. Petroleum Industry.* Washington: Resources for the Future, 1964.

Fisher, F. M., Cootner, P. H., and Baily, M. N. "An Econometric Model of the World Copper Industry." *Bell Journal of Economics and Management Science* 3:568–609, 1972.

Ford Foundation–Mitre Corporation. *Nuclear Power Issues and Choices.* Cambridge, Mass.: Ballinger, 1977.

Forster, B. A. "Pollution Control in a Two-Sector Dynamic General Equilibrium Model." *Journal of Environmental Economics and Management* 4:305–12, 1977.

Førsund, F. R. "Allocation in Space and Environmental Pollution." *Swedish Journal of Economics* 74:19–34, 1972.

Freeman, A. M. "Bribes and Charges: Some Comments." *Water Resources Research* 3:287–8, 1967.

Freeman, A. M. "Air Pollution and Property Values: A Methodological Comment." *Review of Economics and Statistics* 53:415–16, 1971.

Freeman, A. M. "Distribution of Environmental Quality." In *Environmental Quality: Theory and Method in the Social Sciences,* edited by A. V. Kneese and B. T. Bower. Baltimore: Johns Hopkins Press, 1972.

Freeman, A. M. "On Estimating Air Pollution Control Benefits from Land Value Studies." *Journal of Environmental Economics and Management* 1:74–83, 1974.

Freeman, A. M. "The Incidence of the Cost of Controlling Automobile Air Pollution." In *Distribution of Economic Well-Being,* edited by F. T. Juster. Cambridge, Mass.: Ballinger, 1977.

Freeman, A. M. *The Benefits of Environmental Improvement: Theory and Practice.* Baltimore: Johns Hopkins Press, 1979*a*.

Freeman, A. M. *The Benefits of Air and Water Pollution Control: A Review and Synthesis of Recent Estimates.* Washington: Council on Environmental Quality, 1979*b*.

Fuss, M. A. "The Demand for Energy in Canadian Manufacturing." *Journal of Econometrics* 5, 1977.

Fuss, M. A., and Waverman, L. "The Demand for Energy in Canada." Working paper, Institute for Policy Analysis, University of Toronto, 1975.

Gaffney, M. "Concepts of Financial Maturity of Timber and Other Assets." Agricultural Economics Information Series no. 62, North Carolina State College, December 1960.

Gaffney, M., ed. *Extractive Resources and Taxation.* Madison: University of Wisconsin Press, 1967.

Garg, P. C., and Sweeney, J. L. "Optimal Growth with Depletable Resources." *Resources and Energy* 1:43–56, 1978.

Gaskins, D. W., and Teisberg, T. "An Economic Analysis of Pre-Sale Exploration in Oil and Gas Lease Sales." In *Essays in Industrial Organization in Honor of Joe S. Bain,* edited by R. Masson and P. D. Qualls. Cambridge, Mass.: Ballinger, 1976.

Gaskins, D. W., and Vann, B. "Joint Buying and the Sellers Return: The Case of OCS Lease Sales." Unpublished manuscript, University of California, Berkeley, 1975.

Georgescu-Roegen, N. *The Entropy Law and the Economic Process.* Cambridge, Mass.: Harvard University Press, 1971.

Gianessi, L. P., Peskin, H. M., and Wolff, E. "The Distributional Effects of the Uniform Air Pollution Policy in the U.S." Discussion paper D-5, Resources for the Future. Washington: RFF, April 1977.

Gilbert, R. J. "Resource Depletion Under Uncertainty." Unpublished manuscript, Stanford University, 1975*a*.

Gilbert, R. J. "Decentralized Exploration Strategies for Nonrenewable Resource Deposits." Stanford University, 1975*b*.

Gilbert, R. J. "Dominant Firm Pricing Policy in a Market for an Exhaustible Resource." *Bell Journal of Economics* 9:385–95, 1978.

Gilbert, R. J. "Optimal Depletion of an Uncertain Stock." *Review of Economic Studies* 46:47–58, 1979.

Gilbert, R. J., and Goldman, S. M. "Potential Competition and the Monopoly Price of an Exhaustible Resource." *Journal of Economic Theory* 17:319–31, 1978.

Gilpin, A. *Control of Air Pollution.* London: Butterworth, 1963.

Goeller, H. E., and Weinberg, A. M. "The Age of Substitutability." *Science* 191:683–9, 1976.

Goldman, M. *The Spoils of Progress: Environmental Pollution in the Soviet Union.* Cambridge, Mass.: M.I.T. Press, 1972.

Goldsmith, O. S. "Market Allocation of Exhaustive Resources." *Journal of Political Economy* 82:1035–40, 1974.

Gordon, H. S. "The Economic Theory of a Common Property Resource." *Journal of Political Economy* 62:124–42, 1954.

Gordon, R. L. "A Reinterpretation of the Pure Theory of Exhaustion." *Journal of Political Economy* 75:274–86, 1967.

Gould, J. R. "Extinction of a Fishery by Commercial Exploitation: a Note." *Journal of Political Economy* 80:1031–8, 1972.

Gould, J. R. "Total Conditions in the Analysis of External Effects." *Economic Journal* 87:558–64, 1977.

Goundry, G. K. "Forest Management and the Theory of Capital." *Canadian Journal of Economics and Political Science* 26:439–51, 1960.

Grandmont, J. "Temporary General Equilibrium Theory." *Econometrica* 45:535–72, 1977.

Gray, L. C. "The Economic Possibilities of Conservation." *Quarterly Journal of Economics* 27:497–519, 1913.

Gray, L. C. "Rent Under the Assumption of Exhaustibility." *Quarterly Journal of Economics* 28:466–89, 1914.

Grayson, C. J. *Decisions under Uncertainty.* Boston: Harvard Business School, 1960.

Greenley, D. A., Walsh, R. G., and Young, R. A. "Option Value: Empirical Evidence From a Case Study of Recreation and Water Quality." *Quarterly Journal of Economics,* in press.

Grenon, M., ed. *First IIASA Conference on Energy Resources.* CP-76-4. Laxenburg, Austria: International Institute for Applied Systems Analysis, 1976.

Griffin, J. M. "An Econometric Evaluation of Sulfur Taxes." *Journal of Political Economy* 82:669–88, 1974*a*.

Griffin, J. M. "Recent Sulfur Tax Proposals: An Econometric Evaluation of Welfare Gains." In *Energy: Demand, Conservation, and Institutional Problems,* edited by M. S. Macrakis. Cambridge, Mass.: M.I.T. Press, 1974*b*.

Griffin, J. M. "The Effects of Higher Prices on Electricity Consumption." *Bell Journal of Economics and Management Science* 5:515–39, 1974*c*.

Griffin, J. M., and Gregory, P. R. "An Intercountry Translog Model of Energy Substitution Responses." *American Economic Review* 66:845–57, 1976.

Griffiths, J. C. "Exploration for Natural Resources." *Operations Research* 14:189–209, 1966.

Gruver, G. W. "Optimal Investment in Pollution Control Capital in a Neoclassical Growth Context." *Journal of Environmental Economics and Management* 3:165–77, 1976.

Hadley, G., and Kemp, M. C. *Variational Methods in Economics.* Amsterdam: North-Holland, Publishing, 1971.

Haefele, E. T. *Representative Government and Environmental Management.* Baltimore: Johns Hopkins Press, 1973.

Hall, D. C. "A Note on Natural Production Functions." *Journal of Environmental Economics and Management* 4:258–64, 1977.

Halvorsen, R. "Energy Substitution in U.S. Manufacturing." Unpublished manuscript, University of Washington, 1976.

Halvorsen, R., and Ford, J. "Substitution Among Energy, Capital and Labor Inputs in U.S. Manufacturing." In *Advances in the Economics of Energy and Resources, Vol. I,* edited by R. S. Pindyck. Greenwich, Conn.: JAI, Press, 1978.

Hamilton, J. "Effects of Air Pollution on Materials, Vegetation, and Health." In *Available Methods for Estimating the Economic Damages Resulting from Air Pollution.* Submitted to the California Air Resources Board by Public Interest Economics West, 1979.

Hamlen, W. A. "The Optimality and Feasibility of Uniform Air Pollution Controls." *Journal of Environmental Economics and Management* 5:301–12, 1978.

Hamlisch, R., ed. *Economic Effects of Fisheries Regulation.* FAO Fisheries Reports, no. 5. Rome: Food and Agriculture Organisation, 1962.

Hammack, J., and Brown, G. M. *Waterfowl and Wetlands: Toward Bio-Economic Analysis.* Baltimore: Johns Hopkins Press, 1974.

Hanemann, W. M. *A Methodological and Empirical Study of the Recreation Benefits from Water Quality Improvement.* Berkeley: Department of Agricultural and Resource Economics, University of California, Berkeley, 1978.

Hanke, S. H., and Gutmanis, I. "Estimates of Industrial Waterborne Residuals Control Costs: A Review of Concepts, Methodology, and Empirical Results." In *Cost-Benefit Analysis and Water Pollution Policy,* edited by H. M. Peskin and E. P. Seskin. Washington: The Urban Institute, 1975.

Hannesson, R. "Fishery Dynamics: A North Atlantic Cod Fishery." *Canadian Journal of Economics* 8:151–73, 1975.

Hapgood, F. "Risk-Benefit Analysis: Putting a Price on Life." *Atlantic* 243:33–8, 1979.

Harberger, A. C. "The Taxation of Mineral Industries." In *Federal Tax Policy for Growth and Stability,* pp. 439–49. U.S. Congress, Joint Committee on the Economic Report. Washington: U.S. Government Printing Office, 1955.

Harford, J. D. "Adjustment Costs and Optimal Waste Treatment." *Journal of Environmental Economics and Management* 3:215–25, 1976.

Harris, D. P. "An Application of Multivariate Statistical Analysis to Mineral Exploration." Ph.D. dissertation, Pennsylvania State University, 1965.

Harris, D. P. "A Probability Model of Mineral Wealth." *Transactions of the Society of Mining Engineers* pp. 199–216, 1966.

Harris, D. P. "Geostatistics in the Appraisal of Metal Resources." In *Mineral Materials Modeling,* edited by W. A. Vogely. Washington: Resources for the Future, 1975.

Harrison, D. *Who Pays for Clean Air?* Cambridge, Mass.: Ballinger, 1975.

Harrison, D., and Rubinfeld, D. L. "Hedonic Housing Prices and the Demand for Clean Air." *Journal of Environmental Economics and Management* 5:81–102, 1978*a*.

Harrison, D., and Rubinfeld, D. L. "The Air Pollution and Property Value Debate." *Review of Economics and Statistics* 60:635–8, 1978*b*.

Hartwick, J. M. "Intergenerational Equity and the Investing of Rents from Exhaustible Resources." *American Economic Review* 67:972–4, 1977.

Hartwick, J. M. "Exploitation of Many Deposits of an Exhaustible Resource." *Econometrica* 46:201–18, 1978.

Harvard Water Resources Program. *The Design of Water Resource Systems.* Cambridge, Mass.: Harvard University Press, 1962.

Haurie, A., and Hung, N. M. "Turnpike Properties for the Optimal Use of a Natural Resource." *Review of Economic Studies* 44:329–36, 1977.

Haveman, R. H., and Smith, V. K. "Investment, Inflation, Unemployment, and the Environment." In *Current Issues in U.S. Environmental Policy,* edited by P. R. Portney. Baltimore: Johns Hopkins Press, 1978.

Head, J. G. "Public Goods and Public Policy." *Public Finance* 17:197–219, 1962.

Heal, G. "Economic Aspects of Natural Resource Depletion." In *The Economics of Natural Resource Depletion,* edited by D. W. Pearce and J. Rose, pp. 118–39. New York: John Wiley & Sons, 1975*a*.

Heal, G. "The Influence of Interest Rates on Resource Prices." Cowles Foundation research paper no. 407, Yale University, 1975*b*.

Heal, G. "The Relationship Between Price and Extraction Cost for a Resource with a Backstop Technology." *Bell Journal of Economics* 7:371–8, 1976.

Heal, G. "The Long-Run Movement of the Price of Exhaustible Resources." Presented at Fifth World Congress of the International Economic Association, Tokyo, August/September 1977.

Heck, W. W., and Brandt, C. S. "Effects on Vegetation: Native Crops, Forests." In *Air Pollution, Vol. II, The Effects of Air Pollution,* 3rd ed., edited by A. C. Stern. New York: Academic Press, 1977.

Heintz, H. T., Hershaft, A., and Horak, G. C. *National Damages of Air and Water Pollution.* Rockville, Md.: Enviro Control Inc., 1976.

Helliwell, J. F. "The Effects of Taxes and Royalties on Copper Mining Investment Decisions in British Columbia." Mimeographed. Resources paper no. 5, Programme in Natural Resource Economics, University of British Columbia, 1976.

Henderson, C. "The Tragic Failure of Energy Planning." *Bulletin of the Atomic Scientists* 34:15–19, 1978.

Henry, C. "Investment Decisions Under Uncertainty: The 'Irreversibility Effect,'" *American Economic Review* 64:1006–12, 1974*a*.

Henry, C. "Option Values in the Economics of Irreplaceable Assets." *Review of Economic Studies, Symposium on the Economics of Exhaustible Resources* 89–104, 1974*b*.

Herfindahl, O. C. "Some Fundamentals of Mineral Economics." *Land Economics* 31:131–8, 1955.

Herfindahl, O. C. *Copper Costs and Prices: 1870–1957.* Baltimore: Johns Hopkins Press, 1959.

Herfindahl, O. C. *Three Studies in Mineral Economics.* Washington: Resources for the Future, 1961.

Herfindahl, O. C. "Depletion and Economic Theory." In *Extractive Resources and Taxation,* edited by M. Gaffney. Madison: University of Wisconsin Press, 1967.

Herfindahl, O. C., and Kneese, A. V. *Economic Theory of Natural Resources.* Columbus, Ohio: Charles E. Merrill, 1974.

Hirshleifer, J. "Investment Decision under Uncertainty: Choice-Theoretic Approaches." *Quarterly Journal of Economics* 79:509–36, 1965.

Hirshleifer, J. "Investment Decision under Uncertainty: Applications of the State-Preference Approach." *Quarterly Journal of Economics* 80:252–77, 1966.

Hirshleifer, J. "Sustained Yield Versus Capital Theory." In *The Economics of Sustained Yield Forestry: A Symposium,* edited by B. Dowdle. College of Forestry, University of Washington, Seattle, 1974.

Hirshleifer, J., DeHaven, J. C., and Milliman, J. W. *Water Supply: Economics, Technology and Policy.* Chicago: University of Chicago Press, 1960.

Hirshleifer, J., and Shapiro, D. L. "The Treatment of Risk and Uncertainty." In *Public Expenditure and Policy Analysis,* edited by R. H. Haveman and J. Margolis. Chicago: Markham, 1970.

Hnyilicza, E., and Pindyck, R. S. "Pricing Policies for a Two-Part Exhaustible Resource Cartel: The Case of OPEC." *European Economic Review* 2:139–59, 1976.

Hoch, I. "Urban Scale and Environmental Quality." In *Population, Resources, and the Environment,* edited by R. G. Ridker. U.S. Commission on Population Growth and the American Future, research papers, Vol. III. Washington: U.S. Government Printing Office, 1972.

Hochman, E., and Zilberman, D. "Optimal Exploitation of Energy Resources: Solar Power and Electricity Generation in Below Sea Level Basins." Unpublished manuscript, Department of Agriculture and Resource Economics, University of California, Berkeley, 1980.

Hoel, M. "Extermination of Self-Reproducible Natural Resources Under Competitive Conditions." *Econometrica* 46:219–24, 1978a.

Hoel, M. "Resource Extraction, Uncertainty, and Learning." *Bell Journal of Economics* 9:642–5, 1978b.

Hoffman, K. C. "A Uniform Framework for Energy Systems Planning." In *Energy Modelling,* edited by M. Searl. Washington: Resources for the Future, 1973.

Holdren, J. P., Harte, J., and Tonnessen, K. "Environmental Data Bases and Integrated Models as Assessment Tools: A Critical Survey of Accomplishments, Potential and Limitations." In *Proceedings of the Workshop on Integrated Assessment for Energy-Related Environmental Standards.* Lawrence Berkeley Laboratory, November 2–3, 1978. Washington: U.S. Department of Energy, 1980.

Holdren, J. P., Morris, G., and Mintzer, I. "Environmental Aspects of Renewable Energy Sources." *Annual Review of Energy* 5:241–91, 1980.

Hotelling, H. "The Economics of Exhaustible Resources." *Journal of Political Economy* 39:137–75, 1931.

Howe, C. W. "Economic and Social Perspectives Relevant to Forest Policy." Unpublished manuscript, Department of Economics, University of Colorado, February 1976.

Howe, C. W. *Natural Resource Economics.* New York: John Wiley & Sons, 1979.

Hubbert, M. K. "Energy Resources." In *Resources and Man,* pp. 157–242. National Academy of Sciences–National Resource Council. San Francisco: W. H. Freeman, 1969.

Hudson, E. A., and Jorgenson, D. W. "U.S. Energy Policy and Economic Growth, 1975–2000." *Bell Journal of Economics and Management Science* 5:461–514, 1974.

Hughart, D. "Informational Asymmetry, Bidding Strategies, and the Marketing of Offshore Petroleum Leases." *Journal of Political Economy* 83:969–85, 1975.

Humphrey, D. B., and Moroney, J. R. "Substitution Among Capital, Labor, and Natural Resource Products in American Manufacturing." *Journal of Political Economy* 83:57–82, 1975.

Huxley, T. H. "The Herring." *Nature* 23:607–13, April 28, 1881.

Ingham, A., and Simmons, P. "Natural Resources and Growing Population." *Review of Economic Studies* 42:191–206, 1975.

Intriligator, M. D. *Mathematical Optimization and Economic Theory.* Englewood Cliffs, N.J.: Prentice-Hall, 1971.

Isard, W. "Some Notes on the Linkage of the Ecologic and Economic Systems." Unpublished manuscript, University of Pennsylvania, 1969.

Ise, J. "The Theory of Value as Applied to Natural Resources." *American Economic Review* 15:284–91, 1925.

James, E. "A Note on Uncertainty and the Evaluation of Public Investment Decisions." *American Economic Review* 65:200–5, 1975.

Jarrett, H., ed. *Environmental Quality in a Growing Economy.* Baltimore: Johns Hopkins Press, 1966.

Jevons, W. S. *The Coal Question,* 2nd ed. London: Macmillan, 1965.

Johnson, M. H., and Bell, F. W. "Resources and Scarcity: Are There Limits to Growth?" Unpublished manuscript, Department of Economics, George Mason University, 1978.

Jones-Lee, M. W. *The Value of Life: An Economic Analysis.* Chicago: University of Chicago Press, 1976.

Jorgenson, D. W. "Consumer Demand for Energy." Harvard Institute of Economic Research, discussion paper 386, November 1974.

Joskow, P. L., and Baughman, M. L. "The Future of the U.S. Nuclear Energy Industry." *Bell Journal of Economics* 7:3–32, 1976.

Jungenfelt, K. G. "Some Problems in Forestry Economics." Unpublished manuscript, Stockholm School of Economics, 1975.

Kahn, A. E. "Economic Issues in Regulating the Field Price of Natural Gas." *American Economic Review* 50:506–17, 1960.

Kalter, R. J., Stevens, T. H., and Bloom, O. H. "The Economics of Outer Continental Shelf Leasing." *American Journal of Agricultural Economics* 5:251–8, 1975.

Kalter, R. J., and Tyner, W. E. "An Analysis of Contingency Leasing Options for Outer Continental Shelf Development." Unpublished manuscript, Department of Agriculture and Resource Economics, Cornell University, 1975.

Kalymon, B. A. "Economic Incentives in OPEC Oil Pricing Policy." *Journal of Development Economics* 2:337–62, 1975.

Kamien, M. I., and Schwartz, N. L. "A Note on Resource Usage and Market Structure," *Journal of Economic Theory* 15:394–7, 1977a.

Kamien, M. I., and Schwartz, N. L. "Disaggregated Intertemporal Models with an Exhaustible Resource and Technical Advance." *Journal of Environmental Economics and Management* 4(4):271–88, 1977b.

Kamien, M. I., and Schwartz, N. L. "Optimal Exhaustible Resource Depletion with Endogenous Technical Change." *Review of Economic Studies* 45:179–96, 1978.

Kamien, M. I., Schwartz, N. L., and Dolbear, F. T. "Asymmetry Between Bribes and Charges." *Water Resources Research* 2:147–57, 1966.

Kaufman, G. M. *Statistical Decision and Related Techniques in Oil and Gas Explorations.* Englewood Cliffs, N.J.: Prentice-Hall, 1963.

Kay, J. A., and Mirrlees, J. A. "The Desirability of Natural Resource Depletion." In *The Economics of Natural Resource Depletion,* edited by D. W. Pearce and J. Rose, pp. 140–76. New York: John Wiley & Sons, 1975.

Keeler, E., Spence, M., and Zeckhauser, R. "The Optimal Control of Pollution." *Journal of Economic Theory* 4:19–34, 1972.

Kemp, M. C. "How to Eat a Cake of Unknown Size." In *Three Topics in the Theory of International Trade.* Amsterdam: North-Holland, Publishing, 1976.

Kendrick, J. W. *Productivity Trends in the U.S. Economy.* Princeton: Princeton University Press, 1961.

Kneese, A. V. *Water Pollution: Economic Aspects and Research Needs.* Washington: Resources for the Future, 1962.

Kneese, A. V. *The Economics of Regional Water Quality Management.* Baltimore: Johns Hopkins Press, 1964.

Kneese, A. V. "Analysis of Environmental Pollution." *Swedish Journal of Economics* March 1971.

Kneese, A. V. "Natural Resources Policy 1975–1985." *Journal of Environmental Economics and Management* 3:253–88, 1976.

Kneese, A. V. *Economics and the Environment.* New York: Penguin Books, 1977.

Kneese, A. V., Ayres, R. U., and d'Arge, R. C. *Economics and the Environment: A Materials Balance Approach.* Washington: Resources for the Future, 1970.

Kneese, A. V., and Bower, B. T. *Managing Water Quality: Economics, Technology, Institutions.* Baltimore: Johns Hopkins Press, 1968.

Kneese, A. V., and Bower, B. T. *Environmental Quality and Residuals Management.* Baltimore: Johns Hopkins Press, 1979.

Kneese, A. V., and Schultze, C. L. *Pollution, Prices and Public Policy.* Washington: Brookings Institution, 1975.

Kneese, A. V., and Schulze, W. D. "Environment, Health, and Economics: The Case of Cancer." Presented at American Economic Association annual meeting, Atlantic City, September 16–18, 1976.

Knetsch, J. L., and Davis, R. K. "Comparisons of Methods for Recreation Evaluation." In *Water Research,* edited by A. V. Kneese and S. C. Smith. Baltimore: Johns Hopkins Press, 1966.

Kohn, R. E. "Application of Linear Programming to a Controversy on Air Pollution Control." *Management Science* 17:B-609–B-621, 1971*a*.

Kohn, R. E. "Optimal Air Quality Standards." *Econometrica* 39:983–95, 1971*b*.

Kohn, R. E. "Price Elasticities of Demand and Air Pollution Control." *Review of Economics and Statistics* 54:392–400, 1972.

Kohn, R. E. "Input-Output Analysis and Air Pollution Control." In *Economic Analysis and Environmental Problems,* edited by E. S. Mills. New York: Columbia University Press for the NBER, 1975.

Kohn, R. E., and Aucamp, D. C. "Abatement, Avoidance, and Nonconvexity." *American Economic Review* 66:947–52, 1976.

Kolm, S. C. "Les nonconvexities d'externalité." CEPREMAP Rapport no. 11. Paris: CEPREMAP, 1971.

Koopmans, T. C. "Stationary Ordinal Utility and Impatience." *Econometrica* 28:287–309, 1960.

Koopmans, T. C. "On the Concept of Optimal Economic Growth." In *The Econometric Approach to Development Planning,* pp. 225–300. Amsterdam: North-Holland, Publishing, 1965.

Koopmans, T. C. "Some Observations on 'Optimal' Economic Growth and Exhaustible Resources." In *Economic Structure and Development: Essays in Honor of Jan Tinbergen,* edited by H. C. Bos, H. Linnemann, and P. de Wolff, pp. 239–55. Amsterdam: North-Holland Publishing, 1973.

Koopmans, T. C. "Proof for a Case where Discounting Advances Doomsday." *Review of Economic Studies, Symposium on the Economics of Exhaustible Resources* 117–20, 1974.

Krutilla, J. V. "Conservation Reconsidered." *American Economic Review* 47:777–86, 1967.

Krutilla, J. V., and Cicchetti, C. J. "Evaluating Benefits of Environmental Resources with Special Application to the Hell's Canyon." *Natural Resources Journal* 12:1–29, 1972.

Krutilla, J. V., and Eckstein, O. *Multiple Purpose River Development.* Baltimore: Johns Hopkins Press, 1958.

Krutilla, J. V., and Fisher, A. C. *The Economics of Natural Environments:*

Studies in the Valuation of Commodity and Amenity Resources. Baltimore: Johns Hopkins Press, 1975.

Kuller, R. G., and Cummings, R. G. "An Economic Model of Production and Investment for Petroleum Reservoirs." *American Economic Review* 64:66–79, 1974.

Kuznets, S. *National Product Since 1869*. New York: National Bureau of Economic Research, 1946.

Landsberg, H. H., Fischman, L. L., and Fisher, J. L. *Resources in America's Future*. Baltimore: Johns Hopkins Press, 1963.

Lave, L. B., and Seskin, E. P. *Air Pollution and Human Health*. Baltimore: Johns Hopkins Press, 1977.

Lee, T., and Chao, C. "Abundance of Chemical Elements in the Earth's Crust and Its Major Tectonic Units." *International Geology Review* 12:778–86, 1970.

Leland, H. E. "Capital Asset Markets, Production, and Optimality: A Synthesis." Technical report 115, IMSSS, Stanford University, 1973.

Leland, H. E. "Optimal Risk Sharing and the Leasing of Natural Resources." Working paper no. 38, Institute of Business and Economic Research, University of California, Berkeley, 1975.

Leland, H. E., Norgaard, R., and Pearson, S. "An Economic Analysis of Alternative Outer Continental Shelf Petroleum Leasing Policies." Unpublished manuscript, School of Business Administration, University of California, Berkeley, 1974.

Leontief, W. "Environmental Repercussions and the Economic Structure: An Input-Output Approach." *Review of Economics and Statistics* 52:262–71, 1970.

Leopold, L. B. "Quantitative Comparisons of Some Aesthetic Factors Among Rivers." USGS Survey 620. Washington, D.C.: USGS, 1969.

Leung, A., and Wang, A. Y. "Analysis of Models for Commercial Fishing: Mathematical and Economic Aspects." *Econometrica* 44:295–303, 1976.

Lewis, T. R. "Monopoly Exploitation of an Exhaustible Resource." *Journal of Environmental Economics and Management* 3:198–204, 1976.

Lewis, T. R. "Attitudes toward Risk and the Optimal Exploitation of an Exhaustible Resource." *Journal of Environmental Economics and Management* 4:111–19, 1977.

Lieberman, M. A. "United States Uranium Resources—An Analysis of Historical Data." *Science* 192(4238):431–6, 1976.

Lind, R. C. "Special Equilibrium, the Theory of Rents, and the Measurement of Benefits from Public Programs." *Quarterly Journal of Economics* 87:188–207, 1973.

Little, Arthur D., Inc. *Study of Energy-Saving Options for Refrigerators and Water Heaters, Vol. 1, Refrigerators*. Cambridge, Mass.: Arthur D. Little, 1977.

Löf, G., and Kneese, A. V. *The Economics of Water Utilization in the Beet Sugar Industry*. Baltimore: Johns Hopkins Press, 1968.

Long, N. V. "Resource Extraction Under Uncertainty about Possible Nationalization." *Journal of Economic Theory* 10:42–53, 1975.

Long, T. V., and Schipper, L. "Resource and Energy Substitution." *Energy* 3:63–82, 1978.

Lorie, J. H., and Savage, L. J. "Three Problems in Rationing Capital." *Journal of Business* 28:229–39, 1955.

Lotka, A. J. *Elements of Mathematical Biology.* 1924. Reprint. New York: Dover Publications, 1956.

Loury, G. C. "The Optimal Exploitation of an Unknown Reserve." *Review of Economic Studies* 45:621–36, 1978.

Lovejoy, W. F., and Homan, P. T. *Economic Aspects of Oil Conservation Regulation.* Baltimore: Johns Hopkins Press, 1967.

MacAvoy, P. W., and Pindyck, R. S. *The Economics of the Natural Gas Shortage (1960–1980).* Amsterdam: North-Holland Publishing, 1975.

Magat, W. A. "Pollution Control and Technical Advance: A Dynamic Model of the Firm." *Journal of Environmental Economics and Management* 5:1–25, 1978.

Magnus, J. R. "Substitution Between Energy and Non-Energy Inputs in The Netherlands: 1950–1974." University of Amsterdam, November 1975.

Mäler, K. G. *Environmental Economics.* Baltimore: Johns Hopkins Press, 1974.

Malinvaud, E. "Capital Accumulation and Efficient Allocation of Resources." *Econometrica* 21:233–68, 1953.

Manne, A. S. "Waiting for the Breeder." *Review of Economic Studies, Symposium on the Economics of Exhaustible Resources* 47–65. 1974.

Manne, A. S. "ETA: A Model for Energy Technology Assessment." *Bell Journal of Economics* 7:379–406, 1976.

*Man's Impact on the Global Environment: Assessment and Recommendations for Action.* Report of the Study of Critical Environmental Problems. Cambridge, Mass.: M.I.T. Press, 1970.

Manthy, R. S. *Natural Resource Commodities—A Century of Statistics.* Baltimore: Johns Hopkins Press, 1978.

Marcuse, W., et al. "A Dynamic Time Dependent Model for the Analysis of Alternative Energy Policies." In *Operational Research '75,* edited by K. B. Haley. Proceedings of the Seventh IFORS International Conference on Operations Research.

Marglin, S. A. "The Social Rate of Discount and the Optimal Rate of Investment." *Quarterly Journal of Economics* 77:95–112, 1963.

McDonald, S. L. *Federal Tax Treatment of Oil and Gas.* Washington: Brookings Institution, 1963.

McFadden, D., Puig, C., and Kirshner, D. "Determinants of the Long Run Demand for Electricity." In *Proceedings of the Business and Economic Statistics Section, American Statistical Association,* 1977.

McGuire, C. B. "Interest Competition and the Design of Lease Sales for

Western Coal Lands." Unpublished manuscript, Graduate School of Public Policy, University of California, Berkeley, June 1978.

McInerney, J. "The Simple Analytics of Natural Resource Economics." *Journal of Agricultural Economics* 27:31–52, 1976.

McKean, R. N. *Efficiency in Government through Systems Analysis, with Emphasis on Water Resource Development.* New York: John Wiley & Sons, 1958.

McKelvey, V. E. "Mineral Resource Estimates and Public Policy." *American Scientist* 60:32–40, 1972.

Mead, W. J. "Natural Resource Disposal Policy: Oral Auctions Versus Sealed Bids." *Natural Resources Journal* 7:194–224, 1967.

Meade, J. E. "External Economies and Diseconomies in a Competitive Situation." *Economic Journal* 62:54–67, 1952.

Meadows, D. H., et al. *The Limits to Growth.* New York: Universe Books, 1972.

Merklein, H. A., and Howell, F. M. "What It Costs to Find Hydrocarbons in the U.S." *World Oil* October 1973.

Meyer, J. R., and Leone, R. A. "The Urban Disamenity Revisited." In *Public Economics and the Quality of Life,* edited by L. Wingo and A. Evans, Baltimore: Johns Hopkins Press, 1977.

Meyer, R. A. "Externalities as Commodities." *American Economic Review* 61:736–40, 1969.

Mill, J. S. *Principles of Political Economy.* 1848, Reprint. London: Longmans, Green, 1929.

Millecan, A. A. *A Survey and Assessment of Air Pollution Damage to California Vegetation: 1970 through 1974.* Sacramento: California Department of Food and Agriculture, 1976.

Miller, E. M. "Macro-Economic Effects of Resource Discovery and Depletion." *American Journal of Economics and Sociology* 36:241–9, 1977.

Mills, E. S. "Economic Incentives in Air Pollution Control." In *Economics of Air Pollution,* edited by H. Wolozin, New York: Norton and Co., 1968.

Mishan, E. J. "Pareto Optimality and the Law." *Oxford Economic Papers* 19:255–87, 1967.

Mishan, E. J. "The Postwar Literature on Externalities: An Interpretative Essay." *Journal of Economic Literature* 9:1–28, 1971*a*.

Mishan, E. J. "Pangloss on Pollution." *Swedish Journal of Economics* 73, 1971*b*.

Mishan, E. J. "What Is the Optimal Level of Pollution?" *Journal of Political Economy* 82:1287–99, 1974.

Mishan, E. J. "Does Perfect Competition in Mining Produce Optimal Rate of Exploitation?" London School of Economics, 1977.

Mohring, H. "The Costs of Inefficient Fishery Regulation: A Partial Study of the Pacific Coast Halibut Industry." Unpublished manuscript, Department of Economics, University of Minnesota, 1974.

Mount, T. D., Chapman, L. D., and Tyrrell, T. J. "Electricity Demand in the United States: An Economic Analysis." Oak Ridge National Laboratory technical report, June 1973.

Mueller, D. C. *Public Choice*. Cambridge University Press, 1979.

Mumey, G. A. "The 'Coase Theorem': A Reexamination." *Quarterly Journal of Economics* 85:718–23, 1971.

Musgrove, P. "The Distribution of Metal Resources (Tests and Implications of the Exponential Grade-Size Relation)." In *Proceedings of the Council of Economics of the American Institute of Mining, Metallurgical and Petroleum Engineers (AIME)*, pp. 340–471. New York: AIME, 1971.

National Academy of Sciences. *Air Quality and Automobile Emission Control*. Washington: U.S. Government Printing Office, 1974*a*.

National Academy of Sciences/National Academy of Engineering. *The Costs and Benefits of Automobile Emission Control. Air Quality and Emission Control, Vol. 4*. Prepared for the Committee on Public Works, U.S. Senate, serial no. 93–24. Washington: U.S. Government Printing Office, 1974*b*.

National Coal Association. *Coal Facts*. Washington: National Coal Association, 1978.

National Commission on Water Quality. *Staff Report*. Washington: National Commission on Water Quality, 1976.

National Research Council, Commission on Biologic Effects of Atmospheric Pollutants. *Lead: Airborne Lead in Perspective*. Washington: National Academy of Sciences, 1972.

Neher, P. A. "Notes on the Volterra-Quadratic Fishery." *Journal of Economic Theory* 8:39–49, 1974.

Nelson, J. P. "The Demand for Space Heating Energy." *Review of Economics and Statistics* 57:508–22, 1975.

Nelson, J. P. *Economic Analysis of Transportation Noise Abatement*. Cambridge, Mass.: Ballinger, 1978.

Netschert, B. C. *The Future Supply of Oil and Gas*. Baltimore: Johns Hopkins Press, 1958.

Netschert, B. C., Landsberg, H. H. *The Future Supply of the Major Metals*. Washington: Resources for the Future, 1961.

Nichols, A., and Zeckhauser, R. J. "Stockpiling Strategies and Cartel Prices." *Bell Journal of Economics* 8:66–96, 1977.

Niskanen, W. A., and Hanke, S. H. "Land Prices Substantially Underestimate the Value of Environmental Quality." *Review of Economics and Statistics* 59:375–7, 1977.

Noll, R. G., and Trijonis, J. "Mass Balance, General Equilibrium, and Environmental Externalities." *American Economic Review* 61:730–5, 1971.

Nordhaus, W. D. "World Dynamics—Measurement Without Data." *Economic Journal* 83:1156–83, 1973*a*.

Nordhaus, W. D. "The Allocation of Energy Resources." *Brookings Papers* 3:529–70, 1973*b*.

References 264

Nordhaus, W. D. "Resources as a Constraint on Growth." *American Economic Review* 64:22–6, 1974.

Nordhaus, W. D. "The Climatic Impact of Long Run Energy Growth." Presented at the American Economic Association annual meeting, Atlantic City, N.J., August 16–18, 1976*a*.

Nordhaus, W. D. "The Demand for Energy: An International Perspective." In *Proceedings of the Workshop on Energy Demand,* CP-76-1, edited by W. D. Nordhaus. Laxenburg, Austria: International Institute for Applied Systems Analysis, 1976*b*.

Nordhaus, W. D. "A Simulation Model of the Allocation of Energy Resources and Technology." Unpublished manuscript, 1976*c*.

Nordhaus, W. D., and Tobin, J. "Is Growth Obsolete?" In *Studies in Income and Wealth, Vol. 38, The Measurement of Economic and Social Performance,* edited by M. Moss. New York: National Bureau of Economic Research, 1973.

Norgaard, R. B. "Resource Scarcity and New Technology in U.S. Petroleum Development." *Natural Resources Journal* 15:265–95, 1975.

Office of Science and Technology. *Cumulative Regulatory Effects on the Cost of Automotive Transportation.* Washington: U.S. Government Printing Office, 1972.

Olson, M. L. *The Logic of Collective Action.* Cambridge; Mass.: Harvard University Press, 1964.

Opaluch, J. *River Basin Management: The Optimal Control of Water Quantity and Quality.* Ph.D. dissertation, University of California, Berkeley, 1980.

Oren M. E., and Williams, A. C. "On Competitive Bidding." *Operations Research* 23:1972–9, 1975.

Organization for Economic Cooperation and Development. *Economic Aspects of Fish Production.* International Symposium on Fishery Economics, Paris, 29 November to 3 December 1971. Paris: Organization for Economic Cooperation and Development, 1972.

Orr, L. "Incentive for Innovation as the Basis for Effluent Charge Strategy." *American Economic Review* 66:441–7, 1976.

Page, R. T. *Economics of Involuntary Transfers: A Unified Approach to Pollution and Congestion Externalities.* New York: Springer-Verlag, 1973*a*.

Page, R. T., "Failure of Bribes and Standards for Pollution Abatement." *Natural Resources Journal* 13:677–704, 1973*b*.

Page, R. T. *Conservation and Economic Efficiency.* Baltimore: Johns Hopkins Press, 1977.

Page, R. T., and Ferejohn, J. "Externalities as Commodities: Comment." *American Economic Review* 64:454–9, 1974.

Paish, F. W. "Causes of Changes in Gold Supply." *Economica* 5:379–409, 1938.

Pearce, D. W., ed. *The Valuation of Social Cost.* London: George Allen & Unwin, 1978.

Pearce, D. W., and Rose, J., eds. *The Economics of Natural Resource Depletion.* New York: John Wiley & Sons, 1975.

Peirce, W. S. "Factors Affecting Responsiveness to Technological Innovations in Coal Mining." Working paper no. 54, Research Program in Industrial Economics, Case Western Reserve University, 1974.

Peskin, H. M. "Environmental Policy and the Distribution of Benefits and Costs." In *Current Issues in U.S. Environmental Policy,* edited by P. R. Portney, Baltimore: Johns Hopkins Press, 1978.

Peskin, H. M., and Seskin, E. P., eds. *Cost-Benefit Analysis and Water Pollution Policy.* Washington: Urban Institute, 1975.

Peterson, F. M. "Two Externalities in Petroleum Exploration." In *Studies in Energy Tax Policy,* edited by G. M. Brannon. Cambridge, Mass.: Ballinger, 1975.

Peterson, F. M. "A Theory of Mining and Exploring for Exhaustible Resources." *Journal of Environmental Economics and Management* 5:236–51, 1978.

Peterson, F. M., and Fisher, A. C. "The Exploitation of Extractive Resources: A Survey." *Economic Journal* 87:681–721, 1977.

Phelps, E. S., and Riley, J. G. "Rawsian Growth: Dynamic Programming of Capital and Wealth for Intergeneration 'Maximin' Justice." *Review of Economic Studies* 45:103–20, 1978.

Pigou, A. C. *The Economics of Welfare,* 4th ed. London: Macmillan, 1932.

Pinchot, G. *The Fight for Conservation.* New York: Doubleday, Page & Co., 1970.

Pindyck, R. S. "International Comparisons of the Residential Demand for Energy: A Preliminary Analysis." Massachusetts Institute of Technology Energy Laboratory working paper 76–023, September 1976.

Pindyck, R. S. "Interfuel Substitution and the Industrial Demand for Energy: An International Comparison." Massachusetts Institute of Technology Energy Laboratory working paper 77–026, August 1977a.

Pindyck, R. S. "Cartel Pricing and the Structure of the World Bauxite Market." *Bell Journal of Economics* 8:343–60, 1977b.

Pindyck, R. S. "Gains to Producers from the Cartelization of Exhaustible Resources." *Review of Economics and Statistics* 60:238–51, 1978a.

Pindyck, R. S. "Optimal Exploration and Production of a Renewable Resource." *Journal of Political Economy* 86:841–62, 1978b.

Pindyck, R. S. *The Structure of World Energy Demand.* Cambridge, Mass.: M.I.T. Press, 1978c.

Pindyck, R. S. "Uncertainty and the Pricing of Exhaustible Resources." Massachusetts Institute of Technology Energy Laboratory working paper 79–021, 1979.

Pines, D., and Weiss, Y. "Land Improvement Projects and Land Values." Mimeograph. May 1974.

Plott, C. R. "Externalities and Corrective Taxes." *Economica* 33:84–7, 1966.

Plourde, C. G. "A Simple Model of Replenishable Natural Resource Exploitation." *American Economic Review* 60:518–22, 1970.

Plourde, C. G. "Exploitation of Common Property Replenishable Natural Resources." *Western Economic Journal* 9:256–66, 1971.

Plourde, C. G. "A Model of Waste Accumulation and Disposals." *Canadian Journal of Economics* 5:119–25, 1972.

Polinsky, A. M. and Rubinfeld, D. L. "Property Values and the Benefits of Environmental Improvements: Theory and Measurement." In *Public Economics and the Quality of Life,* edited by L. Wingo and A. Evans. Baltimore: Johns Hopkins Press, 1977.

Polinsky, A. M., and Shavell, S. "The Air Pollution and Property Value Debate." *Review of Economics and Statistics* 57:100–4, 1975.

Polinsky, A. M., and Shavell, S. "Amenities and Property Values in a Model of an Urban Area." *Journal of Public Economics* 5:119–29, 1976.

Pontryagin, L. S., Boltyanskii, V. G., Gamkrelidze, R. V., and Mishchenko, E. F. *The Mathematical Theory of Optimal Processes.* New York: Interscience, 1962.

Porter, R. C. "The Long-Run Asymmetry of Subsidies and Taxes as Anti-Pollution Policies." *Water Resources Research* 10:415–17, 1974.

Porter, R. C. "New Approaches to Wilderness Preservation Through Benefit-Cost Analysis." Unpublished manuscript, Department of Economics, University of Michigan, 1978.

Portes, R. D. "The Search for Efficiency in the Presence of Externalities." In *Unfashionable Economics: Essays in Honor of Lord Balogh,* edited by P. Streeten. London: Weidenfeld and Nicolson, 1970.

Portney, P. R. "Toxic Substance Policy and the Protection of Human Health." In *Current Issues in U.S. Environmental Policy,* edited by P. R. Portney, Baltimore: Johns Hopkins Press, 1978.

Portney, P. R., Sonstelie, J., and Kneese, A. V. "Environmental Quality, Household Migration, and Collective Choice." In *The Governance of Common Property Resources,* edited by E. T. Haefele. Baltimore: Johns Hopkins Press, 1974.

Potter, N., and Christy, F. T. *Trends in Natural Resource Commodities: Statistics of Prices, Output, Consumption, Foreign Trade and Employment in the United States 1870–1957.* Baltimore: Johns Hopkins Press, 1962.

Quirk, J. P., and Smith, V. L. "Dynamic Models of Fishing." In *Economics of Fisheries Management: A Symposium,* edited by A. D. Scott, pp. 3–32. Vancouver: Institute of Animal Resource Ecology, University of British Columbia, 1970.

Radetzki, M. "Metal Mineral Resource Exhaustion and the Threat to Material Progress: The Case of Copper." *World Development* 3:123–36, 1975.

Ramsay, W. *Unpaid Costs of Electrical Energy—Health and Environmental Impacts of Coal and Nuclear Power.* Baltimore: Johns Hopkins Press, 1978.

Ramsey, F. P. "A Mathematical Theory of Saving." *Economic Journal* 38:543–59, 1928.

Ramsey, F. P. *The Foundations of Mathematics and Other Logical Essays.* London: Routledge and Kegan Paul, 1931.

Randall, A. "Market Solutions to Externality Problems: Theory and Practice." *American Journal of Agricultural Economics* 54:175–83, 1972.

Randall, A., Ives, B., and Eastman, C. "Bidding Games for Valuation of Aesthetic Environmental Improvements." *Journal of Environmental Economics and Management* 1:132–49, 1974.

Rausser, G. "Technological Change, Production, and Investment in Natural Resource Industries." *American Economic Review* 64:1049–59, 1974.

Rausser, G., and Lapan, H. "Natural Resources, Goods, Bads, and Alternative Institutional Frameworks." *Resources and Energy* 2:1–32, 1979.

Rawls, J. *A Theory of Justice.* Cambridge; Mass.: Harvard University Press, 1971.

Recart, V. A. "Optimal Exploitation Strategy for a Mineral Deposit." M.S. thesis, University of California, Los Angeles, 1972.

Renshaw, E. F. "Should the Federal Government Subsidize Industrial Pollution Control Investments?" *Journal of Environmental Economics and Management* 1:84–8, 1974.

Ricardo, D. *Principles of Political Economy and Taxation.* 1817. Reprint. London: Everyman, 1926.

Richardson, H. W. *Economic Aspects of the Energy Crisis.* Lexington, Mass.: Lexington Books, 1975.

Richels, R. G. "R&D Under Uncertainty: A Study of the U.S. Breeder Reactor Program." Ph.D. dissertation, Harvard University, 1976.

Richels, R. G., and Weyant, J. P. "Models for Energy Technology Assessment." *Advances in Energy Systems and Technology* 2:179–260, 1979.

Ridker, R. G. *Economic Costs of Air Pollution.* New York: Praeger, 1967.

Ridker, R. G., ed. *Population, Resources, and the Environment.* Vol. III of research reports, U.S. Commission on Population Growth and the American Future. Washington: U.S. Government Printing Office, 1972.

Ridker, R. G., and Henning, J. A. "The Determinants of Residential Property Values with Special Reference to Air Pollution." *Review of Economics and Statistics* 49:246–57, 1967.

Robinson, C. "The Depletion of Energy Resources." In *The Economics of Natural Resource Depletion,* edited by D. W. Pearce and J. Rose, pp. 21–55. New York: John Wiley & Sons, 1975.

Rødseth, A., and Strøm, S. "The Demand for Energy in Norwegian Households with Special Emphasis on the Demand for Electricity." Institute of Economics research memorandum, University of Oslo, April 1976.

Rogerson, W. P. "Aggregate Expected Consumer Surplus as a Welfare Index with an Application to Price Stabilization." *Econometrica* 48:423–36, 1980.

Rose-Ackerman, S. "Effluent Charges: A Critique." *Canadian Journal of Economics* 6:512–28, 1973.

Rosenberg, N. "Innovative Responses to Materials Shortages." *American Economic Review* 63:111–18, 1973.

Rosenfeld, A. H. "Some Potentials for Energy and Peak Power Conservation in California." LBL-5926, Lawrence Berkeley Laboratory, University of California, Berkeley, 1977.

Rosenfeld, A. H., Goldstein, D. B., Lichtenberg, A. J., and Craig, P. P. "Saving Half of California's Energy and Peak Power in Buildings and Appliances." Unpublished manuscript, Department of Physics, University of California, Berkeley, 1978.

Rothkopf, M. H. "A Model of Rational Competitive Bidding." *Management Science* 15:362–73, 1969.

Rowe, R. D., d'Arge, R. C., and Brookshire, D. S. "An Experiment on the Economic Value of Visibility." *Journal of Environmental Economics and Management* 7:1–19, 1980.

Ruff, L. E. "The Economic Common Sense of Pollution." *The Public Interest* 19:69–85, 1970.

Russell, C. S. "Model for Investigation of Industrial Response to Residuals Management Actions." *Swedish Journal of Economics* 73:134–56, 1971.

Russell, C. S. *Residuals Management in Industry: A Case Study of Petroleum Refining.* Baltimore: Johns Hopkins Press, 1973.

Russell, C. S., and Spofford, W. O. "A Quantitative Framework for Residuals Management Decisions." In *Environmental Quality Analysis: Theory and Method in the Social Sciences,* edited by A. V. Kneese and B. T. Bower. Baltimore: Johns Hopkins Press, 1972.

Russell, C. S., and Spofford, W. O. "A Regional Environmental Quality Management Model: An Assessment." *Journal of Environmental Economics and Management* 4:89–110, 1977.

Russell, C. S., and Vaughan, W. J. "A Linear Programming Model of Residuals Management for Integrated Iron and Steel Production." *Journal of Environmental Economics and Management* 1:17–42, 1974.

Russell, C. S., and Vaughan, W. J. *Steel Production: Processes, Products, and Residuals.* Baltimore: Johns Hopkins Press, 1976.

Salant, S. W. "Exhaustible Resources and Industrial Structure. A Nash-Cournot Approach to the World Oil Market." *Journal of Political Economy* 84:1079–93, 1976.

Sampson, A. A. "A Model of Optimal Depletion of Renewable Resources." *Journal of Economic Theory* 12:315–24, 1976.

Samuelson, P. A. "The Pure Theory of Public Expenditure." *Review of Economics and Statistics* 36:387–9, 1954.

Samuelson, P. A. "Discussion." *American Economic Review* 54:93–96, 1964.

Samuelson, P. A. "Economics of Forestry in an Evolving Society." *Economic Inquiry* 14:466–92, 1976.

Sandmo, A. "Discount Rates for Public Investment Under Uncertainty." *International Economic Review* 13:287–302, 1972.

Sandmo, A. and Dreze, J. H. "Discount Rates for Public Investment in Closed and Open Economies." *Economica* 38:395–412, 1971.

Sawyer, J. W. *Automotive Scrap Recycling: Processes, Prices, and Prospects.* Baltimore: Johns Hopkins Press, 1974.

Schaefer, M. B. "Some Aspects of the Dynamics of Populations Important to the Management of the Commercial Marine Fisheries." *Bulletin of the Inter-American Tropical Tuna Commission* (La Jolla, California) 1:25–56, 1954.

Schaefer, M. B. "Some Considerations of Population Dynamics and Economics in Relation to the Commercial Marine Fisheries." *Journal of Fisheries Research Board of Canada* 14:669–81, 1957.

Schanz, J. L. *Resource Terminology: An Examination of Concepts and Terms and Recommendations for Improvement.* Palo Alto: Electric Power Research Institute, 1975.

Scherer, C. R. "Operational Management Models for Commercially Harvested Fisheries." Engineering Systems Department, University of California, Los Angeles, 1976.

Schipper, L., and Lichtenberg, A. J. "Efficient Energy Use and Well-Being: The Swedish Example." *Science* 194:1001–13, 1976.

Schmalensee, R. "Option Demand and Consumer's Surplus: Valuing Price Changes under Uncertainty." *American Economic Review* 62:813–24, 1972.

Schmalensee, R. "Resource Exploitation Theory and the Behavior of the Oil Cartel." *European Economic Review* 7:257–79, 1976.

Schramm, G. "Design of a Resource Allocation Function." *Canadian Journal of Economics* 5:515–30, 1972.

Schulze, W. D. "The Optimal Use of Nonrenewable Resources: The Theory of Extraction." *Journal of Environmental Economics and Management* 1:53–73, 1974.

Schulze, W. D., and d'Arge, R. C. "The Coase Proposition, Information Constraints, and Long-Run Equilibrium." *American Economic Review* 64:763–72, 1974.

Schurr, S. H., and Netschert, B. C. *Energy in the American Economy, 1850–1975: An Economic Study of its History and Prospects.* Baltimore: Johns Hopkins Press,1960.

Scitovsky, T. "Two Concepts of External Economies." *Journal of Political Economy* 62:143–51, 1954.

Scotchmer, S. "Estimating the Value of Amenity Improvement Using Property Values." In *Available Methods for Estimating the Economic Damages Resulting from Air Pollution.* Submitted to the California Air Resources Board by Public Interest Economies West, 1979.

Scott, A. D. "Notes on User Cost." *Economic Journal* 63:368–84, 1953.

Scott, A. D. *Natural Resources: The Economics of Conservation.* Toronto: University of Toronto Press, 1955a.

Scott, A. D. "The Fishery: The Objectives of Sole Ownership." *Journal of Political Economy* 63:116–24, 1955*b*.

Scott, A. D., ed. *Economics of Fisheries Management: A Symposium.* Vancouver: Institute of Animal Resource Ecology, University of British Columbia, 1970.

Shaw R. "The Simple Analytics of Natural Resource Economics: A Correction." Department of Political Economy, University of Aberdeen, 1977.

Sims, W. A. "The Response of Firms to Pollution Charges." *Canadian Journal of Economics* 12:57–74, 1979.

Singer, D. A. "Mineral Resource Models and the Alaskan Mineral Resource Assessment Program." In *Non-Fuel Mineral Models: A State of the Art Review,* edited by W. Vogely. Baltimore: Johns Hopkins Press, 1976.

Singer, D. A., Cox, D. P., and Drew, L. J. "Grade and Tonnage Relationships Among Copper Deposits." U.S. Geological Survey professional paper 907-A. Washington: U.S. Government Printing Office, 1975.

Singleton, F. D., Jr., Calloway, J. A., and Thompson, R. G. "An Integrated Power Process Model of Water Use and Waste Water Treatment in Chlor-Alkali Production." *Water Resources Research* 11:515–25, 1975.

Slichter, L. B. "Some Aspects, Mainly Geographical, of Mineral Exploration." In *Natural Resources,* edited by M. R. Huberty and W. L. Flock, pp. 368–412. New York: McGraw-Hill, 1959.

Small, K. A. "Air Pollution and Property Values: A Further Comment." *Review of Economics and Statistics* 57:105–7, 1975.

Smith, F. A. *The Economic Theory of Industrial Waste Production and Disposal.* Ph.D. dissertation, Northwestern University, 1968.

Smith, F. A. "Waste Material Recovery and Re-Use." In *Population, Resources, and the Environment,* edited by R. G. Ridker. Washington: U.S. Government Printing Office, 1972.

Smith, R. S. "The Feasibility of an 'Injury Tax' Approach to Occupational Safety." *Law and Contemporary Problems* 38:730–44, 1974.

Smith, R. S. *The Occupational Safety and Health Act: Its Goals and Its Achievements.* Washington: American Enterprise Institute, 1976.

Smith, V. K. "The Implication of Common Property Resources for Technical Change." *European Economic Review* 3:469–79, 1972.

Smith, V. K. *Technical Change, Relative Prices, and Environmental Resource Evaluation.* Baltimore: Johns Hopkins Press, 1974.

Smith, V. K. "Detrimental Externalities, Nonconvexities, and Technical Change." *Journal of Public Economics* 4:289–95, 1975.

Smith, V. K. "Natural Resource Scarcity: A Statistical Analysis." *Review of Economics and Statistics* 61:423–7, 1979*a*.

Smith, V. K., ed. *Scarcity and Growth Reconsidered.* Baltimore: Johns Hopkins Press, 1979*b*.

Smith, V. L. "Economics of Production From Natural Resources." *American Economic Review* 58:409–31, 1968.

Smith, V. L. "On Models of Commercial Fishing." *Journal of Political Economy* 77:181–98, 1969.

Smith, V. L. "Dynamics of Waste Accumulation: Disposal Versus Recycling." *Quarterly Journal of Economics* 86:600–16, 1972.

Smith, V. L. "The Primitive Hunter Culture, Pleistocene Extinction, and the Rise of Agriculture." *Journal of Political Economy* 83:727–55, 1975.

Smith, V. L. "Control Theory Applied to Natural and Environmental Resources: An Exposition." *Journal of Environmental Economics and Management* 4:1–24, 1977.

Solow, R. M. "Richard T. Ely Lecture: The Economics of Resources or the Resources of Economics." *American Economic Review* 64:1–14, 1974*a*.

Solow, R. M. "Intergenerational Equity and Exhaustible Resources." *Review of Economic Studies, Symposium on the Economics of Exhaustible Resources* 29–45, 1974*b*.

Solow, R. M., and Wan, F. Y. "Extraction Costs in the Theory of Exhaustible Resources." *Bell Journal of Economics* 7:359–70, 1976.

Southey, C. "Policy Prescriptions in Economic Models. The Case of the Fishery." *Journal of Political Economy* 80:769–75, 1972.

Spence, A. M. "Blue Whales and Applied Control Theory." In *Systems Approaches and Environmental Problems,* edited H. W. Gottinger. Gottingen: Vandenhoeck and Ruprecht, 1973.

Spofford, W. O., Russell, C. S., and Kelly, R. A. "Environmental Quality Management: An Application to the Lower Delaware Valley." Research paper R-1, Resources for the Future. Washington: RFF, 1976.

Stanford Research Institute. *Assessment of Economic Impact of Air Pollutants on Vegetation in the U.S.: 1969 and 1971.* NTIS publication number PB 224 818, 1973.

Stankey, G. H. "A Strategy for the Definition and Management of Wilderness Quality." In *Natural Environments: Studies in Theoretical and Applied Analysis,* edited by J. V. Krutilla. Baltimore: Johns Hopkins Press, 1972.

Starrett, D. A. "Fundamental Nonconvexities in the Theory of Externalities." *Journal of Economic Theory* 4:180–99, 1972.

Starrett, D., and Zeckhauser, R. J. "Treating External Diseconomies— Markets or Taxes?" In *Statistical and Mathematical Aspects of Pollution Problems,* edited by J. W. Pratt, pp. 65–84, New York: Marcel Dekker, 1974.

Steele, H. "Cost Trends and the Supply of Crude Oil in the United States: Analysis and 1973–1985 Supply Schedule Projections." In *Energy: Demand, Conservation, and Institutional Problems,* edited by M. S. Macrakis, pp. 303–17. Cambridge, Mass.: M.I.T. Press, 1974.

Steiner, P. O. "Percentage Depletion and Resource Allocation." In *Tax Revision Compendium,* pp. 949–66. U.S. Congress, House Committee on Ways and Means. Washington: U.S. Government Printing Office, 1959.

Stiglitz, J. E. "Growth with Exhaustible Natural Resources: Efficient and Optimal Growth Paths." *Review of Economic Studies, Symposium on the Economics of Exhaustible Resources* 123–37, 1974a.

Stiglitz, J. E. "Growth with Exhaustible Natural Resources: The Competitive Economy." *Review of Economic Studies, Symposium on the Economics of Exhaustible Resources* 139–52, 1974b.

Stiglitz, J. E. "The Efficiency of Market Prices in Long-run Allocations in the Oil Industry." In *Studies in Energy Tax Policy,* edited by G. M. Brannon, pp. 87–94. Cambridge, Mass.: Ballinger, 1975.

Stiglitz, J. E. "Monopoly and the Rate of Extraction of Exhaustible Resources." *American Economic Review* 66:655–61, 1976.

Straszheim, M. "Hedonic Estimation of Housing Market Prices: A Further Comment." *Review of Economics and Statistics* 56:404–6, 1974.

Strotz, R. H. "The Use of Land Rent Changes to Measure the Welfare Benefits of Land Improvements." In *The New Economics of Regulated Industries: Rate Making in a Dynamic Economy,* edited by J. E. Haring. Los Angeles: Economic Research Center, Occidental College, 1968.

Suzuki, H. "On the Possibility of Steadily Growing per Capita Consumption in an Economy with a Wasting and Non-Replenishable Resource." *Review of Economic Studies* 43:527–36, 1976.

Sweeney, J. L. "Economics of Depletable Resources: Market Forces and Intertemporal Bias." *Review of Economic Studies* 44:125–42, 1977.

Talbot, L. M. "Maximum Sustainable Yield: An Obsolete Concept." Presented at the Technical Session on Living Marine Resources, 40th North American Wildlife and Natural Resources Conference, Pittsburgh, Pa., March 17, 1975.

Taylor, L. D. "The Demand for Electricity: A Survey." *Bell Journal of Economics* 6:74–110, 1975.

Thaler, R., and Rosen, S. "The Value of Saving a Life: Evidence from the Labor Market." In *Household Production and Consumption,* edited by N. E. Terlecky. New York: Columbia University Press, 1976.

Thompson, R. G., and Young, H. P. "Forecasting Water Use for Policy Making: A Review." *Water Resources Research* 9:792–9, 1973.

Thompson R. G., et al. *Environment, Energy, and Capital in the Electric Power Industry.* Houston: Gulf Publishing Company, 1976.

Tietenberg, T. H. "Specific Taxes and Pollution Control: A General Equilibrium Analysis." *Quarterly Journal of Economics* 87:503–22, 1973.

Tietenberg, T. H. "Derived Decision Rules for Pollution Control in a General Equilibrium Space Economy." *Journal of Environmental Economics and Management* 1:3–16, 1974a.

Tietenberg, T. H. "On Taxation and the Control of Externalities: Comment." *American Economic Review* 64:462–66, 1974b.

Tietenberg, T. H. "The Design of Property Rights for Air Pollution Control." *Public Policy* 22:275–92, 1974c.

Tolley, G. S. "The Welfare Economics of City Bigness." *Journal of Urban Economics* 1:324–45, 1974.

Tullock, G. "The Social Rate of Discount and the Optimal Rate of Investment: Comment." *Quarterly Journal of Economics* 78:331–6, 1964.

Tullock, G. "Monopoly and the Rate of Extraction of Exhaustible Resources: Note." *American Economic Review* 69:231–3, 1979.

Turvey, R. "On Divergences Between Social and Private Cost." *Economica* 30:309–13, 1963.

Turvey, R. "Optimisation and Suboptimisation in Fishery Regulation." *American Economic Review* 54:54–76, 1964.

Turvey, R., and Wiseman, J., eds. *The Economics of Fisheries;* International Economics Association Round Table in Rome, September 1956. Rome: Food and Agriculture Organisation, 1957.

*Udall, Secretary of the Interior* v. *Federal Power Commission, et al.,* 387 U.S. 428, 1967.

Uhler, R. S. "Petroleum Exploration Dynamics." Unpublished manuscript, Department of Economics, University of British Columbia, 1975.

Uhler, R. S. "Costs and Supply in Petroleum Exploration: The Case of Alberta." *Canadian Journal of Economics* 9:72–90, 1976.

Uhler, R. S., and Bradley, P. G. "A Stochastic Model for Determining the Economic Prospects of Petroleum Exploration Over Large Regions." *Journal of the American Statistical Association* 65:623–30, 1970.

U.S. Department of Commerce, National Marine Fisheries Service, Marketing and Economic Research Branch working papers.

U.S. Department of Commerce, National Oceanic and Atmospheric Administration, Environmental Data Service. *Ocean Data Resources.* Washington: U.S. Government Printing Office, June 1974.

U.S. Department of the Interior. *Final Impact Statement, Proposed Trans-Alaska Pipeline, Vol. 2.* Washington: U.S. Government Printing Office, 1972.

U.S. Federal Energy Administration. *National Energy Outlook 1976.* Washington: U.S. Government Printing Office, 1976.

U.S. President's Materials Policy Commission. *Resources for Freedom,* 5 vols. Washington: U.S. Government Printing Office, 1952.

*U.S. Statutes at Large, Vol. 74,* p. 215 (the Multiple-Use Sustained-Yield Act of 1960, Public Law 86–517).

Usher, D. "An Imputation to the Measure of Economic Growth for Changes in Life Expectancy." In *The Measurement of Economic and Social Performance,* edited by M. Moss. New York: Columbia University Press, 1973.

Van Meir, L. W. "A Study of Policy Considerations in Managing the Georges Bank Haddock Fishery." In *Recent Developments and Research in Fisheries Economics,* edited by F. W. Bell and J. E. Hazelton, pp. 197–209. Dobbs Ferry, N.Y.: Oceana Publications, 1967.

Varaiya, P. P. *Notes on Optimization.* New York: Van Nostrand Reinhold, 1972.

Ventura, E. M. "Operations Research in the Mining Industry." In *Progress in Operations Research,* edited by D. B. Hertz and R. T. Eddison, pp. 229–327. New York: John Wiley & Sons, 1964.

Vickrey, W. S. "Counterspeculation, Auctions and Competitive Sealed Tenders." *Journal of Finance* 16:8–37, 1961.

Vickrey, W. S. "Discussion." *American Economic Review* 54:88–92, 1964.

Victor, P. *Pollution: Economy and Environment.* Toronto: University of Toronto Press, 1972.

Viscusi, W. K. "Labor Market Valuations of Life and Limb: Empirical Evidence and Policy Implications." *Public Policy* 26:359–86, 1976.

Viscusi, W. K., and Zeckhauser, R. J. "Environmental Policy Choice under Uncertainty." *Journal of Environmental Economics and Management* 3:97–112, 1976.

Vogely, W. A. *Mineral Materials Modelling: A State-of-the-Art Review.* Baltimore: Johns Hopkins Press, 1976.

Vousden, N. "Basic Theoretical Issues in Resource Depletion." *Journal of Economic Theory* 6:126–43, 1973.

Waddell, T. E. *The Economic Damages of Air Pollution.* Socio-economic Environmental Studies Series EPA 600/5-74-012. Washington: U.S. Environmental Protection Agency, May 1974.

Walters, A. A. *Noise and Prices.* Oxford: Clarendon Press, 1975.

Wantrup, S. V. C. *Resource Conservation: Economics and Politics.* Berkeley: University of California Press, 1952.

Weinstein, M. C., and Zeckhauser, R. J. "Use Patterns for Depletable and Recycleable Resources." In *Review of Economic Studies, Symposium on the Economics of Exhaustible Resources* 67–88, 1974.

Weinstein, M. C., Zeckhauser, R. J. "The Optimal Consumption of Depletable Natural Resources." *Quarterly Journal of Economics* 89:371–92, 1975.

Weisbrod, B. "Collective-Consumption Services of Individual-Consumption Goods." *Quarterly Journal of Economics* 78:471–7, 1964.

Weitzman, M. "The Optimal Development of Resource Pools." *Journal of Economic Theory* 12:351–64, 1976.

Wellisz, S. "On External Diseconomies and the Government-Assisted Invisible Hand." *Economica* 31:345–62, 1964.

Wenders, J. T. "Asymmetry between Fees and Payments and the Rate of Change in Pollution Abatement Technology." Unpublished manuscript.

Wieand, K. F. "Air Pollution and Property Values: A Study of the St. Louis Area." *Journal of Regional Science* 13:91–5, 1973.

Wilen, J. E. "Common Property Resources and the Dynamics of Over-exploitation: The Case of the North Pacific Fur Seal." Mimeographed. Resources paper no. 3, Research Programme on Natural Resource Utilization, University of British Columbia, September 1976.

Williams, J., ed. *Carbon Dioxide, Climate, and Society.* Oxford: Pergamon Press, 1978.

Wilson, E. O. *Harvard Magazine* January-February 1980.

Wilson, R. "Price Formation Via Competitive Bidding." Unpublished manuscript; School of Business Administration, Stanford University, 1975*a*.

Wilson, R. "On the Incentive for Information Acquisition in Competitive Bidding with Asymmetrical Information." Stanford University, 1975*b*.

Wilson, R. "Comment on David Hughart, Informational Asymmetry, Bidding Strategies and the Marketing of Offshore Petroleum Leases." Unpublished manuscript, School of Business Administration, Stanford University, 1976.

Yohe, G. W. "Substitution and the Control of Pollution: A Comparison of Effluent Charges and Quantity Standards Under Uncertainty." *Journal of Environmental Economics and Management* 3:312–24, 1976.

Zeckhauser, R. J. "Resource Allocation with Probabilistic Individual Preferences." *American Economic Review* 59:546–52, 1969.

Zeckhauser, R. J. "Uncertainty and the Need for Collective Action." In *Public Expenditure and Policy Analysis,* edited by R. Haveman and J. Margolis. Chicago: Markham Publishing, 1970.

Zeckhauser, R. J., and Fisher, A. C. "Averting Behavior and External Diseconomies." Kennedy School discussion paper no. 41D. Cambridge, Mass.: Harvard University, April 1976.

Zellner, A. "Management of Marine Resources: Some Key Problems Requiring Additional Analysis." In *Economics of Fisheries Management: A Symposium,* edited by A. D. Scott, pp. 109–15, Vancouver: Institute of Animal Resource Ecology, University of British Columbia, 1970.

Zilberman, D., and Just, R. "A Dynamic Putty-Clay Model of Pollution Control." Working paper no. 32, California Agricultural Experiment Station, Giannini Foundation of Agricultural Economics, University of California, Berkeley, August 1980.

Zimmerman, M. B. "Modeling Depletion in a Mineral Industry: The Case of Coal." *Bell Journal of Economics* 8:41–65, 1977.

Zupan, J. M. *The Distribution of Air Quality in the New York Region.* Washington: Resources for the Future, 1973.

# AUTHOR INDEX

Acton, J.P., 212
Adams, F.G., 118
Adar, Z., 202
Adelman, M.A., 67
Agria, S.R., 67
Allais, M., 67
Almon, C., 26
Alterman, J., 116
Anderson, K.B., 162
Anderson, K.P., 73, 135
Anderson, R.C., 67
Arrow, K.J., 26, 53, 64, 69, 70, 72, 135, 137, 138
Atkinson, S.E., 198, 205, 228
Aucamp, D.C., 176
Ayres, R.U., 165, 168

Bailey, M.J., 211, 212
Baily, M.N., 44
Banks, F.E., 73
Barger, H., 101
Barnett, H.J., 91, 100, 101, 102, 103, 112, 113, 127
Bator, F., 128
Baughman, M.L., 118
Baumol, W.J., 70, 168, 174, 176, 185, 186, 187, 193, 195, 199, 201
Beckman, M.J., 73
Beddington, J.R., 78
Bell, F.W., 101
Berck, P., 78, 87
Berndt, E.R., 117, 120

Beverton, R.J.H., 78, 79, 80
Bieniewski, C.L., 96
Blitzer, C., 40
Blomquist, G., 212
Bloom, O.H., 66
Bohm, P., 175, 187
Boulding, K.E., 165
Bower, B.T., 189, 196, 226, 227, 228, 229
Bradford, D.F., 176
Bradley, P.G., 67, 124
Bramhall, D.E., 195
Brandt, C.S., 209
Brannon, G.M., 67
Brauch, E.F., 96
Brewer, D., 149
Brobst, D.A., 94, 97, 99
Brooks, D.B., 97
Brookshire, D.S., 206, 226
Brown, G.M., 59, 78, 83, 88, 103, 107, 112, 141
Buchanan, J., 183
Budnitz, R., 161
Burness, H.S., 68
Burt, O.R., 78, 82, 149
Butlin, J., 83

Calloway, J.A., 121, 227
Calvo, G., 72
Campbell, W.M., 66
Capen, E.C., 66
Cazalet, E.G., 125
Chang, S., 64

Chao, C., 99
Chapman, D., 117, 228
Cheung, S.N.S., 87
Christy, F.T., 87, 89, 102, 104
Cicchetti, C.J., 135, 137, 140, 141, 149
Clapp, R.V., 66
Clark, C.W., 79, 80, 82, 83, 85, 87, 88
Clawson, M., 146
Coase, R.H., 179–81, 183, 193
Commoner, B., 234
Comolli, P.M., 169
Conley, B.C., 213
Conrad, R.F., 68
Cooper, B.S., 212
Cootner, P.H., 44
Cowing, T.G., 124
Cox, D.P., 97
Cox, J.C., 67
Crabbé, P.J., 16, 67
Cremer, J., 40
Crocker, T.D., 206, 208
Crommelin, M., 66
Cropper, M.L., 224
Crutchfield, J.A., 82, 87
Cumberland, J.H., 204
Cummings, R.G., 23, 29, 78, 82, 124, 129

Dales, J.H., 199
d'Arge, R.C., 73, 165, 168, 169, 183, 226
Darmstadter, J., 116
Dasgupta, P., 39, 48, 56, 72
David, E.L., 219
Davidson, P., 67
Davis, R.K., 146, 229
DeHaven, J.C., 70
Demsetz, H., 182
Deshmukh, S.D., 64
Devarajan, S., 64, 109, 110
Dolbear, F.T., 184, 194
Dorfman, N.S., 226
Dorfman, R., 26, 226
Dowdle, B., 86
Drew, L.J., 97
Dreze, J.H., 70
Dunkerly, J., 116

Eastman, C., 226
Eckstein, O., 70

Ehrlich, A.H., 76, 97, 165
Ehrlich, P.R., 76, 97, 165
Epple, D., 67
Erickson, G.K., 66
Etheridge, D., 227

Faustman, M., 78
Feldstein, M.S., 70
Ferrar, T.A., 199
Field, B.C., 59, 103, 107, 112
Fischman, L.L., 97, 115, 116
Fishelson, G., 202
Fisher, A.C., 29, 59, 64, 83, 109, 110, 112, 129, 135, 138, 140–1, 147, 148, 149, 150, 152, 176
Fisher, F.M., 44, 124
Fisher, J.L., 115
Ford, J., 117, 120
Forster, B.A., 169
Forsund, F.R., 198
Freeman, A.M., 137, 194, 205, 206, 210, 217, 219, 220, 223, 224, 225, 226
Fuss, M.A., 117, 118, 120

Gaffney, M., 65, 67, 78
Garg, P.C., 73
Gaskins, D.W., 66
Gianessi, L.P., 226
Gilbert, R.J., 40, 48
Gilpin, A., 164
Goeller, H.E., 19
Goldman, M., 237
Gordon, H.S., 78, 79, 87
Gordon, R.L., 23
Gould, J.R., 84, 176
Goundry, G.K., 78
Grandmont, J., 52
Gray, L.C., 13, 16, 67
Grayson, C.J., 65
Greenley, D.A., 137
Gregory, P.R., 117, 120
Grenon, M., 67
Griffin, J.M., 117, 118, 120, 202, 228
Gruver, G.W., 169
Gutmanis, I., 228

Hadley, G., 26
Haefele, E.T., 226
Hall, D.C., 79
Halvorsen, R., 117, 120

Hamilton, J., 205, 206, 207, 209, 212, 214
Hamlen, W.A., 198, 205
Hamlisch, R., 89
Hammack, J., 78, 141
Hanemann, W.M., 146
Hanke, S.H., 225, 228
Hannesson, R., 79, 83
Hapgood, F., 211, 212
Harberger, A.C., 67
Harford, J.D., 200
Harris, D.P., 67, 97
Harrison, D., 219, 221, 224, 226
Harte, J., 205
Hartwick, J.M., 29, 72
Haurie, A., 73
Haveman, R.H., 229
Head, J.G., 167
Heal, G., 22, 29, 47, 48, 50, 56
Hearon, W.M., 227
Heck, W.W., 209
Heintz, H.T., 216
Helliwell, J.F., 67
Henderson, C., 119
Henning, J.A., 218
Henry, C., 137, 138
Herfindahl, O.C., 16, 19, 23, 65, 101, 112
Hershaft, A., 216
Hirshleifer, J., 70, 86
Hnyilicza, E., 42
Hoch, I., 224
Hochman, E., 78
Hoel, M., 48, 87
Holdren, J.P., 97, 161, 165, 205
Holt, S.L., 78, 79, 80
Homan, P.T., 67
Horak, G.C., 216
Hotelling, H., 23, 39, 65, 67, 146
Howe, C.W., 78, 95
Howell, F.M., 109
Hubbert, M.K., 62, 63, 96
Hudson, E.A., 125
Hughart, D., 66
Humphrey, D.B., 101
Hung, N.M., 73

Ingham, A., 73
Intriligator, M.D., 26
Isard, W., 205
Ives, B.C., 226

Jacoby, H., 226
James, E., 137
Jevons, W.S., 99, 100, 101
Johnson, M.H., 101
Jones-Lee, M.W., 212
Jorgenson, D.W., 118, 125
Joskow, P.L., 118
Jungenfelt, K.G., 78
Just, R., 169

Kahn, A.E., 68
Kalter, R.J., 66
Kalymon, B.A., 40
Kamien, M.I., 39, 56, 194
Kaufman, G.M., 65, 97
Kay, J.A., 39, 67
Keeler, E., 169
Kelly, R.A., 226, 228
Kemp, M.C., 26, 48
Kirshner, D., 116
Kneese, A.V., 65, 128, 165, 168–9, 174, 183, 184, 185, 189, 191, 192, 196, 205, 226, 227, 228, 229, 230
Knetsch, J.L., 146
Kogiku, K.C., 73, 169
Kohn, R.E., 176, 228
Kolm, S.C., 176
Koopmans, T.C., 46, 48, 69
Korbach, R.J., 204
Krutilla, J.V., 70, 112, 128, 129, 133, 135, 140–1, 147, 148, 150, 152
Kuller, R.G., 124
Kurz, M., 26, 69

Landsberg, H.H., 97, 115, 116
Lapan, H., 169
Lave, L.B., 205, 210, 211, 216, 218
Lee, T., 99
Leland, H.E., 54, 66
Leone, R.A., 224
Leontief, W., 205
Leopold, L.B., 141
Lewis, D.H., 198, 205, 228
Lewis, T.R., 38, 47
Lichtenberg, A.J., 116
Lieberman, M.A., 96
Lind, R.C., 53, 70, 137, 219
Lof, G., 227
Long, N.V., 48

Long, T.V., 121
Lotka, A.J., 80
Loury, G.C., 48
Lovejoy, W.F., 68

MacAvoy, P.W., 68, 124
Magat, W.A., 191
Magnus, J.R., 117, 120
Mäler, K.G., 169, 174
Manne, A.S., 125
Manthy, R.S., 104
Marglin, S.A., 69, 70
McDonald, S.L., 68
McFadden, D., 116
McGuire, C.B., 66
McInerney, J., 82
McKean, R.N., 70
McKelvey, V.E., 94
Mead, W.J., 66
Meade, J.E., 128
Meadows, D.H., 91, 234
Meeraus, A., 40
Merklein, H.A., 109
Meyer, J.R., 224
Meyer, R.A., 168
Mill, J.S., 24, 69, 127, 128
Millecan, A.A., 208
Miller, E.M., 73
Milliman, J.W., 70
Mills, E.S., 194, 195
Mintzer, I., 161
Mirrlees, J.A., 39, 67
Mishan, E.J., 50, 164, 184, 185
Moroney, J.R., 101
Morris, G., 161
Morse, C. 91, 100, 101, 102, 103, 112, 127
Mount, T.D., 117
Mueller, D.C., 226
Mumey, G.A., 183
Munro, G.R., 83, 85

Neher, P.A., 85
Nelson, J.P., 219, 224
Netschert, B.C., 115, 124
Niskanen, W.A., 225
Noll, R.G., 165
Nordhaus, W.D., 18, 50, 66, 98, 103–4, 106, 117, 118, 124, 165, 224
Norgaard, R.B., 101, 108, 124
Norton, V., 129

Oates, W.E., 168, 174, 176, 185, 186, 187, 193, 195, 199, 201
Olson, M.L., 183
Opaluch, J., 26
Oren, M.E., 66
Orr, L., 191

Page, R.T., 68, 73, 113, 169, 174, 180
Pearce, D.W., 206
Pearson, S., 66
Peirce, W.S., 101
Persse, F.H., 96
Peskin, H.M., 206, 226
Peterson, F.M., 29, 49, 83
Phelps, E.S., 72
Pigou, A.C., 69, 127–8, 164, 179
Pinchot, G., 1
Pindyck, R.S., 29, 40–2, 44, 59, 64, 68, 116, 117, 118, 120, 124
Pliska, S.R., 64
Plott, C.R., 173
Plourde, C.G., 83, 87, 169
Polach, J., 116
Polinsky, A.M., 219
Porter, R.C., 153, 195
Portes, R.D., 176
Portney, P.R., 192, 226
Potter, N., 102, 104
Pratt, W.P., 94
Puig, C., 116

Quirk, J.P., 85

Radetzki, M., 95, 101
Ramsay, W., 161
Ramsey, F.P., 68, 69
Randall, A., 180, 226
Rausser, G., 82, 169
Rawls, J., 71–2
Renshaw, E.F., 196
Ricardo, D., 24, 100, 101
Rice, D.P., 212
Richardson, H.W., 92
Richels, R.G., 124, 125
Ridker, R.G., 116, 218
Riley, J.G., 72
Robinson, C., 93
Rødseth, A., 118
Rogerson, W.P., 53
Rose-Ackerman, S., 198
Rosen, S., 212, 214, 215

Rosenberg, N., 101
Rosenfeld, A.H., 123, 159, 160
Rothkopf, M.H., 66
Rowe, R.D., 226
Rubinfeld, D.L., 219, 221, 224, 226
Ruff, L.E., 184, 185
Russell, C.S., 226, 227, 228, 229

Salant, S.W., 40
Sampson, A.A., 73
Samuelson, P.A., 53, 78, 137, 167, 171
Sandmo, A., 70
Sawyer, J.W., 227
Schaefer, M.B., 78, 79
Schanz, J.L., 94
Scherer, C.R., 82
Schipper, L., 116, 121
Schmalensee, R., 40, 137
Schultze, C.L., 191, 192, 196
Schulze, W.D., 23, 29, 73, 183, 205, 226
Schurr, S.H., 101, 115
Schwartz, A.K., 227
Schwartz, N.L., 39, 56, 194
Scitovsky, T., 128
Scotchmer, S., 205, 206, 220, 223, 224, 225
Scott, A.D., 49, 67, 68, 78, 87
Seskin, E.P., 205, 206, 210, 211, 216, 218
Shapiro, D.L., 70
Shavell, S., 219
Shaw, R., 82
Sidgwick, H. 68
Simmons, P., 73
Sims, W.A., 227, 228
Singer, D.A., 97
Singleton, F.D., 227
Slichter, L.B., 67
Smith, F.A., 73, 165
Smith, R.S., 212
Smith, V.K., 104–5, 112, 113, 124, 133, 149, 229
Smith, V.L., 26, 78, 83, 85, 88, 169, 191
Solow, R.M., 22, 29, 50, 72–3, 162
Sonstelie, J., 226
Southey, C., 80, 87
Spence, A.M., 78, 169

Spiegleman, R.D., 67
Spofford, W.O., 226, 228
Stankey, G.H., 132
Starrett, D.A., 176
Steele, H., 96
Steiner, P.O., 68
Stevens, T.H., 66
Stiglitz, J.E., 39, 48, 50, 56, 65, 73
Stoutjesdijk, S., 40
Straszheim, M., 224
Strøm, S., 118
Strotz, R.H., 219
Stubblebine, W.D., 183
Suzuki, H., 73
Sweeney, J.L., 39, 67, 73

Talbot, L.M., 79
Taylor, L.P., 116
Teisberg, T., 66
Teitelbaum, P., 116
Thaler, R., 212, 214, 215
Thompson, A.R., 66
Thompson, R.G., 121, 227
Tietenberg, T.H., 169, 198, 199
Tobin, J., 224
Tolley, G., 224
Tonnessen, K., 205
Trijonis, J., 165
Tullock, G., 39
Turvey, R., 87, 89, 180
Tyner, W.E., 66
Tyrrell, T.J., 117

Udall, S., 142–3
Uhler, R.S., 65, 67, 110–1
Usher, D., 212, 215

Vann, B., 66
Varaiya, P.P., 26
Vaughan, W.J., 227
Vickrey, W.S., 53, 66, 137
Victor, P., 165, 205
Viscusi, W.K., 153, 212
Vogely, W.A., 124
Vousden, N., 73, 135

Waddell, T.E., 216
Walsh, R.G., 137
Walters, A.A., 219
Wan, F.Y., 29
Watts, C.M.K., 78

Waverman, L., 117, 118, 120
Weinberg, A.M., 19
Weinstein, M.C., 23, 29, 39, 46, 73
Weisbrod, B., 137
Weitzman, M., 29, 40
Wellisz, S., 183
Wenders, J.T., 191
Weyant, J.P., 124, 125
Whinston, A.B. 199
Wilen, J.E., 78, 165
Williams, A.C., 66
Williams, J., 165
Wilson, E.O., 76
Wilson, R., 66

Wiseman, J., 89
Wolff, E., 226
Wood, D., 117, 120
Wright, W.D.C., 67, 78

Yohe, G.W., 202
Young, H.P., 227
Young, R.A., 137

Zeckhauser, R.J., 23, 29, 39, 46, 73, 137, 153, 169, 176
Zellner, A., 80, 82
Zilberman, D., 78, 169
Zimmerman, M.B., 96
Zupan, J.M., 226

Index does not include all authors appearing in list of references.

# SUBJECT INDEX

Coase theorem
  demonstration of, 179–81
  strategic behavior and, 182–3
  transaction costs and, 181–2
common property
  in exhaustible resources, 64–5
  in renewable resources, 76–8,
    86–9
crustal abundance (of a mineral),
    98–100

elasticity of expectations (and re-
    source market instability),
    50–2 energy
energy
  conservation of, 121–3, 159–62
  demand for, 114–23
  models, 114–15,124–5
  substitutability of other factors
    for, 119–23
exhaustible resources
  backstop for, 18–20
  and cartel behavior, 37, 39–44
  cost of extraction of, 23–4, 28,
    29–32, 57–60, 100–2
  exploration for, 55–60, 63–7
  and externalities, 21, 64–7
  and income distribution, 22, 67–
    8
  information about, 63–7
  instability in markets for, 49–52
  and intertemporal equity, 68–72
  leasing of, 65–6

and monopoly, 37–9
  price behavior over time of, 17–
    20, 28, 30–2, 40–2, 55–6, 59–
    62, 102–7
  rate of depletion of, 20, 37–9,
    42–3, 46–9, 62–3
  recycling of, 73
  substitutability of other factors
    for, 72–4, 119–23
  taxation of, 67–8
  and uncertainty, 44–8
extractive output, cost of
  biases in data on, 111–13
  historical behavior of, 100–2
extractive output, price of
  biases in data on, 111–13
  historical behavior of, 102–7
  relation to theoretical behavior
    of, 107
externalities, see exhaustible re-
    sources and externalities; pol-
    lution

Hell's Canyon hydroelectric pro-
    ject, 140–62
  conservation alternative to, 159–
    60
  difficulties in benefit-cost analy-
    sis of, 143–7
  discussion of findings of benefit-
    cost analysis of, 153–62
  findings of benefit-cost analysis
    of, 147–53

Hell's Canyon hydroelectric project (*cont.*)
history of, 141–3
physical setting of, 141
recreation benefits of, 147–9
recreation benefits of preserved project site, 149–53
thermal alternative to, 155–9

irreversibility
and benefit-cost analysis, 128–9, 133–9
of resource development in a natural environment, 128–33
and uncertainty, 136–9

materials balance (model of pollution), 165
mineralogical threshold, 99–100

nonconvexity (and control of pollution externality), 176–9

oil and gas exploration, cost of, 107–11
OPEC, 40–4
optimal control
method of, 26
relation to optimal depletion of, 32–4
optimal depletion (of exhaustible resources), 12, 14–16, 22, 27–8
and competitive equilibrium, 17, 23, 25, 34–6, 52–5
option value, 136–8

pollution
benefits of control of, 204-26
comparative analysis of policies to control, 179, 184–203
and control of externalities, 166–79
costs of control of, 226–31
direct controls on, 190–3
distribution of benefits and costs of control of, 226
and economic growth, 230–1, 235–6
historical concern for, 127–8, 164–5
permit auction for, 198–203, 239

under socialism, 236–7
subsidy to reduce, 193–6
tax on, 171–6, 184–93, 196–8
pollution control
general equilibrium models, 168–9
health benefits, estimates of, 212, 215–18
health benefits, methods of estimating, 209–11, 213,15
property values, and pollution, 218–25
public good
definition of, 167, 175
role in pollution policy of, 174–6

renewable resources
distinction between exhaustible and, 75–7
extinction of, 75–8, 85, 87
growth law for, 79–81
maximum sustainable yield of, 80, 85–6
optimal use of, 81–6
steady state in exploitation of, 77, 83–4
rent
definition of, 14, 58
relation to exploration cost of, 58, 107–10
*see also* royalty
reserves
definition and determinants of, 94–100
as inventory, 97–8
of oil, 92–3
reswitching, 153
royalty
behavior over time of, 16–19, 27–30
definition of, 14, 19, 58
*see also* rent

social discounting (and exhaustible resource use), 68–70

tonnage-grade distribution of a mineral, 95–7

welfare criteria (and exhaustible resource use), 71–2